death by cyanide

death by cyanide

THE MURDER OF
DR. AUTUMN KLEIN

Paula Reed Ward

ForeEdge

ForeEdge
An imprint of University Press of New England
www.upne.com
© 2016 Paula Reed Ward
All rights reserved
Manufactured in the United States of America
Designed by Eric M. Brooks
Typeset in Dante by Passumpsic Publishing

For permission to reproduce any of the material in this book,
contact Permissions, University Press of New England, One Court
Street, Suite 250, Lebanon NH 03766; or visit www.upne.com

Library of Congress Cataloging-in-Publication Data
available upon request

5 4 3 2 1

to all my boys

contents

Illustrations appear
following page 130.

acknowledgments

I would like to thank all those who helped in the conception and execution of this project—from providing even the most mundane of details to sharing huge parts of their lives with me. It could not have happened without each one of them.

This book is a culmination of the work of many, including Lillian Thomas, who is a superb editor and friend; the *Post-Gazette*, which gave me the gift of time to do research and reporting in the early stages; my dear friend Patti Hippler, who can copyedit with the best of them; my best friend, Pamela Walck, who knows how to calm my madness; my sister Janet Sardon, who unfailingly makes me laugh and supports me; my sister Lisa Ford, who sent words of encouragement every day; and my agent, Jane Dystel, of Dystel and Goderich, who took a chance on me sight unseen.

Among those who deserve individual thanks are Neil and Suzanne Alexander for the amazing work they do through their Live Like Lou foundation, and Mike Manko from the Allegheny County District Attorney's office, who really is a very patient man.

To the Klein family, I think about you often and wish you peace and happiness in your lives.

And of course, my most immense gratitude goes to Jim, Logan, and Gavin for not only tolerating me throughout this ordeal—Jim is inevitably right—but for encouraging me, too. I could not imagine a world without you, your love, and fun.

All of the information in this book was obtained through interviews, court documents, medical records, e-mails, and trial testimony.

death by cyanide

prologue

ON WEDNESDAY, APRIL 17, 2013, Dr. Autumn Klein worked a fifteen-hour day. At 11:18 p.m., she sent her husband a message to let him know she was about to make the half-mile walk from the University of Pittsburgh Medical Center (UPMC) Presbyterian to their home.

"Okay," Robert Ferrante responded. "Be safe."

And she was. But shortly after she got home, she collapsed in the kitchen.

"Hello, hello, please, please, please, please," Bob said frantically to the 911 dispatcher. "I'm at 219 Lytton Avenue. I think my wife is having a stroke! She's staring."

"Listen to me, is she awake?" the dispatcher asked.

"Yes, yes."

"Is she breathing?"

"Yes, she's breathing."

He spoke to his wife: "Honey, sweetheart, are you okay?" But Autumn couldn't respond.

Instead, she began to moan, a horrific, guttural groaning that filled the room as the dispatcher ran through standard queries for a possible stroke victim, oblivious to the sounds.

Have her try to smile, he told Bob. Ask her to raise her arms above her head.

She could do neither.

"Oh, God help me, God help me," he pleaded. "Now, she's just now, it's like she's almost gonna throw up," he told the dispatcher. "She's not breathing normally now. Big, huge breaths.

"Oh, please, have them hurry. Sweetheart, sweetheart, I love you very much," Bob begged. "Please don't do this. Please, please, sweetheart, sweetheart."

The dispatcher asked if anything like this had happened before. There had been fainting spells, Bob said, and Autumn had been tired.

"My wife's trying to get pregnant again," he volunteered, noting that she had been on several medications.

"Oh, Jesus, Jesus, Jesus, Jesus, Jesus," Bob cried. "Where the hell is somebody?"

Finally, nearly twelve minutes after the call began, paramedics arrived.

1 ·················

saving one of their own

THEY HAD NO IDEA what was wrong.

Their patient, a forty-one-year-old female, was lying on the kitchen floor unresponsive, after, her husband said, she'd collapsed suddenly while complaining of a headache. Immediately, they began their assessment. She was breathing and had a pulse.

Steve Mason got a quick summary from Bob and asked him about a big ziplock bag of white powder on the counter. It was creatine, he said, that his wife was taking for infertility. As they spoke, Mason's partner, Jerad Albaugh, got his attention.

Their patient was crashing—her pressure and pulse were dropping fast.

"She's not responding," Albaugh said.

The men loaded her on a gurney and rushed her to their ambulance parked in front of the home. They called ahead to the hospital and raced the half mile there, with Albaugh unable to do anything other than start an IV during the short trip.

They pulled up to the emergency entrance of UPMC Presbyterian (Presby) at 12:21 a.m., an hour and three minutes after Autumn had walked out. She lay prone on the gurney, her arms contorted and her face twisted up and over her left shoulder.

Emergency department (ED) resident Dr. Andrew Farkas met the stretcher in the hallway. The patient's eyes were open and glassy, and her breaths were shallow—she was struggling to breathe. There was a vacant look on her face.

They rushed her to curtain area thirty-two in the ED, where her heart rate was measured in the low forties, and her blood pressure was barely moving at forty-eight over thirty-six. Although her pupils were reactive to light, the patient—whom they now knew was a Presby neurologist—was unresponsive.

The team of nurses and technicians assisting Farkas put in another IV to push fluids to try to boost Autumn's blood pressure. Her respirations were starting to slow—as low as four per minute—and Farkas knew immediately she needed to be put on a ventilator to help her breathe. He inserted the breathing tube into her mouth and down her trachea, then ran to get his ED attending physician, Dr. Thomas Martin.

Just two minutes after Farkas checked his patient's pupils, Martin checked them again. They were no longer reacting to light.

Farkas had ordered a broad panel of blood tests, gases, and chemistries be sent out to check Autumn's organ function. The problem, though, was that because she was so slim, the staff was having trouble getting a blood draw from her arm. Using a larger needle, they moved to the femoral artery in her leg, but still couldn't successfully take her blood.

As the staff continued to work on Autumn, her husband arrived with his friend and colleague, Dr. Robert Friedlander, who had driven him there. Farkas pulled back the curtain surrounding the bed where Autumn lay, the vent pushing air in and out of her lungs.

Bob took a long look and then screamed, "No!"

Farkas continued his assessment while he listened to Bob describe what had happened at the house. Autumn had been complaining of headaches in recent weeks, and when she arrived home from work that night she said she wasn't feeling well. Her husband described her grasping her head in her hands and dropping to the floor.

Farkas and Martin suspected she was having a brain hemorrhage. They needed to get a CT scan of her head immediately, so they momentarily scrapped their plans for the blood draw to move her to the 3-D imaging machine.

It was only one hundred feet from her bed, but Autumn's pressure was below sixty, and her pulse was in the thirties. Just putting her in the scanner was too risky. Ignoring protocol, Martin went in with her. Draped in a protective vest, he pushed epinephrine every one to two minutes to keep her heart pumping.

As the scan ran, the images immediately appeared on a computer monitor in the control room.

They were normal.

"It looks completely clear," Farkas said. "There's no explanation for her symptoms. There's no evidence of any disease state whatsoever."

The emergency team then switched focus, trying to think of what else could cause such a dramatic decline so fast. They ordered additional CT scans of Autumn's chest, abdomen, and pelvis. Her EKG showed no abnormalities in her heart's electrical activity. There was no aneurysm in her abdomen. She had no aortic tear that could have caused blood to spill into her chest cavity. There was no blood clot in her lungs.

The treatment team had no idea what was wrong.

At 1:20 a.m., Martin paged the hospital's on-call intensivist—a doctor who works exclusively with intensive-care patients. Dr. Lori Shutter returned the page.

"This is Tom Martin. I'm one of the ED docs."

"Yeah," Shutter answered. "What do you need?"

"I have a patient down here. You may have heard of her: Autumn Klein. She's one of our neurology attendings."

"Autumn?" Shutter responded. Autumn was her colleague, neighbor, and friend.

"Yeah. She got here around midnight. I've been working on her since then, and I just need help. I don't know what's going on."

Shutter hung up the phone, thinking to herself, "What the fuck would have happened to Autumn? She's younger than me. What could have happened?" The critical-care physician told the fellow she was working with that she was needed in the ED and rushed to the elevators to make the trip down the nine floors to the ground level of the hospital.

She quickly walked around the corner to the trauma room where Autumn lay, a huge team of nurses, technicians, and doctors working on her. Bob, Friedlander—the chair of neurosurgery—and Autumn's neurology chair, Dr. Lawrence Wechsler, were there, as well.

"Bob, what's going on?" Shutter asked.

He said Autumn had collapsed at home.

Martin was at the bedside, still pushing syringes full of epinephrine to try to sustain Autumn's blood pressure. He told Shutter about her condition, the need to intubate her, and the puzzling fact that all the CT scans were clear.

"I can't figure out what's happening."

The nurses were still having difficulty getting blood from Autumn, who at nearly five foot seven weighed only 107 pounds. Everyone agreed she needed to have a central line placed in her chest so that they could more quickly administer medications and draw blood.

Using an ultrasound to locate the patient's internal jugular vein—

the largest in the neck—Farkas inserted a triple-lumen catheter. As he placed the tube inside the vein, the blood that came out was bright red—noticeably so, since venous blood, which has less oxygen in it, should be much darker. The resident alerted Martin to what he'd seen, wondering if he'd accidentally placed the line in an artery, where the blood should be a much brighter red. But the more experienced physician had seen the ultrasound and knew the catheter was in the right location. Further, Farkas did a manometer test, placing a plastic tube over the needle to see what would happen to the blood inside. If it pulsed up, then the line was in an artery. If it dropped down, then the tube was in a vein. When Farkas held the line up, Autumn's blood dropped back down. It was in a vein.

Martin dismissed his resident's concerns, and Farkas used stitches to secure the catheter in place.

The treatment team, which now included a neurologist, a cardiologist, and an intensive-care-unit physician, had received Autumn's initial lab results, looking at her electrolytes, white blood cell count, hemoglobin, red blood cell volume, and coagulation factors. Again, they were normal. The only things that came back abnormal were the patient's pH and oxygen levels. There was a lot of acid in her blood, indicating a severe metabolic dysfunction, and her oxygen levels were in the five hundreds—more than double what they should have been. Autumn's cells were unable to use the oxygen in her blood, but the doctors didn't know why. They continued to give her sodium bicarbonate and increased the ventilator speed to make her breathe faster to try to lower the acid levels. They were also still pushing huge doses of epinephrine regularly.

"We've been doing this a long time," Martin said. "We need to come up with some ideas."

Shutter suggested running a toxicology screen that would check for a standard set of drugs and poisons. As the team was treating Autumn, they heard her husband talk about her.

"She really enjoyed what she was doing," he said. "She loved her job, and she would never want to survive if she couldn't be herself and continue her work."

At 2:17 a.m., as the physicians continued to try to stabilize her, Autumn lost her pulse and went into cardiac arrest. They called a code. A respiratory therapist disconnected the ventilator and began bagging her manually as a team of technicians and nurses took turns performing chest compressions. Each person got up on top of Autumn, straddling her. They clasped their hands one over the other with arms fully extended, pounding on her chest to try to compress it one to two inches with each pump.

Martin had his hand on Autumn's femoral artery in her groin to ensure her blood was still circulating with each compression.

"Shit. Bloody secretions," Martin exclaimed as he saw bloody fluid coming up from the breathing tube. They suspected her ribs had been broken from the compressions and maybe punctured her lungs.

For twenty-two minutes, they took turns performing CPR, continuing to push adrenaline to try to sustain her heart and blood pressure.

"This has been going a long time," Martin said. "This isn't going well. Do you think we should call this?"

"We probably should, but I'm not going to be the one to go out and tell the husband," Shutter responded. She told Martin she couldn't tell Bob they let his wife die. "Do you mind going out to talk to him?"

Shutter took over running the code as Martin went to speak to Bob. He sobbed at the news.

She replaced Martin in feeling for Autumn's femoral pulse and was struck for the first time by how small the woman was, lying on the bed wearing nothing but a pair of pink, animal-print panties.

"No one should ever be in this position with a friend of theirs," Shutter thought to herself, a wave of despair flashing through her as she looked at her hand in her friend's groin. Just as quickly, though, she told herself to stop staring.

"The next round is when we'll stop if she's not back," she told the team.

They gave Autumn another round of epinephrine and started a last set of compressions. About thirty seconds in, Martin returned to the room.

"Her husband understands we're going to call it," he said.

A short time later, a nurse keeping track of the time announced, "It's been two minutes."

Everyone stopped what they were doing.

"Oh, my gosh, there's a pulse," Shutter said. "Someone confirm."

A touch to Autumn's carotid artery confirmed.

Her heart was beating—not well, but like a quivering bag.

Using electric paddles, they shocked the heart with 120 joules—equivalent to being hit in the chest with a baseball thrown at fifty miles per hour.

The shock steadied the heart rate, though it remained very slow.

She was not conscious or responsive. But she was alive.

"Now what do we do?" Shutter asked. "What's the next step?"

The treatment team knew they needed to take measures to ensure Autumn's heart continued beating, and so they paged the on-call cardiothoracic surgeon. As the physicians discussed their ideas, about 3:00 a.m., Friedlander suggested he and Bob go get a cup of coffee.

When the cardiothoracic surgeon and his fellow arrived, they discussed a few different options, including placing Autumn on extracorporeal membrane oxygenation (ECMO), which is a type of dialysis, or installing an intra-aortic balloon pump.

The physicians worried that, because of their patient's small frame, they would not be able to place the ECMO lines. The tubing for the procedure is the size of a small garden hose and must be pushed several inches into the patient's veins and arteries.

Dr. Jay Bhama decided they should do the balloon pump, but as they made their plans—and discussed whether Autumn could sustain a trip to the cardiac cath lab—her vitals again began to fall.

"While you guys are standing there, we're losing her blood pressure," said Dr. Jeremiah Hayanga, who was working with Bhama that night.

They immediately decided they had to go with ECMO, which removes blood from the body, filters and puts oxygen in it, and then returns it so the organs can use the oxygenated blood to continue to function. The physicians knew it was possible that Autumn could lose her limbs from the procedure because they would not get proper blood flow with the large lines inside of her.

But without it, they knew, she would die.

There was no time to get to an operating room, so the doctors called the emergency ECMO team on the hospital's second floor, telling the perfusionist to bring all of the equipment directly to the emergency department. Within minutes, the team wheeled the eighteen-inch-wide, thirty-six-inch-tall machine to Autumn's bedside.

Hayanga and Bhama worked together.

They prepped both the right and left femoral regions. Using a scalpel, they nicked the skin on each side, and then used a dilator cathe-ter to widen the holes to accommodate the width of the tubes. Once they were big enough, they fed an eleven-inch-long plastic tube up into the femoral vein on the left and into the femoral artery on the right. When they turned on the ECMO machine, it would work by drawing the blood out of the femoral vein, running it through the filtration and oxygenation system, and then return it to Autumn's body through her right femoral artery.

They then stitched the tubes into place.

Once Autumn was on ECMO, the staff was able to maintain her heart rate at sixty to seventy beats per minute. They gave her a transfusion of two units of packed red blood cells and planned to cool her body because hypothermia can help recovery after cardiac arrest. However, doctors noted that she was already four degrees cooler than the thirty-three degrees Celsius that is recommended.

When Bob and Friedlander returned to the emergency room thirty minutes after they'd left, they learned Autumn was on ECMO.

Bob appeared to relax at the news, and Martin worried that he'd given the man false hope. Although her heart was beating, Autumn's condition remained grave.

Throughout the night, the physicians talked about what they thought might have caused their colleague's collapse. They suggested a number of ideas, including Brugada syndrome, which is an abnor-mal heart rhythm, and even the possibility of an electrical brain storm, which is when brain cells fail to properly discharge energy, causing a surge of it through the brain.

They consulted local, national, and international experts to try to get the best information possible to guide her care.

At 5:30 a.m., it was agreed that Autumn could be moved from the ED to the cardiothoracic intensive-care unit (CTICU) on the second floor of the hospital. Two nurses, a respiratory therapist, and two members of the ECMO team transported her to CTICU bed number two.

On arrival, the staff removed Autumn's white-gold wedding band to return to her husband and hooked her up to a continuous EEG machine with thirty-two small electrodes placed around the head to measure her brain activity. There was none.

Although her heart was now beating steadily, the doctors treating her knew the prognosis was poor.

Dr. Frank Guyette, a consultant with the hospital's post–cardiac arrest team who evaluated Autumn at 8:21 a.m., noted that her blood pressure was still just seventy over thirty. Her pupils were not responding to light. She had no gag reflex. Her extremities showed no spontaneous movement, and there was no response to painful stimuli.

He put her chances of a meaningful recovery at less than 4 percent.

Later that morning, Dr. Jon Rittenberger, another member of the post–cardiac arrest team at Presby, took over Autumn's care. He noted that she was "profoundly comatose" with a "flat, nonresponsive EEG," but said that from a "neuro prognostic standpoint, it is simply too early to tell."

The doctors treating Autumn agreed that it would not be fair to fully assess her brain activity until she had been properly rewarmed since the cooling protects brain function. Shutter spoke with a colleague at Yale, who suggested they give their patient at least seventy-two hours at average body temperature before reaching any conclusions. She passed that information along to Bob.

"Don't call things too early," she told him. "You never know."

Autumn herself, when having her first appointment with her new family physician in Pittsburgh in June 2012, noted that if she ever entered a persistent neurovegetative state, "she would like to give herself a trial of intensive and ICU care for about a week, but if there is no impact and no improvement, then she prefers not to have measures taken to prolong her life."

Rittenberger, still stumped by what precipitated Autumn's collapse, called his colleague, Dr. Clifton Callaway, an emergency physician, who was traveling. He filled him in on the case and recounted the patient's symptoms—including the bright-red blood in the central line —and noted that she still had very high levels of acid, even with improved blood flow and increased levels of oxygen.

Callaway suggested running a test for cyanide toxicity, even though the chances of that causing the collapse were slim.

"Please also note that due to her profound acidosis on initial arrival, we had added on a toxicologic screen along with serum alcohols and cyanide (although this is unlikely)," Rittenberger wrote in Autumn's chart.

The blood was drawn at 2:32 p.m. on April 18, and the tube sent to Quest Diagnostics in Chantilly, Virginia, to be tested.

About two hours later, Bob met with a social worker at the hospital. He told the woman that his wife's parents had arrived in Pittsburgh from their home in Baltimore, but that he was uncertain if they planned to visit their daughter.

In the meantime, his in-laws had been waiting at the couple's home since about 5:30 a.m. to go to see Autumn. Her elderly parents, Lois and Bill, had driven through the night from their home in Towson, Maryland, after receiving a call from their son-in-law. Bob told them he did not want to take them to see their daughter until his adult children, Michael and Kimberly, arrived from Boston and San Diego.

The whole family finally went to the hospital that evening.

When the group entered Autumn's room in the cardiac intensive-care unit, her grave condition was obvious.

Lois saw all the flat lines on the monitors attached to her daughter and knew she was gone.

Kimberly Ferrante, a physician, also noted that her stepmother was not on any sedation, which is usually necessary for someone who is intubated—unless there's no brain activity.

She knew it was a poor prognosis.

Over the next two days, Autumn's family members spent their time shuttling back and forth from the couple's home to the hospital. Because they were unable to walk substantial distances, Lois and Bill were unable to get to the hospital themselves. Instead, Michael, who busied himself by trying to help his dad around the house and with his six-year-old half-sister, Cianna, during those few days, drove them.

Lois and Bill sat for hours at a time at the bedside.

They felt like they were being left out of the discussions about their daughter's care and condition. When Bob met with his wife's doctors, he would include Kimberly, but not the Kleins.

This angered Lois, who simply inserted herself into the conversations. When Bob met with the doctors in the hallway, Lois forced her way in, determined not to be ignored.

She was further frustrated by her son-in-law's behavior during the discussions with the doctors. Instead of letting them talk about their suspicions, Bob kept making his own diagnoses. "Don't you think this is what it is?" he would ask.

The team of physicians continued to talk about what might have caused such a drastic, untreatable condition. Autumn had been in touch with her family physician six weeks earlier, noting that she had been having significant hair loss and that she thought she might need to have her hormone levels checked, but otherwise, there were no medical complaints reported.

At the hospital, Bob told several people he believed his wife had suffered an electrical brain surge.

"Autumn's two-year history of headache-migraine may have caused this," he wrote in an e-mail to Friedlander on April 20. "While we were certain of four events that I witnessed, there may have been more that she did not discuss or were subclinical. There remains the hypothesis that this was myogenic and that there was a defect in the heart."

As it became clear that Autumn was not going to recover, Sharon King, her cousin and best friend with whom she'd grown up in Baltimore, asked Lois to hold her cell phone up to Autumn's ear so that she could speak with her from her home in Seattle.

On Friday evening, Sharon spoke to the woman with whom she'd shared her childhood dreams and memories, telling her that she loved her, that she needed her to wake up.

"I need you. Cianna needs you,'" she said.

The family started talking about Autumn's wishes to be an organ donor. Intensive-care physicians treating her believed that the liver and kidneys could be transplanted.

Bob e-mailed Friedlander: "This may be the last physical gift that she can provide and would be a wonderful one."

There was also talk about an autopsy.

Rittenberger suggested to Bob that if Autumn had died from a heart-rhythm disturbance, then an autopsy ought to be performed. It was likely that such a condition would be genetic, which meant their young daughter could be at risk.

Lois wanted an autopsy. She wanted to know what had happened.

"A healthy forty-one-year-old woman doesn't just come home, drop on the floor, and die."

But Bob said no. He was so insistent that several physicians noted his rejection of the idea of an autopsy in Autumn's chart. He didn't even want a limited one—an external examination and toxicology screening—that would have allowed for genetic testing.

He talked to Shutter about it, suggesting that the ECMO might wash anything out of his wife's system that would point to cause of death.

"What would an autopsy tell us?" he asked.

He reiterated the point in the e-mail to Friedlander: "Discussion with all the principals suggests that autopsy, limited or full, will not resolve this issue. I am unclear whether we will resolve this issue."

But in Pennsylvania, with any unnatural death, the law requires an autopsy. Whether he wanted it or not, the Allegheny County Medical Examiner's Office was going to do one.

As Autumn entered her third day in the hospital, her status remained unchanged.

"Autumn's EEG remains without any activity and has been so twenty-four hours after rewarming. The ICU team is ready to call her death," Bob wrote to Friedlander. "The fact that the EEG has not change[d] suggests little chance of recovery. Bedside brainstem exam is negative. It would be wonderful to get another CT, but they are unable to take her off ECMO to do this. Unclear whether her heart would sustain the workload."

Bob took Cianna to the hospital to see her mother Saturday morning. For the two previous days he had sent his daughter to school to try to sustain normalcy and told her that Autumn had gone away to a meeting but would return soon. By Saturday, though, he explained to his little girl that her mom had a medical problem, was very ill, and was in the hospital.

"Cianna was there all morning," Bob wrote in his e-mail to Friedlander. "That was the best thing to do. She was pleased to see her mom, but when she left she commented that she did not think that mommy would be coming back home. This is all so very sad to me. It breaks my heart."

Bob agreed that day to remove Autumn from life support.

At 11:06 a.m. on April 20, Rittenberger performed the first of two required brain-death exams on Autumn, with her parents and Bob at her side. He called to her, announcing his presence. She did not respond. He pinched her. There was nothing. He checked her pupils, shining a light directly into her eyes. No response.

No gag reflex.

A doll's-eye reflex—where the patient's eyes spontaneously move to the side when the head is moved in the opposite direction—was absent.

And Autumn showed no reaction when he dripped cold water into her ear canal.

At 12:10 p.m., he declared her brain dead.

Fifteen minutes later, Dr. Joseph Darby, a critical-care physician, conducted the same tests with the patient's parents at her bedside.

He also took Autumn off the ventilator for a full five minutes.

"Throughout the entirety of my observations to my examination, I observed no respiratory efforts whatsoever," he wrote.

Autumn was pronounced dead at 12:31 p.m. on April 20 but remained on the equipment to keep her heart beating and her lungs breathing.

That afternoon, staff from the Center for Organ Recovery and Education (CORE) met with Bob to obtain permission for organ donation. The family remained with Autumn throughout the evening.

Then, at 2:26 a.m. on April 21, staff arrived in the room to prep her for organ harvesting, and she was transported to the operating room.

The surgery began at 3:00 a.m. and ended two hours later.

Her body arrived at the medical examiner's office six hours after that.

2 ∎ ∎ ∎ ∎ ∎ ∎ ∎ ∎ ∎ ∎ ∎ ∎ ∎ ∎ ∎ ∎ ∎ ∎
who was autumn klein?

AUTUMN JOINED THE STAFF at UPMC in July 2011, moving her practice in women's neurology from Brigham and Women's Hospital—a part of the Harvard medical system in Boston—to Pittsburgh.

Both she and Bob, a well-known neuroresearcher who studied ALS (amyotrophic lateral sclerosis, a.k.a. Lou Gehrig's disease) and Huntington's disease, had been recruited by the University of Pittsburgh. But Autumn, at forty-one, was up and coming, whereas Bob, who was twenty-three years older, was contemplating retirement.

Autumn had done a dual MD/PhD program at Boston University, and her passion was helping women with neurological problems, especially problems in pregnancy. She had founded Brigham's Women's Neurology Program and did the same in Pittsburgh. Most of her patients were pregnant or postpartum, and she was board certified in epilepsy and headache—the two most common neurological problems in pregnancy.

She was a sought-after speaker both nationally and internationally and won a number of grants to study the role of antiseizure medications in pregnant women and their babies. Autumn also studied the effect of oral contraceptives on migraines.

She carried a grueling work schedule that often had her in the hospital and her medical offices for twelve hours a day, while also editing and writing in scholarly journals and books. Despite all of those demands on her, she also took time with her patients. It was one of the reasons that she was so well-loved by them.

Wende Corcoran was one of those patients.

In March 2010, Corcoran had a seizure in her right arm and the right side of her face while at a Chicago airport traveling for her work for a Rhode Island nonprofit. She described a feeling of her face being tugged violently down from the inside. From the outside, it drooped. Her arm contorted, forming her hand into a claw that she couldn't control. It happened a few more times between March and May, lasting anywhere from ten seconds to a minute. She never lost consciousness.

When her husband witnessed it, Corcoran was hospitalized in Providence for three days. She saw several neurologists, who could find nothing wrong.

"They all believed I was faking it. Every one of them," she said. "They—literally—accused me of wanting to get on disability because it's easy to fake."

It was suggested that she see a neurologist at Brigham and Women's in Boston. Autumn greeted Corcoran in the waiting room of the Patriot Place office and took her back to the exam room.

"She took my hand. 'Let me guess, the people that don't believe you are all males?'"

"I said, 'Yes, 100 percent of them.'"

"'That it's in your head? You're making it up?' Autumn asked. 'I'm here to tell you, whatever you're having isn't registering electronically. [But] there's a lot we don't know about the brain.'"

"'I believe you.'"

Autumn explained that even if she were not the right doctor for Corcoran, she would ensure she found the one who was. It turned out that she needed to see a specialist in movement disorders. Autumn continued to keep in touch with Corcoran, by e-mail and calls, and eventually, they learned that she had a condition called pseudo brain tumor, where the body makes too much brain and spinal fluid. The buildup put pressure on the parts of Corcoran's brain controlling her face and arm. A spinal tap—which an intern in Rhode Island originally suggested but was dismissed by the male neurologist—showed that her pressure was five times what it should have been.

Since her diagnosis, Corcoran has been seizure free.

Autumn's dedication to her patients was recognized by her colleagues. In a tribute to her in the February 2014 issue of *Continuum*, they wrote, "She had a passion for her clinical mission to bring expertise to the care of women with neurologic problems and to help them achieve both their family and medical goals. She understood that patient education was essential for excellent care, and she dedicated herself to the role of an available and supportive physician. She gave patients time, and she listened as she sought to help them understand their illnesses so they might become their own advocates."

In Dr. Lawrence Wechsler's 2013 annual report on UPMC's Department of Neurology, he referred to Autumn as "a consummate teacher of residents and medical students" who "communicated her passion for her work in every lecture." Acknowledging her dedication to patients, Wechsler called her "a shining light" in neurology.

AUTUMN WAS BORN November 30, 1971, in Baltimore.
Her parents had begun dating when Lois asked Bill for a ride home from their duck-pin bowling league, and they got married in 1964.

Seven years later, Autumn was born. She was their only child.

The family spent the first few years of Autumn's life on one side of a row house in the city; the other side belonged to Lois's sister's family, which included four children. One of the kids, Sharon, was just seventeen months older than Autumn, and the girls were best friends. Sharon and Autumn were so close that they developed their own language so their families couldn't understand them.

Sharon had her own bed in Autumn's room and spent weekend mornings with the family. Lois, who worked for the IRS, cooked breakfast while Bill, an electrician, played music from the 1950s and danced the girls around the kitchen. Autumn and Sharon often played "Best Mall," which was a carefully designed place with a medical clinic where their stuffed animals served as patients. Autumn, who always played the doctor with Sharon as her assistant, gave Cupcake, Sharon's beloved Pillsbury Doughboy, new teeth made out of white nail polish. Autumn removed the tongue from her own stuffed animal, Mousy, so that Mousy couldn't tell on whatever it was Autumn had done in front of her.

Autumn wasn't a shy child, but she wasn't terribly outgoing either. She was low-key, caring. And intelligent.

Autumn was raised in a strict home with a warm, easygoing father and a mother who was both loving and stern. Sharon considered Aunt Lois's lap one of the most comforting places on the planet.

Autumn's childhood included lots of trips to the local roller-skating rink with her dad and regular family vacations in Ocean City.

She was a good kid and didn't cause trouble for her parents.

The Kleins valued education and fretted about their daughter's safety and the idea she could be exposed to drugs. They enrolled Autumn in St. Paul's School for Girls for sixth grade. The Episcopal private school just a few miles from home would be perfect, Lois thought

—it had only about fifty girls in each grade level, and would be a safer environment than public school.

At St. Paul's, Autumn excelled, and in the seventh grade, a biology class piqued her interest in the sciences. Furthering that, her teacher's husband worked at Johns Hopkins University and took Autumn to work with him the following summer. In high school she got involved in yearbook and the drama club. She loved being on the stage. Even though Sharon went to a different high school, Autumn got her on the stage crew at St. Paul's, helping with set designs and lighting.

The two remained inseparable.

By the time Autumn began her senior year in high school, she was starting to come into her own. She was known as an exceptional student with a maturity beyond her age. She again bonded with a teacher, Bette Kenzie, who taught AP biology and was head of the upper school.

Autumn would regularly drop by her teacher's office to chat, and Kenzie used the seventeen-year-old as a sounding board for issues within the school. At graduation, Autumn gave Kenzie a clock that she cross-stitched for her, featuring a scene of children playing on the top and a red schoolhouse on the bottom. Kenzie kept it, hanging it in her dining room after she retired.

Autumn dated a boy named Tim a year ahead of her in high school. When he decided to go to Amherst College in western Massachusetts, it was important to Autumn that she be able to get into the small, prestigious, liberal arts school as well. She got early acceptance in 1989.

That fall, Autumn arrived at Amherst—a tall, terribly thin girl, with big, eighties-style curly hair.

She moved into a single room—like all the girls on the second floor of Morrow—where she became part of a group of eight on that side of the hallway that became fast friends. She lived next to a girl from Long Island named Emmy Ludwig.

During that first week in late August, the group of friends, including three guys from the floor below, sat on Memorial Hill, a beautiful, serene spot on campus overlooking the school's soccer fields. There they talked about how their lives were just beginning, that they had the world on their plate, that they could do anything they wanted.

Autumn and Emmy bonded. They both were only children of older parents. They both wished they had a sibling to turn to when their parents were acting crazily. Autumn sometimes said she felt like her parents were disconnected from her generation. Her mother's controlling nature frustrated her even as she strove constantly to live up to the standards set for her.

Although Autumn was able to attend the pricey private school that had only about eighteen hundred students, she did not have a lot of money and was enrolled in work study. Three days a week she would leave early in the morning for Valentine Dining Hall to work in the cafeteria. Her friends knew her to be much more careful with her money than they were.

Autumn knew right away that she would double major in neuroscience and women's studies. She sometimes intimidated her friends with her regimented study habits.

As the first in her family to go to college, Autumn put a lot of pressure on herself to succeed. And because of her tough class load, she had less time than some of her friends to screw around. But she also didn't mind that she might be the one to stay behind to do class work. Autumn didn't get annoyed with her friends who might be going to a party or to "Tap," a school-sponsored party each week where students of all ages were permitted to drink. Instead, she'd encourage them to have fun.

Even when she did go out, Autumn tended to sit back and observe —taking everything in.

Her friends regarded her as focused, mature, kind, and completely nonjudgmental. Although there was a fair amount of drama among those freshmen women—they called themselves "first years" to avoid the sexist term *freshmen*—Autumn always seemed to stay above it, even when she and her boyfriend, Tim, broke up.

She began taking premed classes that first year, including fundamental chemical principles, where she met Karen Kiang, her lab partner. Karen accidentally blew up their experiment, but Autumn just laughed. It cemented their close, lifelong friendship.

Autumn liked Amherst not only because of the area, but also for its history of great literature. Emily Dickinson grew up there, and Robert Frost taught there. Autumn's interest in women's studies likely came from her Aunt Carolyn, Sharon's mom, who served as the president of the League of Women Voters in Baltimore in the 1960s and worked as an activist in the streets of Baltimore.

Autumn was proudly pro-choice, considered herself to be a feminist, and was dedicated to women's rights. She was involved in campus activities like Take Back the Night and support groups for rape victims. Her devotion to women's rights prompted her friends to think about equality too.

Along with all the energy and ambition that fueled Autumn, there were other forces driving her. Her friends worried that she was anorexic. She spent a lot of time on a stationary bike in her room, and often, instead of a full meal, she would eat rice cakes with jelly on them—using a knife to noisily scrape away excess jelly.

Her friends became so concerned they got in touch with Lois to talk to her about their fear that Autumn had an eating disorder.

Lois tackled the problem head-on. She and Bill told Autumn that if she didn't start eating properly, they would make her move home. Autumn ate and stayed at Amherst.

In fact, she rarely returned to Baltimore to visit. She liked that she had moved away. Lois could see her daughter was happy to be gone, but took it in stride, as she felt that this was something lots of teenage girls felt.

In her sophomore year, Autumn was selected to be a resident counselor and moved into Pratt Hall across the small quad from Morrow. She and Tim had broken up, and Autumn began dating another Amherst student a year younger than she. Brian was in a band, and she and her friends used to watch them play at the Tea Lounge on campus.

By then, Autumn was fully engrossed in her major classes, including cell structure, organic chemistry, women and writing in Russia, and construction of gender.

In addition to working at the dining hall, Autumn baked for the student center's café. She was well known for her lemon–poppy seed muffins.

The neuroscience program that Autumn majored in at Amherst—one of the first of its kind in the country—was among the most challenging at the college. Only about a dozen students majored in it each year, and the program used a multidisciplinary approach, combining biology, physics, psychology, and math. Her professors knew her to be a dedicated, serious student, never earning below a B in any class.

During Autumn's senior year, Lois and Bill wanted to surprise their daughter for her twenty-first birthday, so they woke up early that morning to call her. Then, they hopped in their car and made the six-hour drive unannounced to meet her after classes. They tied balloons to her dorm-room door and hid in the stairwell as she arrived.

The plan worked. When they jumped out and yelled "Surprise!" Autumn, puzzled, said "But you just called me this morning."

That same year, Autumn took advantage of a program in western Massachusetts known as the Five Colleges, which allows students enrolled at five different schools, including Amherst, to take classes at any of the other colleges. Autumn did her senior thesis under Geert de Vries, an associate professor of psychology at the University of Massachusetts. Typically, only one or two students each year would take on such a project because of the time demands and difficulty of the work. At the UMass lab, Autumn, who was regarded as serious and intense, would stain samples of rat-brain sections and study them to find a specific substance that showed when the cells dictating male or female were born. She spent hours and hours sitting behind a microscope studying the slides and rarely interacted with the other students.

Although it wasn't published, her "Development of a Sex Difference in the Rat Brain" was a significant step as she began her efforts at earning an advanced degree.

When it was time to start applying for medical schools, Autumn considered Duke, the University of Rochester, and Boston University (BU). She interviewed with all three schools before picking BU. When Autumn told her parents the school she had chosen, they were unhappy. Lois thought the city was unsafe, but her daughter didn't care —she liked the idea of having such a large hospital system in Boston where she would be working.

AUTUMN GRADUATED from Amherst in 1993 and set off for her prestigious, combined MD/PhD program.

The intense workload required at least seven years—two years of medical school first, then three years of PhD work, and finally the last two years of med school, which included rotations through various medical specialties.

In her first year at BU, Autumn met and seriously dated a fellow med student from Greece—even visiting him in Cypress. She talked about moving in with him, but never did. Her friends thought he could be controlling, telling her how to dress and often draping his arm around her like he owned her.

She told Sharon about him in a letter—the same one where she noted she'd been studying for boards, was reading *Anna Karenina* for fun, and was exhausted.

"I'm off to eat and get drunk," she wrote happily.

Ultimately, Autumn broke up with him.

Autumn's friend Karen was a medical student at Yale, and drove to Autumn's place in Brookline to see her about once a month. The two studied together, gulped down heaping bowls of Cheerios, talked about boys, and shopped at Trader Joe's.

When Lois visited, she'd take Autumn frozen containers of spinach —which her daughter loved—so that she'd have it when she wanted.

All through her career at BU, Autumn chose the toughest classes and toughest rotations, always wanting to push herself to be the best. On top of that, she trained for and ran her first marathon—in three hours and forty-eight minutes—in 1997 in Vermont.

She rewarded herself, too, though, by taking her radiology rotation in Paris, where her mom visited for a week. They shopped local markets, walked the city, visited museums and parks, and ate a lot of good food—including, for Lois, mussels for the first time.

Then, during her PhD program, in 1995, Autumn went to work in the lab at the Bedford Veterans Administration (VA) Medical Center.

There, she was assigned to work under Dr. Neil Kowall, a professor of neurology and pathology. Bob Ferrante worked in the lab, as well, and his colleague asked him if he'd be willing to work with the new student. He agreed.

"I'll take her."

3

who was bob ferrante?

BOB FERRANTE WAS BORN October 21, 1948, and raised on a dead-end street in Quincy, a working-class town outside of Boston.

The family—parents and Bob's older siblings, Dianne and James—lived in a brick home with white siding on quiet Theresa Road. His father, James, worked as a pastry chef for Gillette and his mother, Jessica, was a housewife who worked part time as a decorator and seamstress, and later as a receptionist in a doctor's office.

Education was very important in the Ferrante household, as was culture and sports. Jessica, who once played violin in a symphony orchestra, encouraged her children to play, but Bob refused. He did take up the guitar, eventually playing in a number of bands in his teen years during the Beatles era. He took art lessons at the Boston Museum of Fine Arts and loved baseball. The family spent a lot of time traveling by car to visit grandparents on both sides.

Bob's uncle knew the famous Boston Red Sox left fielder Ted Williams and introduced the boy to him. Instead of wanting to emulate the future hall-of-fame slugger, Bob told Williams he wanted to be Frank Malzone, the team's third baseman. Williams's response was to just shake his head.

Bob loved that his father was a pastry chef. For the boy's ninth or tenth birthday, his dad made him a cake constructed of twenty chocolate eclairs piled high atop one another. Bob ate the entire thing by himself in just two days—not sharing with anyone.

James often worked two jobs to bring additional money into the household. The parents preached the importance of hard work to their children, and strove to give their kids a better life than they had—a lesson Bob took with him into adulthood.

After attending public schools through their early years, the Ferrante children went to private high schools, with Bob graduating from the Chauncy Hall School in 1966. He went on to earn his bachelor's degree in 1970 at the University of Bridgeport in Connecticut, as well as a master's degree in neuroscience a year later.

While in college, Bob went on a blind date with a group of friends to the beach. There he met Diane McLaughlin, who was a year older. They began dating and married in August 1971. He was twenty-two. She was twenty-three.

Bob, who had a lifelong interest in science, had strong mentors in college who encouraged him to focus on neuroscience. In the 1970s, the field was exploding, and he wanted to be a part of it. Among his interests were trying to understand clinical symptoms and matching them to areas of brain damage to identify neurological syndromes and enhanced early diagnosis and treatment.

He began his career after graduate school first as a research assistant, then as a senior research assistant, and later as a research supervisor. He focused on neuropathology and for several years worked at the Eunice Kennedy Shriver Center for Mental Retardation in Waltham, Massachusetts.

It was there that he worked for Dr. Thomas L. Kemper, a neurologist who at the time was studying both rats and monkeys. When Kemper decided to move his work to Harvard Medical School, Bob was originally supposed to go with him, but instead ended up at Massachusetts General Hospital, where he spent several years as a clinical laboratory supervisor doing research on Huntington's disease.

Diane taught second and third grade, and was intelligent, loving, and caring. The couple spent the first years of their marriage focused on each other and their careers, and in 1975 bought a large, white, two-story wood-frame colonial in Canton, Massachusetts, about twenty miles outside of Boston. Five years later, their first child, Kimberly, was born. Their son, Michael, followed three years later.

The family enjoyed spending time together, picking wild blueberries and making pies, horseback riding, playing sports, and going on vacation.

Bob had started to apply to medical school and PhD programs, but around the time Michael turned four, it was clear there were problems in the Ferrante marriage. Diane had a family history of bipolar disorder, and it began to manifest in her after their children were born. Bob insisted that they enter counseling, and they did, but to no avail. They last lived together in July 1988 and filed for divorce in Norfolk County, Massachusetts, a month later. Court records indicate that an "irretrievable breakdown of the marriage" occurred on or about September 1,

1987, which included their "different lifestyles, a breakdown in communication leading to a loss of affection."

Bob blamed the divorce on her illness, but Diane told a reporter decades later, "He wanted me barefoot, pregnant, and in the kitchen." Her husband refused to allow her to have a Tupperware party because he didn't want "strangers in the house." She said he had a temper.

As part of their divorce agreement, the couple would share joint physical and legal custody of the children. Bob was responsible for the costs of Michael's child care, clothing, and activities, while Diane bore responsibility for Kimberly's. Diane agreed to move out of the home on Kristin Lane and sold her stake in it to her ex-husband for $100,000 to be paid over three years.

The divorce paperwork included a three-page, single-spaced, itemized list of everything in the house that would go with Diane when she moved out. It included, among the 132 items, their Noritake china service for twelve, two Christmas cactus plants, their family picture, four Kleenex holders, half of the couple's cookbooks, self-help books, and six green placemats.

The divorce agreement called for the children to live with Diane from 6:00 p.m. Sunday to 8:00 a.m. Wednesday, and for Bob to have them the rest of the time, with alternating weekends. However, after the divorce, Diane mostly disappeared from the kids' lives. Bob raised them with the help of his father, who moved into the family home.

"Papa," as he was known, helped drive the children to school, cooked meals for them, had fresh baked goods ready when they got home, and devoted himself to helping his son raise his family. Bob continued to enjoy his children—drawing funny faces on their school lunch bags, coaching Michael's sports teams, and taking Kimberly to horseback-riding lessons. She loved to chase her little brother around the yard with frogs found in the backyard pond.

Daily life was kept on schedule with the help of a three-foot by four-foot corkboard Bob built and hung in the kitchen. Taking up the better part of a wall, the twelve-inch oak squares held everyone's calendars —with notes about school and activities and who needed to be where when. As a single parent, it's how Bob was able to maintain balance. He put his goals of pursuing further education on hold.

All along, Bob continued to be an ideal father, serving in the role of both parents. He coached Michael's sports teams—soccer, basketball, football, and baseball—and kept the household together with Friday night laundry and movie nights. He went to every game, despite his busy schedule.

He knew the other parents at school and participated in group service projects.

Once, in Michael's junior year at Roxbury Latin when he was quarterback of the school football team, the teen came down with mononucleosis. He was desperate to play, and Bob was anguished over his son's plight.

He knew there could be injury to his son's spleen if he were to get hit playing, but he also knew how much the game meant to Michael.

The school headmaster made the decision for them, forbidding Michael from taking the field.

It likely was the right decision—in fact, Michael went on to play football at Bowdoin College in Brunswick, Maine. At the time, Bob was working at the Bedford Veterans Administration Medical Center as a neuropsychologist and researcher. For years, he had been studying Huntington's disease, Alzheimer's, ALS, and other neurodegenerative diseases. He had published dozens of papers, both as the lead author and as a contributor, and in 1985 published his first seminal paper about Huntington's disease in the journal *Science*.

Despite not having an advanced degree, he had already established himself as highly successful in his field. After dozens more publications, Bob was encouraged by the chair of the neurology department to continue his education. He knew that the limitations on his time would prevent him from going to medical school. And so, in 1993, he enrolled in a special program at Boston University School of Medicine in neuropsychology for a PhD in behavioral neuroscience.

Because of his extensive research and work history, he completed his course work in less than a year and was often asked by his professors to help in lecture. Bob completed his dissertation, "Mitochondrial Energy Impairment as a Model for Huntington's Disease," in 1996. As part of his research, he injected the neurotoxin 3-nitropropionic acid, or 3-NP, into rats, which closely mimicked the brain damage observed in Huntington's disease.

In the acknowledgments for his dissertation, Bob thanked the colleagues he had worked with and under, and then wrote, "I am forever indebted to my family, especially my father, James Vincent Ferrante, for their unflagging support, encouragement, and assistance during these past years. Their pride is a source of great satisfaction to me."

The PhD punched Bob's ticket, allowing him to compete with his colleagues and build his own program developing scientific and medical theory. His career was on a steady upward trajectory and he became a sought-after speaker, served on a number of boards in academic and professional roles, and won dozens of grants to further his work.

He served as the principal investigator or project leader for research on creatine therapy, Huntington's disease gene mutation, and dozens of other research projects on other diseases like Parkinson's, Alzheimer's, and ALS—some funded by the National Institutes of Health, the Department of Defense, the Veterans Administration, and independent nonprofits.

His work was designed to develop drug therapies to treat neurological diseases.

"What I loved about my work was discovering something that no one had ever observed before, seeing it for the first time, and then showing it to others," Bob said. "How the meaning of that discovery impacted patients was an important component. Making discoveries that reduce human pain and suffering is the penultimate [*sic*] experience."

4 ···························
the investigation begins

AUTUMN'S BODY, WRAPPED IN a bright-blue zippered bag, arrived at the Allegheny County Medical Examiner's Office at 10:55 a.m. on Sunday, April 21, 2013. The medical examiner's investigator unloaded it from the van, placed it on a gurney, and rolled it through the loading dock and into the sprawling, nondescript building. Before putting the body in a cold room to await autopsy, the investigator paused at a large floor scale, weighed it, opened the bag to expose its contents, and generated a bar code. That code, placed on a bracelet on Autumn's left wrist, would then be matched up to the body bag and to an identification photo of her taken from an overhead camera.

The bag was then closed again, and Autumn was placed into the incoming body cooler—stored at four degrees Celsius.

She remained there for a few hours before Dr. Todd Luckasevic, the forensic pathologist on autopsy coverage that day, got to her. It had been a busy day, with three earlier patients. By the time the body was moved to the exam room at 1:45 p.m., Luckasevic had already autopsied a fifty-year-old man with a brain aneurysm, a fifty-seven-year-old man with heart disease, and a thirty-eight-year-old man with heart disease. His fellow—a physician in training—did the autopsy for a seventy-three-year-old man with blunt-force trauma to the head and neck.

When it was time to start the exam, Luckasevic and the technician working with him that day, Brittany Harmon, discussed whether to perform a full autopsy or just an external exam. Harmon argued that Autumn had been hospitalized for three days, and it was unnecessary to do an internal because she would have had CT scans and other diagnostic testing already completed at Presby. Luckasevic acknowledged that since the hospital physicians could not find a cause for Autumn's collapse, it was unlikely he would during the autopsy. Still, he told Harmon, they would do the full procedure.

"She's young," he told Harmon. "Anybody under sixty."

Autumn's body was pulled from the cooler and rolled into the exam room—a large, brightly lit space set up with four stainless-steel workstations. She was removed from the bag and photographed while Luck-asevic, wearing safety glasses, blue scrubs, a white apron, and white arm sleeves, started with his external exam. He noted the clothing she was wearing and any signs of medical intervention. Using a drawing of a person in an anatomical position with the arms and legs extended from the body, he noted and measured the distinguishing marks that he saw—bruising in Autumn's groin from the ECMO, a breathing tube still in place, a central line at her throat, and the beginnings of a small pressure sore on her buttocks. He made mention, too, of a tiny lady-bug tattoo on the inside of her right ankle.

Once the external exam was completed, Harmon collected the nec-essary fluids for testing—five gray-topped tubes of heart blood, two gray-topped tubes of femoral blood, red-topped tubes of bile and eye fluid, and a yellow-topped tube of urine. She then began her prepara-tions for the internal exam. In most morgues, it is the technician who does the work to open the body, while the pathologist does the dissec-tion of the organs as they are removed. Harmon slid Autumn's body from the gurney where she'd been lying onto the stainless-steel table. A continuous stream of water ran down the table to keep the space as clean as possible.

Because Autumn had been an organ donor, her chest and abdo-men had already been opened, so Harmon worked from there, sim-ply extending the incision to the shoulders in a Y shape. She then went through the process of removing the organs, weighing them, and pass-ing them along to Luckasevic for examination. Autumn had donated her liver and kidneys, so they were no longer there. Her heart, they found, was sitting unattached in her chest.

CORE had initially planned to take it for donation, but a technician claimed to have seen black lesions on it. They were not lesions, Luck-asevic found. They were lymph nodes from surrounding valves and lung tissue. The pathologist was frustrated at the way the heart had been removed—he was worried that evidence of a possible pulmo-nary embolism could have been lost in the sloppy cutting.

Working to the left of the body, Luckasevic set up at his dissection station. Using a large knife, ruler, scissors, scalpel, and long forceps, he examined each organ. He cut a piece from each one and stored it in a black-lidded jar. He then cut smaller sections of the heart and lungs and put them in small, rectangular cassettes about a half inch by one inch; the sections would later be preserved in wax and sliced into paper-thin segments used to make microscopic slides. The pathologist also examined the arteries and valves around Autumn's heart to ensure there was no blockage.

Luckasevic saw nothing abnormal in his examination of the organs other than a benign tumor of about five or six centimeters in her uterus. Because he saw nothing in the heart that could have caused death—and in a young, seemingly healthy woman it is often the heart—Luckasevic called CORE to ask if the organization would cover the cost to send the heart to the Jesse Edwards Heart Registry in Minnesota where a cardiac pathologist could do a more thorough evaluation. CORE agreed. Autumn's brain, too, looked fine, but again, to be sure, Luckasevic sent it out to be examined by a neuropathologist at UPMC.

With the dissection completed, the organs were placed in a red biohazard bag and returned to Autumn's chest cavity. When Harmon sewed closed the incision, the organs were left inside. Autumn was returned to the blue body bag and placed in the outgoing cooler at 3:42 p.m.

McCabe Brothers funeral home was alerted that the body could be released, and it was picked up the next day, April 22, at 2:43 p.m.

Luckasevic, who had not seen anything unusual in his examination, made notes on the autopsy report that both cause and manner of death were undetermined pending the results of the specialists' review of the heart and brain, as well as toxicology results, which likely wouldn't be completed for weeks.

Around the same time that the autopsy was under way, Martin, the emergency department doctor at Presbyterian, accessed his former patient's chart to see what, if anything, he could learn about what happened to her. He saw that a test result for cyanide had been returned to her electronic chart from Quest Diagnostics.

Martin made a mental note of it, but went back to his work.

However, as he was finishing his overnight shift, about 7:00 a.m. on Tuesday, April 23, Martin saw Farkas, who was just coming on after having the weekend off.

"Hey, I think you should take a look at this," Martin told the resident, pointing to the test result.

The cyanide in Autumn's blood measured at 3.4 milligrams per liter. A fatal level.

A few hours later, it occurred to Farkas that since the patient was dead, it was possible no one was monitoring her returning lab work.

At 1:26 p.m., he called the medical examiner's office. Farkas spoke with an investigator, who immediately relayed the test result to Luckasevic, who directed the investigator to contact the hospital and have the records faxed over.

The next step was to call McCabe Brothers funeral home to get Klein's body back for additional testing.

But it was too late.

She had already been cremated.

WHEN LUCKASEVIC LEARNED that Autumn had a high level of cyanide in her system, he was relieved because that meant he had a cause of death. The question became: How did she get it?

He immediately called the analysts in the Allegheny County crime lab to tell them to run their own cyanide test on the blood samples they had collected—once a routine test done on every autopsy, it now had to be specifically requested—and had an investigator in his office contact the Pittsburgh police.

Longtime homicide detective Jim McGee, who was acting sergeant that Tuesday, walked into the unit office about 2:30 p.m. and was handed a white scrap of paper with messages scribbled all over it. One caught his attention: "Hey, the coroner's office called. Something about a woman doctor who might have had high levels of cyanide in her. She's dead and was cremated already."

Working with his partner, Robert Provident, McGee showed him the note.

"Huh, that's interesting."

The men, who were going off-shift at 4:00 p.m., made arrangements to speak with Dr. Karl Williams, the medical examiner, the next morning. When they arrived, the detectives spoke with Luckasevic and Williams and got the rundown on Autumn's case. All they knew for sure was that she was a physician who had a high level of cyanide in her system. They didn't know if she took the poison herself, accidentally ingested it, or if someone gave it to her.

Provident and McGee, who were working other cases as well, spent that afternoon gathering as much background on Autumn and cyanide that they could. They also reached out to UPMC to make plans to interview her colleagues the next day.

In the meantime, about 3:00 p.m. on Wednesday, April 24, Alesia Smith, a toxicology analyst for the medical examiner's crime lab, prepared to run her own cyanide test. She had two whole-blood samples drawn at the hospital to choose from to run the test: one that was taken at 12:48 a.m. on April 18—just minutes after Autumn's admission to the hospital—and another that was drawn about five hours after that. Smith knew the crime lab planned to send the first tube—considered to be the most valuable specimen—to a national laboratory for forensic, quantitative testing, which would report a numerical finding as to how much cyanide was in the body. She chose, then, to test the second-most valuable specimen—the lavender-topped tube of whole blood drawn at 6:00 a.m. Wearing a lab coat, gloves, and safety glasses, Smith began by removing the 2 milliliter sample from the large walk-in refrigerator and walking it to the cyanide–carbon monoxide station in the extraction lab.

Opening a drawer in her workstation, she pulled out a Conway microdiffusion cell and lid—a little white plastic dish with three concentric rings. She set them on the cream-colored countertop and dropped in sulfuric acid, which would pull the cyanide out of the blood, and sodium hydroxide, which would act like a magnet to attract the cyanide pulled from the blood sample and trap it in the center of the Conway cell.

Then she used an electronic pipette to place a 1 milliliter sample of Autumn's blood in the middle ring with the stronger sulfuric acid. She closed the lid, checked the seal, and gently swirled the dish to mix the contents.

Smith got control samples ready, using known concentrations of cyanide, to be sure the test was working properly.

After thirty minutes, she added four drops of sodium hydrogen phosphate and two drops of chloramine T, waited three minutes, and added one drop of pyridine-barbituric acid.

Almost immediately, Autumn's sample turned purple.

"This is, wow. It's a very dark purple," Smith told her boss, who observed the color development test with her.

Purple meant positive for cyanide.

THE NEXT MORNING, McGee and Provident, along with fellow detectives Harry Lutton and Hal Bolin, headed to the UPMC hospital complex to talk to Autumn's colleagues. They visited her office in the Kaufmann Building, inquiring about her state of mind—what was her family life like? What type of work did she do? Could she have been suicidal?

What they heard quickly made them rule out suicide. Autumn's colleagues, who were happy to cooperate, described a woman who loved being a mom to her six-year-old daughter, and who was passionate about her work. Autumn was excited about several research projects she was involved with—and the coworkers said that she would never take her own life. She was also not involved in any projects involving cyanide, so it seemed that an accidental exposure was unlikely.

The detectives also learned that as soon as Martin and Farkas saw the elevated cyanide levels in Autumn's chart, the information spread through the hospital like wildfire—everyone knew.

After spending a few hours talking to Autumn's fellow doctors, the detectives met up for lunch at the nearby Panera to debrief.

They agreed it was time to talk to the husband. Should it be all four of them, Lutton wondered?

They decided Provident, a twenty-five-year veteran, and McGee, on the force for twenty-six, would handle it.

The pair made the short drive in their silver Chevy Impala to the home Autumn had shared with her husband and daughter. They were met at the front door by Bob's adult daughter, Kimberly.

"Dad, the police are here," she called over her shoulder.

Bob, dressed in a light-blue, button-down dress shirt and slacks, came out of the sunroom and led the detectives to the dining room table, where the four of them sat.

"We're here to talk to you about your wife," McGee began. "What can you tell us about what happened that night?" Bob, who was calm and cooperative, answered the detectives' questions without hesitation. He told the detectives he and Klein had been married more than ten years, that they had a daughter together, and that his wife had been trying to get pregnant again—including getting in vitro fertilization from several clinics, most recently in New Jersey. However, he noted that she stopped taking the fertility drugs a few months earlier. She was on a creatine regimen, which he provided for her—often in a sugary drink or on cinnamon toast—to help with fertility.

On the night of the collapse, he told the detectives that he greeted his wife at the back door in the kitchen, and shortly thereafter, she said she felt ill. Bob told the officers he thought it was a seizure or heart attack and that he immediately called 911. After that, Bob described calling his friend and colleague, Dr. Friedlander, to take him to the hospital, and said that he found another colleague to take care of Cianna. He recounted telling the emergency physicians about his wife's fainting spells, as well as the fertility meds she'd been taking.

"Did Autumn ever talk about killing herself?" McGee asked, prompting a gasp from Kimberly.

"Autumn once said she's glad she lives in Pittsburgh because there's a lot of bridges," Bob said.

"But she never tried to kill herself, or made any statements she actually wanted to kill herself?" McGee continued.

"No," Bob answered.

"Do you know what your wife died from?" the detective went on.

"Either a heart attack or brain aneurysm."

The two detectives glanced at each other, and Provident gave a slight nod to his partner.

"It was learned that your wife died of a fatal dose of cyanide," McGee said.

Bob gasped, covering his mouth with his hand.

"Why would she do that to herself?" he asked. "Who would do this to her?"

The detectives were surprised by Bob's reaction—particularly since everyone they'd spoken to in the hospital already knew Autumn had lethal levels of cyanide in her body.

McGee asked Bob whether his wife worked with cyanide in her research, and he said that she did not. They then asked whether he still had the medications of hers that he had taken to the hospital the night of her collapse. He had left them in his office in Scaife Hall, Bob told them.

"I'll take you to the lab and get them for you," Kimberly offered to the detectives.

Before leaving, the detectives collected two large bags of creatine from Bob in the kitchen, as well as three small glass vials with markings on them and two hairbrushes.

McGee left his business card on the dining room table.

"It's an ongoing investigation," he said. "If you have any questions, give me a call."

They then drove Kimberly to the hospital campus a few minutes away and parked at the top of the hill. As she sat in the backseat, she said to the detectives, "This is unbelievable. I can't believe this is happening."

The three of them walked through the medical school to the fifth floor of Scaife Hall, where Kimberly led them into her father's lab and office with his swipe card. The detectives waited in the entryway of the office as Kimberly retrieved a ziplock bag of Autumn's medications, as well as another bag of creatine

They returned to the car, and as they drove back to Bob's home, Kimberly said, "I've been a doctor for five years, and I wouldn't even know how to get cyanide."

A short time later, she asked, "Is my dad a suspect?"

Neither detective responded.

"Do you think my dad needs an attorney?" Kimberly then asked.

McGee glanced at Provident, who was driving.

"I don't know," McGee answered. "Do you think he needs an attorney?"

5 ·
ferrante becomes a suspect

BY THE TIME THE DETECTIVES dropped Kimberly back off at her father's home, their curiosity about whether Bob was involved in his wife's death was piqued. But they still weren't even sure if Autumn had been the victim of foul play. They set out to eliminate both accident and suicide as causes of death.

At 3:30 that afternoon, they went to Friedlander's office at UPMC. They figured that they might have to wait on UPMC's chief of neurosurgery, but the world-renowned physician knew they were coming and met with them quickly.

They spoke in Friedlander's large office. The physician, originally from Caracas, Venezuela, was guarded, only giving as much information as was necessary to answer their questions.

"We're friends," Friedlander said. "I knew Autumn. I know him."

They spent about thirty minutes questioning the doctor, who exuded confidence. He verified the information Bob had provided in their earlier interview about what happened the night of Autumn's collapse without giving them anything much new to go on. It was what they expected.

The next morning, both McGee and Provident decided to head to Bob's lab in Scaife Hall to see if he had any cyanide there. A young woman let them in.

"Is there any cyanide in the lab?" McGee asked her.

"Probably right there," she answered, pointing to a cabinet.

The woman left the detectives flipping through an alphabetized list of chemicals that was attached to the cabinet and was several pages long.

"Look, they've got cyanide here," McGee said, noting that potassium cyanide was included in the list.

A short time later, the woman returned.

"Why are you here? I don't think you should be here," she told them.

"That's fine," McGee answered. "We'll be back."

On Monday, April 29, the detectives headed to the district attorney's office on another homicide case. As they sat down with the prosecutor on that one, assistant district attorney Lisa Pellegrini, McGee filled her in on what they'd been working on.

"You're not going to believe this, but we think we have a cyanide murder," he told her.

Pellegrini, who was just about to leave for a three-day capital litigation conference in State College, told the detectives to gather all of their reports and the documents from the autopsy, and that they would get together on Friday when she returned.

The next morning, the detectives got a phone call from the head of security at the University of Pittsburgh. It had been reported to him that Bob had purchased cyanide two days before his wife's collapse.

The detectives started running down the essential questions:

- How was it acquired?
- Why did he buy it?
- Where did he buy it?
- How does the lab make those kinds of purchases?

They knew they had to get search warrants for the lab and interview the employees there.

On Wednesday, while Pellegrini was still at her conference, KDKA-TV news reporter Marty Griffin broke the story that Autumn had died from cyanide poisoning and that police were investigating. Pellegrini was livid. From her hotel, she called a number of investigators, including the lieutenant in charge of homicide, questioning who might have leaked the information on the case—and why.

"We lost any edge we would have had to go back and reinterview this guy again. We're going to scare away witnesses. What does the police department gain?" she asked.

Pellegrini also called Mike Manko, the district attorney's office spokesman, to see how they might get a handle on the information being released.

When Pellegrini returned to the office Friday morning, there was a meeting among the prosecution team and investigators. There was frustration about the media leaks, and combining that with the complexity of the investigation, it was decided that the district attorney's office would take the lead in the case. Although supervisors in the city homicide unit balked at first, they ultimately conceded. The detectives had already been instructed by their bosses that the case would require everyone's participation, and it remained that way for several weeks—with the exception of McGee, who had scheduled a trip to Key West.

During that initial meeting, the prosecutors and detectives started to formulate a plan of action and began writing the first of what would ultimately be nearly one hundred search warrants. Time was of the essence since news of the investigation had leaked, so they wanted to hit the house shared by Autumn and Bob that night.

Early that evening, a team of about ten detectives arrived at 219 Lytton Avenue. The house was empty. In no rush to knock down the door, the detectives waited, trying to call Bob several times to no avail.

Finally, they noticed that there was an air-conditioning unit in a kitchen window that could be removed for entry. The detectives tried to convince the smallest and lightest guy to go in, but Bolin didn't want anything to do with it. So another homicide detective, Tim Rush, a broad, jovial man, agreed to allow his colleagues to lift him up the four or five feet to get access to the window. He climbed on their shoulders, and two others pushed him through the open window. Everyone else then entered through the now-unlocked back door.

The team of detectives split up, with Lutton taking the basement and Provident taking the upstairs. Members of the mobile crime unit had arrived as well, and they began looking for evidence in the kitchen. Among the items listed on the search warrant was anything that could be used to transport or ingest cyanide, as well as anything that could be used to clean up the poison. Thus, the team collected mops, buckets, vacuum cleaners, cupcakes, shampoos, and hairbrushes.

Bob, who had been out with his sister and Cianna, returned home as the search was going on, meeting Provident in the kitchen. He offered to get the detective something to drink and was cordial and welcoming, even as he asked if he could call his attorney. He went out into the backyard where he called former U.S. attorney J. Alan Johnson, who was now representing him. Johnson said he would be over soon.

After Bob got off the phone, Provident joined him in the backyard. The men talked about baseball and Pittsburgh's Oakland neighborhood, and Bob talked, too, about how magnificent he thought Autumn was, and how much he loved their daughter.

"Wouldn't you agree, that's the most important thing in life—family?" he asked the detective.

He also inquired of Provident where he was from and where he went to school. Provident was a little taken aback—Bob was treating it like a social chat rather than a criminal investigation. As they stood outside, Provident began to feel his allergies kicking in and looked around for the lilac he could smell. He spotted the bush that was triggering his reaction and said, "Doc, you mind if we walk over there? That stuff's killing me."

As they moved away, Bob again asked where Provident was from.

"Why?" the detective responded.

"Because if that stuff's killing you, I'll send you some," Bob answered.

Provident found it to be a bizarre joke from the researcher whose home was being searched in conjunction with a homicide investigation. The longtime detective noted that everything Bob was saying was calculated—like a chess match, where the moves are thought out ahead of time, if for no other reason than wanting to stay in control.

A few minutes later, Bob's attorney and a young associate arrived. Johnson told Provident that Bob had already turned over his and Autumn's cell phones as well as their computers to him, and that he planned to have them mirrored for review and would turn them over to homicide detectives the next day.

Provident called Pellegrini to tell her.

"You tell him he will turn those over to city homicide no later than ten o'clock or we'll execute a search warrant," she responded.

At one point during the search, Lutton asked Bob if he could open a safe kept in the basement. He did, and they found about $35,000 inside. Bob called it his "in case" money.

They closed the safe and left the cash there.

When they were done with the search, Lutton sat at the dining room table and started making an inventory of the items being seized. Bob said, "Are you taking all my vacuum cleaners? I just bought that one."

"We're taking it," Provident answered.

After about two hours at the house, the detectives wrapped up and got ready to leave. By that time, the media were camped out all along the street with cameras trained on the house. Again, information had been leaked—again—further angering the prosecuting attorneys.

The next day, a Saturday, search teams were sent out again. Two detectives went to Autumn's office, another was sent to Bob's office at the Veterans Administration, and Provident and Lutton went to Bob's lab in Scaife Hall.

When they arrived, the two men went first to Bob's office, a space with cream-colored walls on three sides and an accent wall of light blue behind his desk. It also included a large whiteboard with research notes written on it and a small table and two chairs. Decorations included a few family photographs on cherrywood bookshelves and on his desk, a bat enclosed in a case under a picture of star Yankees first baseman Lou Gehrig, and a couple of human skulls.

As they entered, Lutton sat down in Bob's desk chair while Provident looked around.

"Hey," Lutton said to his partner. "Look at this."

Sitting on top of a book in the middle of Bob's desk was a receipt, dated April 15, 2013, for overnight delivery. The total cost, paid for by a credit card in the name of a lab administrator, was $163.94.

It was for one bottle of potassium cyanide.

As the detectives continued their search, they were directed by a lab employee to a cardboard box containing a 250-gram bottle of potassium cyanide. Its safety seal had been broken, and it was no longer in the original packaging like it had been when the product arrived on April 16. It also had been moved from the place Bob had told his research associate, Dr. Jinho Kim, to store it.

With gloved hands, the detectives took the bottle of poison and delivered it to the county crime lab. They also seized a number of computers, glass vials, and containers of creatine, as well as a safe that was under Bob's desk.

THE DETECTIVES WERE READY to make an arrest. But Pellegrini and deputy district attorney Lawrence Claus, who oversaw the homicide unit, urged them to take a step back. Even though they had compelling circumstantial evidence against Autumn's husband, the prosecutors knew that if they moved forward too quickly, they could damage their case. Pellegrini and Claus wanted to make sure detectives ruled out accidental death or suicide before filing any charges. They knew it was going to be a high-profile case and wanted to ensure everything was done right. They also knew that once criminal charges were filed, they would only have a year under Pennsylvania's speedy trial rules to get the case to trial. Instead of losing that time while they still investigated, the prosecutors thought they could continue their search for information before making an arrest.

They also wanted to find a motive. Even though it is not an element of the crime, Pellegrini knew it was human nature to want to understand: Why did he do it?

To help figure that out, they pulled in detectives from within the DA's office who had expertise in financial records and computer and Internet investigations to assist.

Almost immediately, the district attorney's office's Detective Lyle Graber, a retired Pennsylvania state trooper, began gathering information to obtain search warrants to get access to the data contained on the phones and in the computers. To put together probable cause, Graber reasoned that messages on the phones and in e-mails could show planning of the possible crime as well as Autumn's mind-set.

The team of prosecutors and detectives set up what they referred to as their "war room" in Claus's office on the third-floor DA's office in the courthouse. They gathered around a long, cherrywood table for meetings almost daily, surrounded by foam boards with images of Autumn taken from hospital surveillance attached to them with binder clips.

It was there that the prosecution team and detectives listened to the 911 call for the first time—and heard the guttural moans from Autumn as she struggled to breathe on her kitchen floor.

ON MAY 10, Lois and Bill Klein held a memorial service for their daughter at Grace United Methodist Church on North Charles Street in Baltimore.

Titled "A Service of Celebration and Remembrance for the Life of Autumn Marie Klein, M.D., Ph.D.," the program featured a large photograph of Autumn with her hair pulled back and a smile on her face. The service began with an organ selection by Brahms and a number of hymns prior to the opening prayer. Autumn's cousin and best friend, Sharon, read Psalm 23, before a duet of "Amazing Grace" and another reading from Isaiah.

Autumn's close friends, Ellen Bubrick, with whom she worked in Boston, and Karen Kiang, with whom she'd gone to Amherst, spoke to the crowd gathered in the church.

Ellen described meeting Autumn ten years earlier while they were residents together in Boston. "She was all the things I wanted to be:

poised, articulate, successful, resolute, brilliant, beautiful, compassionate, loyal, funny, kind. She was the best friend you could ask for. The kind of friend you could tell the most personal things, things you're afraid of, things you're ashamed of, things that make us human. And you could tell her knowing that she would treat you with loving kindness, and that she wanted to love and support you."

Ellen praised Autumn for always making time for her friends despite a terribly busy schedule. She recalled a "semi-frantic" voice mail that Autumn once left her about attending a bris for her friend's son. She asked Ellen a number of questions about the Jewish circumcision ceremony. "She said, 'Ellen, I need a Jewish consult, stat! . . . Gift or no gift? . . . And what do I wear? . . . Can I just sit in a corner and not look? Call me,'" remembered Ellen.

"It's not just in her work that she left this Earth a better place, though. It is in all of the lives that she touched. She lives on in her beautiful daughter Cianna, in her family, in all of us. To Bob, she loved you dearly, and cherished the family you built together. To Mr. and Mrs. Klein, you must've been so incredibly proud of her, as you should be. And I am so personally grateful, for the gift of having such a wonderful friend in my life. May you be comforted in your memories of her, and in knowing how much good she did in this world. And to Cianna, please always know how much she absolutely loved mothering you. She marveled at every moment watching you grow, always giving us proud, loving updates of every milestone, from going on the potty for the first time all the way to your first manicure just a few months ago. You were the light of her life, and you brought her great happiness and joy."

Ellen recounted her own personal story about the death of her mother, not being able to say good-bye to her, and her fear that her mom didn't know how much she cared for her.

"In her very practical, problem-solving, never fear kind of way, Autumn said, 'Ellen . . . give me a break. Of course she knew you loved her. You loved her and she loved you, that's how it works.' She said, 'She knew you loved her, even if you didn't say it that day.' She offered me that forgiveness, that redemption, that peace. So I pass Autumn's own wise words onto you now. She loved all of you, and she knew you loved her, even if we didn't say it that day. Autumn, may you rest in peace, dear friend. You will always be remembered."

Karen described her first meeting with Autumn—the blown-up chemistry experiment—and their relationship since then.

"As she did then, [until her death] she worked tirelessly, and diligently. She cared for patients in the hospital and clinic during the day, and worked on her research (the grant writing, the book chapters) late into the night. One of the most amazing things about Autumn was that, unlike so many others, she had the confidence from early on to know what she wanted to do and which path she wanted to take. She'd been labeled by her mentors as 'a pioneer in the field' and 'a rising star.' Even in the male-dominated world of medicine, she continued to break the glass ceiling.

"I don't need to go through all of her accomplishments, but the other major point is that she was so humble about them that most of us, including me, are hearing just the half of them now."

Karen then read to those gathered the tributes left on Autumn's memorial page—from patients, colleagues, and students in Pittsburgh and Boston.

Her patients, she said, considered Autumn to be a friend. Her colleagues praised her as warm, energetic, and enthusiastic. Her students remembered her passion and intensity.

"Lastly, and most importantly, she loved and lived for her family," Karen said. "This was apparent in so many ways. Lois and Bill, I hope you know how much she loved you, even if she didn't always show it. Sharon, you were her twin. Bob, you were her rock and best friend. She loved and admired you so much and, like the rest of her life, she knew exactly who was right for her from the very beginning.

"Cianna, you brought your mom such immense joy. In the past few years, the challenge that she and I talked about most frequently was juggling between doctoring and mommyhood. But she always knew which was her priority."

Even though both Ellen and Karen specifically addressed Bob and Cianna in their eulogies, neither of them heard it. They weren't there, despite Bob's telling Lois that they would be. His attorney told him to stay away.

Two Pittsburgh homicide detectives attended the memorial to talk with Autumn's family and friends and gather some background, but they didn't formally talk to Ellen there. She had contacted them early on in their investigation to make sure they knew that there was no way

Autumn would have taken her own life. McGee and Provident scheduled interviews with her and several others at Brigham and Women's Hospital and drove to Boston the week of May 20.

It was there that they learned in even greater detail that Autumn's career was on the rise, and that her research involved working with patients—not with cyanide. She also would never leave her daughter, Ellen told them, and took especially good care of herself out of fear that her much older husband might die, leaving her alone to care for Cianna.

Dr. Thomas McElrath, with whom Autumn had been a close friend and colleague, told the investigators that Autumn was one of the five friends a person would keep in his or her life forever. He described the work the two of them did together and told them about a conference they attended in San Francisco in February 2013.

One night during the trip, McElrath and Autumn were out to dinner when she said her husband sent her a text message saying he was coming to San Francisco. She told McElrath that Bob was not being romantic, but was trying to control her. Autumn said that night that she was planning to leave her husband.

McElrath also shared with the detectives the text messages he had exchanged with Autumn after that. She had been planning to attend a conference in Boston in May and was going to stay at his house. On April 13 at 1:43 p.m., Autumn sent McElrath a message reading, "Change of plans. Husband is coming to Boston. Told me 'to keep me out of trouble.'" McElrath replied, "Oh, dear. Did not know you were in trouble." Autumn wrote back, "I feel like I have been for a while now."

The text messages exchanged with McElrath were enough to give the detectives probable cause to seek search warrants to go through the data contained in her phone.

The morning of May 28, Detective Jackelyn Weibel, with the DA's office, and Pellegrini obtained a sealed search warrant from Common Pleas Judge David R. Cashman to conduct a search for financial records belonging to both Autumn and Bob at their home. Weibel, along with two other detectives from the DA's office, Provident, Lutton, and McGee served the warrant about one thirty that afternoon.

When they arrived, they knocked on the door, announcing they had a warrant. Kimberly answered and called to her father in the back of the house. Weibel explained that they were there to look for financial information, to which Bob responded, "Why are you searching for that?"

Weibel didn't answer, but asked him if he could point them to the location in the house where the couple kept those types of records. He directed them to what he called "the office" upstairs. He and the family dog went outside in the backyard, while Kimberly stayed in the house.

Autumn had a work space on the left side of the large room, and Bob's desk was on the other. The detectives gathered about three or four boxes worth of documents, including income tax returns, bank statements, life insurance policies, and anything else they thought might be able to show a possible motive in the case. Behind Autumn's desk, there was a table, and beneath that, Weibel found a shredder perched on top of a trash can. The detectives discussed whether to take the contents.

"When you do a search warrant, you only get one shot at what's in the house," Detective Keith Andrews said. "If it fits with the warrant, you take it."

After quickly glancing through some of the shredding—it was a straight-cut shredder and not the cross-cut kind—Weibel saw numbers on some of the pages, which could be indicative of financial documents. They agreed to take the materials and dumped them into a single banker's box.

The detectives moved on and searched the bedrooms and spare rooms, and also found safety deposit box keys on the dining room table. They also returned to the safe that the city detectives had seen in the basement during the earlier search.

Lutton said to Bob, "We want to go down and look in your safe."

Bob used the key and opened it for them, and it was completely empty. The $35,000 in cash that had been there during the search earlier in the month was gone.

Lutton asked three or four times, "Where'd the money go?"

Bob never answered, instead telling the detectives that he'd called his attorney and would not be answering any questions. Although Weibel was leading the search for the team, Bob did not address her, instead choosing to talk to the male detectives. After about two hours, the investigators left with five boxes of materials that had been seized, leaving Bob a two-page inventory of everything they'd taken.

The detectives loaded the boxes in their cars and headed back to the investigations office. Weibel started painstakingly going through each of the documents they took, while the shredded materials got tucked underneath her desk, where they remained for several weeks. Using the documents she obtained, Weibel was able to determine that the couple kept their money separate from one another. Autumn primarily used hers to take care of Cianna and her expenses, while Bob sent a lot of his money to his adult children. Autumn used her own money, too, to pay for all of her fertility treatments, which were costly. The couple held a joint account that they used to pay their household expenses.

Using the documents she'd gathered, Weibel then set out to obtain search warrants for the couple's bank and credit accounts and started tracking Bob's credit card statements. She also put everything into a spreadsheet to analyze. Her investigation revealed nothing unusual regarding any life insurance policies or their finances. Bob had accounts totaling some $2.5 million, and it did not appear that the couple was having any financial difficulty.

I N THE WEEKS AFTER Autumn's death, Bob's family returned to their homes, leaving him by himself with Cianna. Seeing that her father was struggling, Kimberly returned to Pittsburgh, offering to quit her fellowship to help her dad. But he insisted against it.

Bob spent his time trying to care for Cianna and create some sense of normalcy for her. However, as he became aware that he was a suspect, it became difficult to do. Cianna was being harassed by fellow students in her kindergarten class, and he felt as though he had become a pariah in his community.

The experience was surreal. He learned from a lawyer whose brother was a detective that investigators first suspected he killed Autumn over money or not wanting to have another child. But, for Bob, both of those ideas seemed ludicrous. He was the one who had the financial means in the relationship, and they were still actively trying to have another baby.

Although the accusations shook him, he and his family believed that he ultimately would be cleared.

As the weeks wore on, the ever-present media trucks parked outside his home frustrated him. It became clear to Bob that he should not remain in Pittsburgh. He was already on leave from his positions with Pitt and the VA, and Cianna was nearing the end of her school year.

He spoke, too, with his new lawyer, William Difenderfer, who agreed that getting away from the intense attention was a good idea.

Bob decided that he and Cianna would join Kimberly in California.

They stayed there for almost a month. Still in talks with his legal team, Bob was starting to feel relief that an arrest was unlikely. He knew that he did not want to remain in Pittsburgh, and he'd already planned to retire. He debated with his family whether to stay in California with Kimberly or move to St. Augustine, Florida, where Bob's sister lived. They decided on Florida and headed there in late June.

Bob enrolled Cianna in a well-known public school and found her a pediatrician and a dentist. He signed her up for art and dance classes, and the young girl began to make new friends.

With each passing week, Bob and his lawyers thought there was less of a chance of arrest.

I N EARLY JULY, as the investigation was continuing, Weibel pulled out the box of shredding and gave it to four interns who were working in the office that summer. She asked them to see what they could do with it and set up work space in the large grand jury room. They dumped the box on a random table and set to work. At first, they separated strips of paper with numbers on them from the ones with words. Weibel also suggested that they look for specific types of paper that might stand out.

The interns found cuttings from a heavy yellow bond paper. Using strips of double-sided Scotch tape on the table, two of the interns and Weibel started to line up the strips. About ten minutes into the process, they realized that what they'd found was a letter—with words and a date. It was addressed to Kimberly, Michael, Cianna, and Bob's sister, Dianne. Weibel wondered if it was going to be a confession, but it was not. It was, instead, a good-bye letter.

My Dearest Dianne, Kimberly, Michael and Cianna
Words cannot express my deep and undying love for each and every one of you for oh so many reasons. You have all been my rock for many years, my reason for living. The memories I have had with each of you and as a family together would carry multiple lifetimes

for any person. I have been very fortunate in having each of you in my life. I want you to remember those times and keep them close to your heart and in your mind, not the horrific and inexplicable events that have happened over the past three weeks. This experience has taken an incredible toll on me, one that I can no longer burden. While I remain steadfastly adamant that I did not take Autumn's life, I no longer have the strength to carry the weight of losing her. Someone who shared all the pleasantries and meaningful events, especially with Cianna, with the added suspicion that I would be the cause. It has been too great a weight for me to carry. I feel as a pariah in my community, even though there are some very special people around me that have my greatest interest at heart. Kim and Mike, I had that strength for you but these are very — are a very different set of circumstances. Please forgive my weakness. Please all of you care for Cianna. I will miss many of the most important events of her life. Let her know how deeply I love her and how important it is for her to belong to this family and that I will be with her in spirit forever. Provide for her the roots and a fertile growing environment so that she may succeed in whatever her endeavors are, despite the loss of both her mom and dad. Be consistent in your love for her and how you interact with her. That will bring her comfort. Lastly, I will miss each and every one of you. Dianne, you and I growing old together and laughing at our experiences. Kim and Mike, your successes in life and your future families. Just being together with all of you and celebrating life. Please keep working hard, as well as not forgetting to enjoy the successes, even the small ones. Sometimes we forget to celebrate the simple things. Bless each of you for your being in my life. I am so sorry for not physically remaining in your lives. I'm with Autumn.   *Love, Dad, "Robby."*

Weibel immediately called Claus to tell him what they'd found. He couldn't believe it.

"Are there more?"

Weibel wasn't sure, so she asked the interns to get back at it. Three of them spent the next three tedious weeks reconstructing a total of ten letters—many of them just copies of each other—ultimately finding letters written by Bob to each of this three children and his sister. Some were signed, some were not.

The interns found every piece of every letter.

Pellegrini was thrilled.

"Holy shit! Now I know he did it. There's case law on it—consciousness of guilt."

The prosecutor also thought that the letters were a ploy—emotional manipulation.

"What a coward. You were brave enough to kill her but couldn't kill yourself?"

As the month of July entered its fourth week, the prosecution team was almost ready to file charges. Dr. Luckasevic, who'd performed the autopsy, had already changed the manner of death from "pending" to "homicide." Pellegrini and Claus were confident that they'd ruled out accidental death and suicide. The only thing left was to get the arrest warrant.

Provident and McGee and Graber and Weibel spent days drafting the affidavit of probable cause—a quirky document that is part official form, part stark presentation of the details of the crime, and part narrative of the investigation. Then the prosecuting attorneys spent even more time editing and redrafting it.

They knew it was a circumstantial case—although a strong one—and so they wanted the affidavit to be as thorough as it could be. That meant they needed to include the details of the night of Autumn's collapse and Ferrante's lab work with cyanide. But they also wanted to incorporate evidence of text messages and e-mails, too—what they believed was his motive.

Although Bob had agreed to turn over his passport through his new attorney, investigators knew he'd been traveling domestically because they'd been tracking his credit card purchases.

Because he was in Florida and had access to a lot of money, Pellegrini worried about his potential to flee the country—or worse, harm Cianna. Difenderfer had asked the prosecutors to alert him if an arrest was imminent so that he could turn his client in. But neither Pellegrini nor Claus would agree to that. It was a homicide, and the defendant didn't get to dictate the terms of arrest.

About 4:00 p.m. on July 24, Pellegrini went to see Judge Cashman again. This time it was to have him sign and seal the arrest warrant.

6 · · · · · · · · · · · ·
life in boston

FOR THOSE WHO KNEW BOB as a dedicated father and talented re-searcher, the idea that he was consulting with lawyers and on the verge of criminal charges for allegedly harming his wife was ludicrous.

He had first met Autumn in the fall of 1995 when he agreed to take her on as a new student in his Bedford VA lab. Autumn, who was in the middle of her MD/PhD program, walked in three weeks late—with a pink stripe in her bright blonde hair and holes in the knees of her jeans.

"What have we gotten ourselves into?" Bob asked himself.

But, he'd later concede, first impressions can be wrong—and his was. He immediately recognized Autumn's dedication to her field and the hard work she put in.

The two developed a close friendship. As time wore on, she told those close to her, including her friend Karen, that she liked him. He had gone from mentor to friend to romantic interest.

Karen questioned Autumn about the circumstances—the guy was twenty-three years older than her, he was a supervisor in the lab.

"Are you sure?" she asked, more than once.

And Autumn always said yes: "He's so attractive and so smart."

Autumn was fully aware of the power dynamic between the two of them, but she felt comfortable in the role of star student and intellectual partner. Bob challenged her, and he had the kind of successful career she wanted for herself.

Autumn knew all about Bob's life—that he raised two children alone—and respected him all the more because of it.

She befriended his kids, taking Kimberly on a tour of Amherst when the teen was looking for colleges and helping to serve as a kind of mentor for her when she, too, chose to major in neuroscience at the school.

Autumn and Bob didn't begin dating until years after they'd met, and by the time she completed her dissertation in 1998, "Beta Amyloid Injections Cause Cortical Injury and Oxidative Damage in the Mouse Cerebral Cortex," they were involved.

"First and foremost, I would like to thank my parents for their enormous support and encouragement and for possessing the stamina to have a child in a mudphud program," Autumn wrote in her acknowledgments. "I would not be where I am today if it were not for you both, and I am forever indebted to you. I only hope that one day I will become as giving, loving and selfless as you both have been."

She went on to thank Dr. Kowall for allowing her to work in his lab and Karen for being a great friend and wonderful human being, and then she acknowledged Bob.

"I would also like to thank Dr. Robert J. Ferrante—this much."

She later told Bob she loved him from the very first day.

To Bob and Autumn, there was no age difference—Autumn was old for her age, and Bob was young for his. She called them "trendsetters" and often said she knew she could not be with someone her own age because they would have been too competitive and selfish in their careers. With Bob, neither was a threat to the other.

Throughout their courtship, they enjoyed hiking and biking: they embarked on an eight-day trip through the Loire Valley to Mont Saint-Michel in Brittany, France, biking more than one hundred miles. They took dance lessons together—including the sensuous South American dances, like the samba. They often drove to their favorite restaurant in Providence, Rhode Island, to savor salad, crème brûlée, and Alsace wine before going to WaterFire, where they enjoyed bonfires on the city's three rivers and the open-air dancing stages.

Bob and Autumn cooked together, too. He often prepared her favorite dish of homemade pasta in a Bolognese sauce with a rich Burgundy wine, and for himself, made-from-scratch pizza—with fig and prosciutto. It would take days to prepare, but he considered cooking to be a labor of love—a way to share with family.

Bob especially loved Autumn's spontaneity and vim and vigor. She would call him out of the blue with plans she'd made for them. "Listen, I have two tickets to the ball game. Red Sox versus Yankees. Tonight. We're going. Meet me there."

"It was great, unexpected and just wonderful."

As Autumn's relationship with Bob evolved, she and Sharon laughed at a childhood joke that might be fulfilled. As kids, they always said they wanted to be old maids together, running a bed and breakfast while Autumn sold cross-stitch. Now, with Autumn contemplating spending her life with a man twenty-three years her senior, and with

Sharon already married to a man seventeen years older than she, the prospect of the two women growing old together could still come true. They got a kick out of that.

Sharon was able to help Autumn through the early hurdles of the relationship. They discussed Bob's two children—Sharon's husband had three from his first marriage—and how to acclimate to the family. Autumn saw how Bob was with his kids—serving as both mother and father. She told Sharon that he spoiled them, and she thought he was overcompensating for their mom leaving.

"You go in delicately, not trying to be a mother," Sharon advised her. "You be you and let them come around when they're ready."

After Bob and Autumn got engaged, she moved in with him, the kids, and Papa, whom she adored. Papa taught her how to make eclairs and biscotti, and she helped in his medical care.

They lived together for a year before the wedding, in the family home that Bob had bought with his first wife. Autumn had her own room.

Leslie Hand, a close friend of Autumn's from Amherst, and her boyfriend visited Autumn and Bob during that time, staying at the house with them. Bob was the expert on "Boston Italian" cooking, and when the couples ate out one evening, he treated everyone to a discourse on the wine, menu, and cuisine. He seemed much older to Leslie and always gave the impression of being in the professor role.

As the wedding date grew near, Leslie asked her friend about their registry.

"Autumn, don't you want your own dishes?" Leslie asked.

"Bob is right. He has perfectly fine dishes from his first marriage. We'll just use those," Autumn said.

ON FRIDAY, MAY 18, 2001, Bob and Autumn married in a small, candle-lit ceremony at the Old North Church in Boston.

Lois suggested the historic Episcopal church founded in 1722 because it was neutral ground for both of them—Bob was Catholic and Autumn was Methodist.

Autumn wore a fitted, straight gown with elegant beadwork, her hair swept up with a long veil, and Bob wore a traditional black tuxedo. She searched Boston high and low for a bouquet of sweet peas because that was Bob's nickname for her.

Sharon, who hand-quilted a runner for the couple with their names embroidered on it with sweet peas and a ladybug, served as matron of honor and Michael, who was then eighteen, stood as his father's best man. About fifty close friends and relatives attended the ceremony and then headed to a small Italian restaurant nearby for the reception. They had a live band and gave out as favors a customized CD, called "Love across Generations," featuring songs from Diana Krall, Sam Cooke, Billy Joel, Dean Martin, Perry Como, Barry White, Celine Dion, and Savage Garden.

Among their guests was the Reverend Dr. F. Washington Jarvis, the headmaster at Michael's school, who gave the couple a piece of his grandmother's china as a wedding gift. Each year afterward, Bob sent Jarvis a Christmas card with a picture of the piece placed in a different setting. Jarvis was moved by the thoughtfulness and the steadfast devotion Bob showed in taking the trouble each year to mark the gift and its importance to him.

Bob and Autumn waited until all their guests had left before the two of them climbed into the back of a limousine for a ninety-minute drive to Kennebunkport, Maine. There, they checked into the White Barn Inn, a luxury resort where they spent the weekend.

Although Autumn's family and friends had reservations about her marrying a man so much older than she was, none of them ever interfered. Lois believed that she had no right to tell her daughter whom she should or should not love. She thought Bob was a decent man.

Everyone knew that part of Autumn's attraction to Bob was his intellect. Sharon said the pair "matched brain pans." She thought that was what Autumn needed.

Autumn loved her husband's intelligence, his maturity, his success in his field, and his station in life. To him, her drive to understand medicine was infectious. He encouraged her in her work, knowing what it would take to become a successful physician and researcher. He didn't object to her working an eighty- or one-hundred-hour week—in fact, he was completely supportive of her drive and the work she did to advance her career.

Two days after they married, on a Sunday afternoon, Autumn graduated magna cum laude from Boston University with her MD and PhD.

Bob presented her with her diploma.

After that, Autumn began her one-year internship at Brown University, about thirty-five minutes from their Canton home, and later went on to do her neurology residency at Partners—a program combining the hospitals of Harvard Medical School, Brigham and Women's, and Massachusetts General—where she became chief resident in 2004.

She rewarded herself for all her hard work with a powder-blue BMW z3 convertible. And even as she built her career, she continued to stay active at Amherst as well, serving as an alumni mentor through the career center for years and returning to guest-lecture in the neuroscience program.

Some in her family thought Autumn would pick neurosurgery as her specialty. But she didn't.

"It's not challenging enough," Autumn told Sharon on the phone one day. She chose neurology because she wanted to be the one to make the diagnoses. She wanted to be the one to say what needed to be done by the surgeon. Autumn loved the idea of solving the puzzle, and she and Bob would spend their evenings together talking about patients and symptoms and possible diagnoses—helping each other learn. There wasn't a day that went by that the couple didn't discuss their work. Once, as they stopped at the Hoover Dam on the way to hike the Grand Canyon, Bob spotted a woman and told Autumn his diagnosis of her from fifty yards away. Later, Autumn ran into the woman in a restroom and struck up a conversation with her. Bob had been right.

Autumn ultimately chose to specialize even further, narrowing her field to women's neurology, a passion that began during her time at Amherst. She struck up a friendship with a visiting professor, Dr. Karen Roos, who was editor in chief of the journal *Seminars in Neurology*, which was based at the Indiana University School of Medicine. Roos instantly liked Autumn, who was completely engaged and was genuinely interested in whatever person she talked to. Everyone felt the same, including patients. There was no negativity in her, it seemed, and everyone found her easy to love.

When Enia Alberto, who had epilepsy, got pregnant at age thirty-two, her doctor told her she should terminate the pregnancy because her seizure medications would harm the baby. Six other physicians she spoke to advised the same.

By the time she went to see Autumn, Alberto was in her second month of pregnancy. By that point, she was having grand mal seizures every other day. Everyone was telling her not to keep the baby.

But Autumn was different.

"Women who have seizures deserve to be mothers like everyone else," Autumn told her. She promised to walk through the journey with Alberto and do her best to help her.

When Alberto said that she felt like she was alone against the world, Autumn wouldn't hear it. "Hey, I'm here. You're not alone," she'd say.

Autumn kept track of Alberto's meds and adjusted the levels regularly, checked up on her obstetrics visits and her ultrasounds, and saw her every month. Autumn believed Alberto could have the baby, and made her believe it, too.

Although Alberto's seizures continued throughout the first trimester, they stopped in the second. And Alberto gave birth to a perfectly healthy baby boy.

The day after Ryan was born at Brigham and Women's, Autumn visited them at the hospital. The women looked at the baby, and at each other.

"Look at him. He's here. He's beautiful," Autumn said.

IN THE SPRING OF 2006, Bob was slated to give two lectures in Switzerland, and Autumn joined him. They visited Zurich and Lausanne, and one evening during the trip enjoyed a romantic alfresco dinner along the shores of Lake Geneva. Autumn excused herself from the table and returned a few minutes later with a wide smile. She took Bob's hands and kissed him.

"I just tested positive," she said. "We are having a baby."

The next several months were full of happiness and nervous anticipation. Bob was relaxed and excited, singing to Autumn's pregnant belly every night and feeling the baby move around inside.

Although Autumn had always believed that women didn't need to have children to feel complete, by the time she was in her mid-thirties, she knew she wanted to have a baby. She gave birth to Cianna Sophia Marie Ferrante in January 2007.

Autumn was in love with motherhood, particularly taking pleasure in sharing with her close friend Karen the joys and frustrations she experienced during Cianna's early years when she learned Karen was pregnant.

"You are going to have so much fun with this. Work will seem like the most boring thing in your life," Autumn wrote in an e-mail to her friend, who was living in Melbourne, Australia. In another, she said of Cianna, "She is so cute, I just want to hug her and kiss her all the time."

She talked about the time it took to bond with Cianna, too.

"Everyone talks about the 'bonding' like you instantly feel like you should be totally gaga over this little thing—well, you are, I was, but whether it is the hormones or everything else going on, my mommy love didn't fully kick in for a few months. It is kind of hard to explain, I loved Cianna, but not like I do now."

In another message from December 7, 2009, Autumn wrote, "I declined going to a meeting today on a topic I found very interesting, only to sit home and happily play with Play-Doh and make hot chocolate after traipsing in the snow. Cianna loves making Play-Doh spaghetti and feeding us all."

But she also wrote about the difficulty in trying to balance work and family.

"Bob is always annoyed [because] he thinks I work too much and get home too late and don't spend enough time with the baby, but hey, when she is sick or wants someone, she comes to me, so I must be present enough."

That topic was a recurring one for Autumn.

She often asked Roos how she was able to balance her professional life with her two daughters. Roos told her she'd try to do her work with her daughters, and so Autumn began taking Cianna with her to the office.

The little girl would play on the floor or color while Autumn wrote and edited. In one e-mail to Karen, she wrote: "I thought I was a total freak because I was not THAT into her when she was born, but one day it just clicked and now I want to have a ton, it is silly. I never thought of myself as too emotional, in fact, as a resident, I prided myself on being able to keep my emotions under complete control, but now, as a mom, I am like a total nut sometimes. Cici, as we speak, is coloring my *Epilepsia* journal in technicolor and I find it the most adorable thing in the entire world. WEIRD—yes, years ago, who woulda thought?!"

Although Bob, who was fifty-eight when Cianna was born, had been hesitant to have another child, he took to fatherhood the second time around enthusiastically. The couple balanced their jobs so that

Bob was home with Cianna in the afternoons after day care and into the evening for dinner and bath time, while Autumn got her off and ready in the mornings.

When Autumn would return home for dinner, Bob often had music playing as he cooked, and she would join him, dancing around their open floor plan with Cianna sandwiched between them like peanut butter.

Cianna became best friends with the little girl who lived across the street, Jessica, who was three weeks older.

The girls played outside together constantly, and Bob would join in the fun, playing tag and hide and seek, pushing them on the swings, and taking hundreds of photographs of them and their friends. It was clear that he very much enjoyed spending time with Cianna, although on weekends, the little girl became Autumn's responsibility almost exclusively.

DESPITE HER HAPPINESS with motherhood, there were frustrations in Autumn's life.

She hated that she had to spend as much as three hours of her day commuting from their home in Canton to work because of the notoriously snarled traffic around Boston.

Still, she made the most of it by using her drive home to first take care of patient calls and then call Sharon to chat. Those calls would be regularly interrupted two and three times by Bob, calling Autumn to check to see where she was.

"Five minutes farther down the road than last time," she'd tell him. The repeated calls from Bob frustrated Sharon. She asked Autumn pointedly why he kept calling.

"He just wants to know where I am," Autumn would answer.

Sharon told her that Bob was trying to exert power and control over his wife—that it was a form of domestic abuse.

But Autumn brushed it off. It was petty, and she wanted to stay focused on the big picture.

When Sharon and Jeff would visit the couple in Boston, they never felt completely at ease with Bob.

Even though Bob and Autumn had been together since the late 1990s, he never went with Autumn back home to Baltimore—not even for Sharon's mom's funeral. He didn't go with Autumn, either, when she visited Sharon and Jeff in Denver or, later, Seattle, even for Sharon's wedding, with Autumn as the maid of honor.

Sharon saw Bob as someone who always wanted to be in control. He was never wrong. You couldn't challenge him, and if you did, he was determined to win.

Lois and Bill often complained that Bob always had his nose in his computer and would not interact with them when they'd visit—four to five times each year.

Autumn would remark, too, about other things Bob did that annoyed her, including that he was an obsessive housekeeper.

"I can't even put my teacup down without him coming up behind me and telling me where it belonged," Autumn said.

BY AUGUST 2008, AUTUMN was ready to have another child, but Bob wanted to wait. He had been hesitant to have Cianna and got frustrated when people would ask if he was the girl's grandfather. However, he ultimately agreed to the idea, and in January 2010, they began to try naturally. After a year with no success, the couple turned to fertility specialists and in vitro fertilization (IVF).

In mid-2010, Autumn and Bob were contemplating a move to Pittsburgh. The University of Pittsburgh Medical Center wanted Autumn to join the neurology practice and start a women's program, and the University of Pittsburgh wanted Bob to move his research lab in Boston to Scaife Hall.

The idea of moving to Pittsburgh, where there would be less backbiting among her colleagues, more money, and a significantly shorter commute, appealed to Autumn.

She also knew that Bob would likely retire within a few years, and once that happened, she would be the sole breadwinner of the family. A bigger salary in a city with a lower cost of living was enticing.

On January 25, 2011, Bob signed a contract to move his lab, valued at $3 million, along with nine grants in his name, to the University of Pittsburgh.

7

life in pittsburgh

IN MAY 2011, AUTUMN AND BOB bought a stately $590,000 home in Schenley Farms, a beautiful, historic neighborhood just a few minutes' walk from their new jobs with UPMC and the University of Pittsburgh.

Autumn quickly settled in to her new position as head of women's neurology at the hospital system while Bob moved his entire lab, including three mice colonies, from the Veterans Administration Medical Center in Bedford, Massachusetts, to Scaife Hall in Oakland.

For years, he had been designing and conducting experiments seeking treatment for Huntington's disease, ALS, and other neurodegenerative diseases.

Getting the highly regarded researcher and his multimillion-dollar, 2,500-foot, state-of-the-art lab was a coup for Pitt. At the time, he was in the second year of a five-year plan to move drugs to treat Huntington's disease to the next level of testing.

Again, researchers were tasked with injecting the drugs into mice that carried genes for Huntington's disease.

Patricia Cipicchio, who started with Bob at the Bedford VA in July 2010, moved with the lab to Pittsburgh.

Cipicchio was a full-time research assistant put in charge of the R6/2, or Huntington's, colony of mice, where her duties included preparing and administering the drugs, managing their breeding, and conducting genotyping. Once the mice were adults—at thirty days old —the lab could start treating them with the drugs being tested. The R6/2 mice would start to show symptoms of becoming ill about thirty days after that.

She was also responsible for killing them—which in labs is called *sacrificing*. Mice were killed not just in the course of experiments, but also were sacrificed if they weren't the right genotype or sex because it was so costly to keep them alive.

Once the animals were dead, Cipicchio had to prepare brain tissue by freezing, slicing, and staining the samples to measure differences in the mice's brain anatomy. It got to her sometimes, and the ethics of what was being done in the lab were on her mind all the time.

Because the researchers' jobs entailed observing the mice as they became ill, they knew when the severely sick ones were near death.

Once or twice, when Bob walked into the animal house, which was located at UPMC Montefiore—about a five-minute walk from the lab—the mice got agitated. Cipicchio knew that it took little to disturb the already frail mice, ill with symptoms that mimicked the effects of crippling diseases.

Bob joked about his effect on the mice.

He was an early riser who needed just a few hours of sleep each night and would typically arrive at the lab before 6:30 a.m. Bob's work was to conceive and design the experiments, while occasionally checking in on the researchers' progress.

He was a demanding boss who wanted things done his way. He was also a little odd, but willing to joke with those he trusted—including teasing Cipicchio about the color of her nail polish. Once he changed her computer desktop background to seahorses.

After Bob had announced the lab would move to Pittsburgh, he told all of his employees that he'd changed his mind, they were staying in Boston, and their jobs were safe.

It was an April Fool's joke.

He didn't much care whether others thought he was funny.

Bob was an engaged mentor to the younger research assistants in the lab, taking an interest in their work and helping them advance.

Although he was private about most aspects of his personal life, he talked about Cianna all the time.

Bob's reputation in his field was superb, and because of that, he had access to a lot of resources. He was also passionate about his work.

In 2010, Bob and three others, including Rick Silverman at Northwestern University, collaborated to win a $1.69 million grant over three years from the Department of Defense to attempt to identify drugs to treat ALS. Those working in the Silverman lab would synthesize compounds and then send them to another lab to test with cells that were engineered to have a mutation in a gene found in some ALS patients to see whether any would inhibit the production of aggregated proteins—which is what happens in the brains of ALS patients. Then, the best compounds would be sent to Bob to test in the mice he'd developed with the same genetic mutation as the one found in some ALS patients. If the research was successful, the lives of the mice would be extended with the treatment.

Then, in the fall of 2011, Friedlander began to seek out donors to fund additional work on ALS in the lab.

He introduced Bob to Neil and Suzanne Alexander. The couple had become active in the ALS community after Neil was diagnosed with the debilitating disease at age forty-six. Bob began to court the couple, soliciting grant money to fund his research.

The Alexanders were desperate for an answer to the disease, and Bob had the credibility in his field to try to find one. They found him slightly off-putting as he sought money from them, but they knew he was a talented researcher and represented hope for them and others with ALS.

By mid-2012, the couple had agreed to sign on by providing $50,000 for the lab to hire a postdoctoral fellow and for Neil to participate in the research by providing spinal fluid and skin cells for the lab to use to grow stem cells, and the researchers mapped his brain.

To show them the progress being made, Bob sent photographs to the Alexanders of Neil's skin cells growing into fibroblasts, which would be converted into motor neurons.

Bob also participated in events for the couple's nonprofit, Live Like Lou, including going to the zoo with Cianna and to a Pirates game at which Neil threw out the first pitch.

When the Friedlander/Ferrante lab celebrated its grand opening on the fifth floor of Scaife Hall with a reception in the brand-new, state-of-the-art facility, Autumn joined her husband at the event. Their new life in a new city had begun.

BOTH AUTUMN AND BOB took to Pittsburgh. They loved that they could walk everywhere, go to the many museums and libraries, and play in the park.

For Autumn professionally, she was able to balance treating patients with research and writing. She liked her new colleagues, who seemed to her to be more down to earth and less status conscious than those in Boston.

"I like the easier lifestyle here. A bit different in that every other person is not some big shot somebody-or-other, but I kind of like that. I was getting tired of the over privileged. I feel like I deal with real people, real issues here," she wrote in an e-mail to a friend.

Although Bob's salary decreased, Autumn's tripled, and the city was much more affordable than Boston. She could run her own program. Besides treating her own patients, she served on the patient post–cardiac arrest team and read EEGs for neurology patients.

She was awarded two private foundation research grants to look at managing seizures in pregnant women with epilepsy and was applying for others through the National Institutes of Health. Much like in Boston, Autumn had a huge patient population, and the patients loved her.

She had a five-minute commute, and that meant she could spend more time with Cianna, who would often go with Bob to meet her mom for dinner on nights when she worked late. Autumn took her daughter to see her first ballet, *The Nutcracker*, in Pittsburgh, and it seemed that she'd gotten the professional/personal balance she'd wanted.

By the next summer, though, old issues resurfaced. Autumn was working extraordinary hours, and she was frustrated by her inability to get pregnant. By that time, doctors had isolated the problem to Autumn's eggs, and they encouraged her to gain weight and take time off work. They also suggested that the couple use a donor egg, but she refused.

Autumn didn't believe she was getting the support she wanted and needed from her husband. She had gone through repeated IVF cycles, requiring multiple, daily injections into her stomach and buttocks. Bob didn't help. Autumn gave herself the shots.

They considered adoption, but Autumn told her friend that adoption agencies viewed their age difference as a problem. It was a lonely time.

In a diary entry dated July 30, 2012, she wrote: "I am here writing now because I am not sure who I can talk to about things. I just found out today my third IVF cycle failed. This time not even fertilization. I am not sure where to go from here. I just know that I am incredibly unhappy. Yet I am not sure why. I have wanted another child for years. But is what I want another child or what that represents to me? Why do people have children? Are they a representation of self? Do they represent more love in life? More satisfaction? More pleasure? Do I want another child because these things are lacking in my life? It is not clear to me. I just feel like something is missing in my life. I think that thing missing is love."

In late August, Karen visited from Australia with her family. Autumn and Bob took them on a full tour of the city, going up one of the city's famous inclined plane railways, eating ice cream on Pittsburgh's Mount Washington and the legendary sandwiches at Primanti Brothers, and taking them for a walk along the North Shore by the stadiums.

But during the few private moments that Karen and Autumn had over those days, Autumn shared her feelings about Bob and their marriage. Although her husband had agreed to go forward with IVF, Bob also told Autumn that if they had another child, she would be fully responsible for everything it might need.

"It's going to be my kid," Autumn told Karen.

She worried about money, too. Autumn was frustrated with her husband for always giving money to his adult children, who by that point were already established with their own careers—Michael in investment management, and Kimberly as a physician. Michael was getting married in September, and Autumn was unhappy that Bob was paying so much toward the event, especially given that Michael had a well-paying job in Boston.

Autumn was concerned especially, she said, because Bob was talking about retiring within a few years, which would leave Autumn as the sole income earner in the family. She had just finished paying off her medical-school loans and fretted about spending money on what would be her fourth round of IVF—out of pocket instead of from insurance. She was so concerned, she ordered her fertility meds from Canada.

Autumn noted, too, that Bob's brother, who had dementia, recently had to be relocated, and Bob was concerned that he could be diagnosed with it as well.

Karen could see for herself what was happening—like the day Bob chastised Autumn for putting something into the dishwasher incorrectly.

WITHIN A MONTH of Karen's visit, Autumn started to plan to leave her marriage.

She told Sharon.

"I don't know what else to do," Autumn said. "I see myself alone in a couple years. It's just gotten so bad, you have no idea. It's just gotten so bad these last few months."

Autumn told Sharon she loved her husband, and that she'd suggested marriage counseling. Twice during phone calls with Sharon, Autumn had Sharon ask her husband, Jeff, a clinical psychologist, if there was a specific gene for compassion.

"Because if there is," Autumn said, "then Bob is lacking it."

She started telling Bob how she felt—in e-mails.

On February 9, 2013, Autumn wrote: "So, yet again, thanks for not asking about what my conversation with [Reproductive Medicine Associates of New Jersey] was. I hate to say it, Bob, but through this entire mess, while in body you have done your duty, you have not been there for me. Sorry I am angry about all of this. Both not having another kid and your lack of interest. Yes, this is what has been telling me you do not want another kid. Anytime you want something, you are like a dog with a bone. In this case, you have not asked pertinent questions until the last minute or after it is all over. Too little and too late. It is clear you are not interested. You showed more interest in that [Huntington's disease] researcher who got in trouble. I realize now I have been alone in this entire emotional journey. I'm going to speak my mind as you do and be angry because . . . the only means of conversation you seem to get is anger. You stink at picking up on almost all other emotions, and I am sorry I, right now, I just cannot talk to you in person. I can't even speak to you without getting angry.

"Every time we have done, I have not produced nearly enough eggs, and my embryos have arrested. [The] genetic evidence shows that this is a mitochondrial failure, embryos arresting in the way mine have. He definitely recommends not continuing IVF. My eggs will never— will likely never recover from this until they genetically determine, if they can, what the mitochondrial lesion is. He is trying to determine this. The only thing he can recommend is CoQ-10. It has not shown improvement in having babies, but does show improvement in helping the eggs if I want to try and get pregnant naturally. He also feels this is something that likely will affect Cianna and for her to freeze her eggs at 30 since this is inherited. Other than slightly early menopause, I likely will have no other medical repercussions, he thinks. I have to get ultrasounds to follow up on the cysts in the next few months. I have an appointment with my gyne in April. I will probably get an IUD at that time. I don't know where I want to go from here. I don't know what else to say, Bob."

A few days later Autumn confided to McElrath that she wanted out of the marriage. They were in San Francisco together for the conference, and he was the person she turned to. On February 18, 2013, Autumn sent her husband another e-mail with the subject line "Us."

"I think at some point in the near future we should go out to talk. I really don't know where to begin with all that has been going on in life recently and in my head. I have tried to talk to you but can't. I have written you many letters I have not sent. I don't know where things are going to go, and you may not like what you hear, but I think it is about time we talked."

Five hours after he received that message, police later found out, Bob did a Google search for "divorce pittsburgh pa," and the day after, he searched "does increased vaginal size suggest wife is having sex with another."

During that same time period, Sharon's nephew died.

Both Autumn and Sharon were going to the services in Baltimore, and they planned to talk extensively during the visit because Autumn didn't want to discuss her marriage troubles on the phone.

Sharon and Jeff had already agreed they would head to Pittsburgh in the summer to help Autumn move. They would talk logistics in Baltimore.

But then, Bob decided to make the trip for the funeral, too. It was the first time in the twelve years they were married that Bob accompanied Autumn back home.

During the visitation and wake, he was polite, cordial, and pleasant to be around.

He spoke with Jeff, telling him that "being married to Autumn is the greatest thing in my life."

But Jeff knew about the problems in the marriage and that Autumn wanted out.

Sharon and Autumn never got the chance to talk, and at the wake, on February 21, 2013, Bob made the family leave early to head back to Pittsburgh. As they headed out of the church fellowship hall, Autumn turned to Sharon with a look that mixed sadness and frustration over not being able to talk.

It was the last time Sharon ever saw her.

8 · · · · · · · · ·
the arrest

WITH THE ARREST WARRANT signed and sealed on July 24, investigators alerted the U.S. Marshals Service and sheriff's deputies in St. Augustine that they would be in Florida the next day to arrest their suspect.

Law enforcement agents in Florida agreed to sit on Dianne Ferrante's house on Silo Road, where Bob and Cianna had been living, until detectives from Pittsburgh arrived.

Lutton and Provident left Pittsburgh police headquarters about 5:00 a.m., heading first to pick up Bill and Lois, who were staying at a nearby hotel. The Kleins, who had obtained an emergency custody order to have Cianna return with them to live, were going to fly with the investigators down to Florida to bring the little girl home. As the detectives left headquarters, they noticed that reporters were already camped out, waiting for the suspect to be brought into custody. Although the arrest warrant had been sealed, the *Pittsburgh Post-Gazette* had learned that it had been issued and published a front-page story about it that morning.

As soon as the detectives' flight landed in St. Augustine, they dropped the Kleins off at a nearby hotel. Then they learned that Bob was no longer at his sister's house.

Difenderfer, who had only learned about the arrest warrant from a newspaper reporter late the night before, called Pellegrini at 8:00 a.m. to confirm an arrest warrant had been issued. She refused to answer, and he consequently refused to tell her where his client was.

He immediately called Bob, telling him an arrest was imminent and to get back to Pittsburgh immediately to turn himself in. Difenderfer didn't want to have to deal with him being arrested in a different jurisdiction and having to be extradited.

Bob, who had planned that day to take Cianna to her first pediatric checkup in Florida and then to an alligator farm, instead told his young daughter that he had to go back to Pittsburgh to help people there understand why her mommy had died.

She looked at him with fear and dejection—a look that stayed with him as he set out on the road about 9:00 a.m. with a heavy heart and unsettled feeling in his stomach.

A short time later, Provident and Lutton pulled up at Dianne's home —a large ranch with a pond set on several acres in a rural area of St. Augustine about ten minutes off Interstate 95—to question the sister and take custody of Cianna.

More than fifteen armed marshals and sheriff's deputies in assault gear carrying rifles had already made a soft entry at the home, knocking on the door and announcing they had an arrest warrant for her brother.

Dianne was crying and on the brink of hysterics when Provident and Lutton arrived. She called a local attorney, who told the detectives they could not take Cianna, claiming that the girl was now a resident of Florida and that the Pennsylvania custody order carried no authority. There was a flurry of phone calls between the Florida attorney, Pellegrini, and others before it was agreed that the Pennsylvania order was binding.

Provident spent several minutes trying to calm Dianne, explaining to her that Cianna, who had been at her home for several weeks, would be safe going to Baltimore with her grandparents. Once things calmed down, another officer went to pick up Lois and Bill and drove them to the house. When they arrived, Dianne was kind to the Kleins and helped them gather up Cianna's belongings from her room, which was filled with movies and dolls. It was the first time the six-year-old had gotten to see her grandparents alone since her mother had died. She was ecstatic.

WHEN PELLEGRINI LEARNED that Bob was not at his sister's house, she called Difenderfer back, furious.

"Where is he?" she shouted.

Difenderfer asked again if there was a warrant, and the prosecutor confirmed there was.

He told her Bob was on the road back to Pittsburgh. "As soon as he gets here, we will fucking turn him in."

Let him turn himself in at my office, he requested.

"He doesn't get to dictate," Pellegrini snapped. "Now he's a fugitive. Don't play this game with me. Tell him to pull over and tell us what mile marker he's at, and we'll come get him."

Difenderfer refused.

"This is obstruction," she barked. "You're not negotiating his surrender."

But by the time they hung up, Difenderfer thought he had convinced the prosecution to let Bob turn himself in.

"Okay. You win. We'll meet you in the parking lot," Pellegrini said.

But she had no intentions of letting that happen. There was a nationwide notice for law enforcement agencies to be on the lookout (BOLO) for him and his silver Hyundai Sonata as he traveled northbound from Florida. Police were using GPS to ping his phone, which was being repeatedly turned on and off.

In the meantime, Provident and Lutton drove the Kleins and Cianna back to their hotel and then took the family out to dinner at an Italian place recommended by the staff. Cianna, who ordered buttered noodles, called the detectives "Mr. Bob" and "Mr. Harry," and chattered away to Grandma and Grandpap. She drew pictures and ate her noodles.

She told the detectives that her mommy had a heart attack and went to heaven, and that she was staying with her grandparents until her father got back from a business trip.

She was a sweet kid.

A T 5:52 P.M., West Virginia state police received a BOLO from Pittsburgh police that they were looking for a suspect, providing a description of Bob's car and its license-plate number. Sergeant Chuck Tupper, who was on duty that night, went to mile marker nine on the turnpike and sat in the median. At 6:30 p.m., license-plate-recognition technology along the highway alerted officers that Bob's vehicle had just gone through a tollbooth in Beckley, near mile marker twelve, headed north.

"Want us to pick him up?" a West Virginia trooper asked McGee.

"Yes."

At 6:50 p.m., troopers on Interstate 77 stopped traffic and started a rolling roadblock at mile marker thirty—using their patrol cars to box in the vehicle they were after.

Bob, who had never been so afraid in his life, called Difenderfer.

"There's police all around me. No lights on yet. Oh my God, Bill. There's a bunch of them."

"Just pull over," Difenderfer instructed.

Bob did as he was told, moving his car to the shoulder of the road and exiting with his hands above his head as instructed. He then walked backward toward Tupper as instructed.

With guns drawn, the troopers took Bob into custody.

Difenderfer blasted the prosecutor's manhunt for his client as "over the top and unnecessary," called the DA's office unprofessional, and said that the characterizations of his client as trying to flee were completely fabricated.

"It was a media statement. It was 100 percent sleazy," he said.

A short time after Bob's arrest, he appeared, wearing a blue button-down shirt and jeans, before a magistrate judge in Raleigh County, West Virginia, where he was informed of the charge against him. He was then taken to the Southern Regional Jail, where he was held for four nights until a hearing the following Monday. At that brief proceeding, he agreed to waive extradition.

The next morning, Lutton and Provident drove to West Virginia to pick him up. A couple of nights in jail didn't seem to have softened him up—as soon as he was brought out to them, Bob demanded, "Where's my wallet?"

He launched into more demands for more belongings when Lutton stopped him.

"Mr. Ferrante, you have the right to remain silent. We're not allowed to talk to you. I think you should exercise that right."

Bob shut up.

That afternoon, he appeared—unshaven and in a white, collared shirt under a red jumpsuit—before Judge Cashman for arraignment in a video conference from the Allegheny County Jail.

Squinting into the camera, he listened to the judge and shuffled through paperwork.

He was charged with a single count of criminal homicide.

THE PROSECUTORS BELIEVED they had found their motive, and they laid it out in their long affidavit of probable cause: Bob believed that his wife had been cheating on him.

"Investigators have discovered evidence that shows that within weeks of the victim's death, Ferrante confronted the victim three times as to whether she was having an affair. Further, evidence has been uncovered that reflects that the victim intended to have a conversation with Ferrante, and that Ferrante would 'not like the discussion.'" The document, which identified the witnesses by number instead of name, included the statements from McElrath about his conversations with Autumn and her plans to leave her husband, as well as statements from Farkas, her initial treating physician. He was identified as witness number one in the affidavit.

"Witness number one, who was present at Presbyterian Hospital, reported that Ferrante's reaction upon seeing the victim on the exam table seemed fake and like 'bad acting.' Witness number one said that in his/her ten years of experience in the medical field, he/she has never seen anyone act the way Ferrante did. Witness number one reported that Ferrante began speaking about the victim in the past tense while the doctors were still actively treating her."

The affidavit then continued, "Witness number three, who was present in the hospital that night, reported that Ferrante began asking about whether an autopsy should be performed before the victim was pronounced deceased. Witness number three reported that Ferrante said he did not believe an autopsy would help because any toxins in her blood would have been washed out. Witness number three found it strange that Ferrante would be talking about toxins being washed out of the victim's blood."

Witness number four was quoted in the affidavit as saying that Bob spoke about his wife in the past tense, and that on April 19, while Autumn was still actively being treated, Bob said, "I'm going to spend the last night with the love of my life."

In addition to describing Bob's behavior in the hospital that night, the affidavit outlined the 911 call and what he told the dispatcher, including his request that his wife be transported to UPMC Shadyside —a mile farther away and not a trauma center—because "her folks are down at Shadyside, maybe that would be the best place to take her." The affidavit noted that Autumn's parents were in Baltimore at the time.

As they had talked about previously, the investigators included in the affidavit their reasoning for ruling out suicide, including that Autumn had been making both short- and long-term plans in the hours and days leading up to her collapse. She had talked to a friend about planning a camping trip, to Sharon about visiting her in Washington, and to her husband about flight reservations for the two of them. In addition, five hours before she became ill, Autumn texted Bob to ask if he could fix her car because she needed it the next morning, and just three hours before, she e-mailed a group of colleagues about a meeting in Boston scheduled for May 9.

"The victim was described by several witnesses as being health conscious. Witnesses reported that the victim would take extra care of herself to ensure she stayed healthy because she worried that if something happened to her husband, who was much older, her six-year-old daughter would be alone if she was not there. It was learned that the victim's career was on the rise, and she was becoming a well-known doctor in her field. It was described to investigators that the victim was very passionate about her work and deeply cared for her patients. She was not described by any witness as having suicidal tendencies. After a careful review of the information collected from witnesses, investigators ruled out suicide as the cause for the victim's death."

Although it had previously been leaked to the media that Bob had bought cyanide through his research lab just before his wife's death, the affidavit, for the first time, laid out the details of that order. "Witness number seven reported that on April 15, 2013, Ferrante approached him/her for assistance in purchasing cyanide. Witness number seven is responsible for the purchasing of all chemicals and materials for the laboratory. He/she reported that on this day, Ferrante approached him/her and asked whether it would be possible to order a chemical and receive it the next day. He/she informed Ferrante that it would be possible and that he would have to use a credit card. Ferrante informed witness number seven that he wanted the best and purest cyanide he could get. After selecting the cyanide he wanted, Ferrante said, 'It's that easy, huh?'"

According to the affidavit, of the 145 chemicals purchased for Bob's lab, only the cyanide was not related to a project or grant number. "It is clear that at the time Ferrante placed the order for overnight delivery of cyanide, there were no active or pending projects that necessarily involved the use of cyanide, let alone any that required cyanide for overnight delivery."

The affidavit also addressed creatine, including a text-message exchange between Autumn and Bob from the day she collapsed.

At 1:05 p.m., Autumn texted her husband regarding a potential migraine. "I have an aura. According to my calendar, I ovulate tomorrow." Three minutes later, he wrote back, "Perfect timing. Creatine :o)."

Autumn wrote back, "Right." And Bob said, "I'm serious. It will make a huge difference. [I'm] certain of it."

"I'm sure I hope so. Mild [headache] right now," Autumn replied.

"Creatine will take care of that as well :o)."

Autumn replied at 2:36 p.m., "Will it stimulate egg production too?"

Bob responded, again, with a smiley face.

According to the Allegheny County crime lab, the affidavit said, the bottle of potassium cyanide that Bob had ordered on April 15 and asked his research associate to store the next day had been analyzed. It was missing 8.3 grams.

9 ■ ■ ■ ■ ■ ■ ■ ■ ■
the fallout

IN THE DAYS IMMEDIATELY AFTER Ferrante's arrest, there was a flurry of court activity related to both Cianna and the family's assets.

While temporary orders had been granted giving custody of Cianna to Bill and Lois and freezing Ferrante's assets, both matters had to be handled in court proceedings.

On August 5, Difenderfer and Claus squared off before Judge Cashman to argue the issue.

Claus, who had specialized in white-collar financial investigations throughout his career, displayed a chart for the court listing all of the various accounts belonging to Autumn and Bob, including those that belonged only to Ferrante that were spread across fifteen different institutions and totaled about $2.5 million. The prosecutor also noted that Autumn had $150,000 split among three life insurance policies, and that money belonging to either her or to the couple jointly totaled just under $900,000. If Ferrante were to be convicted, the prosecution would seek restitution from him for Autumn's medical bills, which added up to more than $400,000 for her three-day hospital stay. In addition, Claus noted, Cianna and the Kleins could potentially file a wrongful-death lawsuit against Ferrante, resulting in damages of as much as $10 million in Autumn's lifetime lost wages.

Claus asked that all of the money belonging to Autumn or to the couple jointly be frozen by the court under Pennsylvania's Slayer's Act, which prohibits a person convicted of killing someone from financially benefiting from the crime.

Difenderfer told the judge that he had never been involved in a homicide case where the prosecution worried about medical-bill restitution. He accused them of attempting to be bill collectors for the insurance company. But Claus responded that in white-collar cases, assets are protected for potential restitution all the time.

Difenderfer told Cashman that this case was different—these weren't ill-gotten gains.

"The embezzled money or the stolen money is probably the source of the funds that they are seeking for restitution, and they don't want anything to happen to that. That makes sense if I am stealing from a bank, and I have $100,000 or $5 million in an account, and they seize that so I don't get rid of it or do anything. In this case, none of the proceeds were being dissipated by the defendant. As a matter of fact, all the proceeds through the estate management with the Kirkpatrick and Lockhart firm was devising a way to set up a trust for [the] children. None of the money was intended to be stolen or hidden or in any bank accounts like that. It is all there, and that wasn't the intent at all. I mean, the money and the source of all this money is from a long, very successful career of my client, as well as his wife. That is a lot different than 'we do this in white-collar crimes.'"

Difenderfer conceded, though, that he understood the request to protect the assets. He agreed temporarily to the freeze, asking—and receiving—permission to return to the issue later. To ensure his client could pay trial costs and fees for experts and investigators, all parties agreed that one account, containing just under $280,000, would remain available to the defendant.

At that same hearing, Pellegrini asked the court to issue a gag order in the case, which would prevent both sides—and any involved parties—from discussing it with the media. Difenderfer said he had no intention of trying the case in the press.

"I did, obviously, grant some interviews, and I think that I made every effort to not talk about the facts of the case at all. I don't intend to do that, and I will not do that," Difenderfer said. "I will tell the court, though, that due to the leaks in the Pittsburgh police department that the press knew more about this case as it was going on than I, and sometimes I think even the district attorney's office, [knew] . . . and the whole point of [Ferrante] coming from Florida to Pittsburgh and how that went down and how it occurred was absolutely wrong and extremely prejudicial to the defense. And responding to that is appropriate."

Cashman granted the order.

At the same time, the Kleins were worried about keeping Cianna. In the emergency petition for temporary custody that they filed the day before Ferrante's arrest, they accused their son-in-law of purposely keeping Cianna away from them with no explanation and of trying to "transfer" custody of her to other relatives. They further said that keeping Cianna from her grandparents could be seriously detrimental considering that her mother had died and her father was accused of killing her.

Their petition claimed that Lois and Bill had a "very close and frequent" relationship with Cianna and that they could take immediate custody of her. By having full custody, they claimed that they would protect the girl from "nefarious attempts of [the] father and his relatives to influence her testimony and memory relating to the events surrounding the death of her mother."

The district attorney's office, at the time, said the girl could be a material witness in the case. However, Michael Ferrante and his wife, Nicole, were seeking sole legal and primary custody as well. In their complaint, the couple, who lived in Wellesley, Massachusetts, argued that living in their home would be in Cianna's best interest. Among the reasons they listed were that they were age-appropriate guardians for her—they noted that Lois was seventy-eight and Bill was seventy-six, that Michael and Nicole had a close relationship with Cianna when she lived in Boston and even after she moved to Pittsburgh, and that with Nicole working as a nurse practitioner, she would be able to provide good care for the girl.

The filing said that both Lois and Bill were "elderly and in declining health, struggling to get in and out of their vehicles and preparing food" for Cianna, and accused them of engaging in "alienating behaviors by isolating [Cianna] from the paternal family."

"[The Ferrantes] will provide a positive atmosphere without criticizing the child's father or mother and will insulate the child from the child's father's likely murder trial," wrote attorney Christine Gale.

At a hearing on the issue on August 7, Cashman found that Michael and Nicole Ferrante did not have standing to seek custody, since under Pennsylvania law, the only people who do are parents, grandparents, and those people who have been identified as acting in loco parentis, or standing in for a parent.

Because of that decision, the Ferrantes filed a separate private dependency action with the court, but that meant, in the meantime, custody remained with the Kleins. Lois and Bill, who had both long since retired, also filed a motion seeking child support from Ferrante.

With that settled, the Kleins moved on to handling their daughter's affairs. Autumn had died without a will, and because Ferrante had been charged with his wife's death, he could not serve as the estate administrator. That meant the Kleins needed to be granted permission from the Register of Wills to start the probate process so that they could close Autumn's bank accounts and handle insurance policies to help pay for Cianna's care.

While these civil issues continued, the criminal court proceedings were just starting.

10 · · · · · · · · · · · ·
legal wrangling

EVEN THOUGH DETECTIVES had spent two months investigating Ferrante before they arrested him, they still had plenty to do.

They sought search warrants to access the couple's cell phones and computers and continued to review hospital surveillance video and key-card records.

At the same time, both the prosecuting and defense attorneys started laying the groundwork for the intense pretrial battles that were to come.

Difenderfer, who had been practicing law in Pittsburgh for thirty years, had a reputation. He was either very confident or very cocky, depending on who was giving the description. A big man who always wore a nice suit, he was known for his courtroom swagger. He was old school, often playing coy before pouncing on a witness. But he rarely made enemies. In fact, when cops found themselves in legal trouble, they often hired Difenderfer—even though he was so often the guy defending the people they arrested.

He liked high-profile cases and was known for taking them. He'd represented a number of notorious defendants, including Richard Baumhammers, who killed six people in a hate-fueled rampage across several Pennsylvania communities. Although he lost the case, he earned a reputation as one of the best criminal defense attorneys in Pittsburgh.

Difenderfer was also smart enough to pay attention when a colleague suggested he get a woman on the team, which would help with public perception at the trial. He turned to Wendy Williams, a longtime defense attorney who excelled in writing motions and getting into the detailed discovery results. She also understood technology better than he did.

The Ferrante case was outside of Difenderfer's comfort zone. He'd never had a case that required so much medical and chemical knowledge, or one that required so many expert witnesses and technical terminology.

Difenderfer started making regular visits to his client, who had been denied bail, at the jail. By January, he was visiting him at least three hours a day, three to four days each week. Difenderfer spent more time with Ferrante at the jail, trying to master the science and medical terminology, than he'd spent with every other client he'd represented in his career—combined.

For Pellegrini, the fall of 2013 was dedicated to the trial of another man accused of killing his ex-wife. She spent weeks working to convict John Minch of first-degree murder before going on to focus exclusively on Ferrante's case. A prosecutor since 1997, she became a part of the DA's homicide unit in 2001. During her career up until that point, she had handled 103 cases, going to trial in sixty-six of them and obtaining guilty pleas for the rest. At trial, she lost just thirteen times.

Pellegrini had a reputation for being tough, well prepared, protective of her victims' families, and occasionally overly dramatic. In the year before the Ferrante case, Pellegrini's work had focused on cases involving children. She tried and convicted a woman of drowning her two-year-old son, and earned a conviction of a man accused of beating his girlfriend's eleven-year-old son to death.

Before the Ferrante case, the most high-profile case Pellegrini had been involved in was against Richard Poplawski, a man who stockpiled weapons and ammunition and then shot and killed three Pittsburgh police officers responding to his home for a domestic dispute with his mother. She'd been the second chair, though, to the prosecutor then heading the homicide unit.

This time, she was leading the charge. Initially, Pellegrini worked with both Claus and Kee Song on the prosecution team. But as the idea of a financial motive was eliminated, it became clear that Claus—and his expertise in white-collar crime—would not be needed at trial. That left Pellegrini, Song, and several interns in the DA's office dedicated to the prosecution.

After the criminal charge was filed, Pellegrini and Song began their preparations for the preliminary hearing, at which a judge would decide whether they had enough evidence to go to trial. In the end, it didn't matter. After asking for three postponements, Difenderfer agreed to waive.

The case was going to trial.

FOLLOWING THE FIRST pretrial hearing—one of at least seven—on November 6, the defense received the initial batch of discovery—in the form of electronic records. In the meantime, Pellegrini was doing everything she could to educate herself on cyanide poisoning. She researched the most recent cyanide cases across the country and called prosecutors in Maryland, Illinois, and Cleveland who had dealt with the poison. She contacted medical examiner's offices as well.

At the same time, Jennifer Janssen, the chief toxicologist for the Allegheny County crime lab, was contacting forensics laboratories across the country to see if any of them had an existing test to detect the presence of another neurotoxin, 3-nitropropionic acid—or 3-NP.

During their investigation, detectives learned that Ferrante had done a significant amount of research with the substance, which is used to cause cell death.

On December 10, investigators interviewed Dr. Jinho Kim, Ferrante's research associate, who asked them if Autumn's blood had been tested for 3-NP, which he described as a neurotoxin that "could make someone appear tired and sick as it inhibits mitochondria at a cellular level."

"Kim explained that he did not wish to be accusatory but had recalled something odd which also occurred during March and April of 2013." Ferrante had asked Kim to order the chemical three times during that period, first saying he needed a new bottle because what they had in the lab had lost its potency. In an affidavit, the detectives wrote: "Kim was also told by Ferrante that he (Ferrante) had 'loaned' the 3-NP to University of Pittsburgh neurosurgery professor Dr. Edward Dixon. Ferrante later told Kim that Dixon returned the 3-NP to Ferrante at an unknown later date." But it continued, "Dr. Dixon was later interviewed regarding the 3-NP and stated that [he] had never asked for or received 3-NP from Ferrante, as described by Dr. Kim."

On December 16, Graber sought a sealed search warrant seeking all containers of 3-NP, all records associated with it, and any of Ferrante's research projects in 2012 and 2013 that would use it, as well as testing records, lab notes, orders, and invoices.

A review of Pitt's orders showed 3-NP was ordered on Ferrante's behalf on March 6, March 12, and April 3.

Kim, who had seen Autumn the day of her collapse, thought she did not look well, and asked her twice if she was ill. The prosecution team wondered whether Ferrante had been dosing his wife with the 3-NP—either to make her appear to be ill or to kill her—but when that process took too long, he turned to cyanide.

Despite her efforts, Janssen quickly learned that no lab, including the FBI, had a test that could be used to detect 3-NP.

The prosecution agreed to focus its work, instead, on the cyanide.

Talking to the prosecutor in Cleveland, Pellegrini found the person who would become her lead expert witness at trial, Dr. Christopher Holstege, a professor of emergency and pediatric medicine with a specialty in toxicology at the University of Virginia. She sent him all of Autumn's medical records, as well as relevant documents from the case, asking him to render an opinion on the woman's cause of death.

By December, the prosecutors in the DA's office were in full swing —starting to go through all of the evidence they'd received and deciding what needed to be turned over to the defense. Because of the huge volume of electronics that they'd seized, there were terabytes of data that needed to be examined.

On the defense side, Difenderfer also knew that sifting through all of that discovery would take an eternity. He and Williams hired two technology-litigation firms to help speed up the process. In addition, in mid-December, Difenderfer asked Common Pleas President Judge Jeffrey A. Manning, who would preside over the criminal case, whether his client could be permitted access to a computer in the jail to be able to help his attorneys review the computer records provided in discovery. Manning agreed to the arrangement, and Ferrante was ultimately permitted to work on the computer for eight hours a day.

B Y EARLY JANUARY 2014, prosecutors were confident that they had a strong circumstantial case. And then they got their first big break related to the computer evidence. Graber, who had been responsible for seeking all of the search warrants for the electronic evidence, had gotten a sealed search warrant on December 23 for a MacBook Air laptop computer belonging to Ferrante that was found in his car when he was arrested. The next day, that computer was delivered to Pennsylvania state trooper Donald Scott Lucas, whose expertise was in computer crimes. On January 3, 2014, Lucas contacted Graber and alerted him that "there's something you might be interested in."

As he reviewed the forensics report from the laptop, Graber found a

Google search done on April 25—four hours after detectives informed Ferrante that his wife had died from cyanide poisoning. It read, "would ecmo or dialysis remove traces of toxins poisons."

Graber immediately called Pellegrini. She was ecstatic.

"I can't believe it," she exclaimed. "If he Googled this, there's got to be more."

But Graber thought—since he'd already combed through thousands of e-mails, text messages, and computer records—that the search about ECMO was probably the last useful thing that they would find.

BY EARLY JANUARY, the defense lawyers were becoming concerned about having enough money to represent their client. On January 8, Difenderfer filed a motion asking Judge Manning to lift the freeze on Ferrante's assets—including $30,000 the detectives seized from a safe-deposit box. In the motion, Difenderfer wrote that he anticipated that the case would be very complex, requiring the review of thousands of documents and the hiring of several experts and investigators.

"The commonwealth has two attorneys and their entire office and support staff available at their disposal to work on this case, as well as a budget that allows them to hire experts and investigators without prior court approval," he wrote. "Defendant should not have to seek court release/approval of his own funds for the use in his defense."

But in the district attorney's response, prosecutors said that Ferrante had a history of moving large amounts of money around and highlighted those transactions. On May 15, 2013, he transferred $50,000 held in a joint account with Autumn into his own individual account. Between May 23, 2011, and April 9, 2013, he transferred $126,050 from joint and individual accounts to his daughter Kimberly—including $100,000 in one transfer on February 25, 2013. And he transferred $130,455 to his son, Michael, again including $100,000 on February 25, 2013. The filing also noted that $30,000 in cash was placed in two safe-deposit boxes on May 15, 2013, with Kimberly's name added as a co-owner three days later.

The freeze on the funds, the filing said, was necessary because of "the fact that defendant routinely transferred large sums of money to his adult children [that] shows that the defendant could readily deplete his assets and/or make them unavailable to the jurisdiction of the court of Common Pleas of Allegheny County. The use of safe deposit boxes to hide large sums of cash and property and the joint-titling of said boxes demonstrates that the defendant has the wherewithal and desire to make his considerable assets unavailable to the jurisdiction of the court. The fact that defendant had contemplated relocation and/or custody litigation in various foreign states strongly suggests that the defendant has the motivation to structure his legal and/or financial affairs so that he is beyond Pennsylvania jurisdiction."

But in his response, Difenderfer discounted all of the prosecution arguments.

The transfers of cash to Ferrante's adult children were done while Autumn was still alive and without any evidence of objection by her. The safe-deposit boxes, he wrote, also contained family items with sentimental value, as well as personal records. The cash—$26,000, not $30,000—had been saved for home remodeling. "It defies logic that this is 'suspicious.' Rather, it was actually prudent to remove these items from the house to safeguard them, especially when so much attention had been drawn to defendant and the residence following his wife's death. If defendant was truly trying to hide these assets, he would not have put the safe-deposit box in his name."

As for Ferrante contemplating moving to Florida, Difenderfer wrote, that made sense.

"In the months before defendant was charged, he was not permitted to work and locked out of his office at UPMC and the VA, as he was a 'person of interest' in this suspected homicide. Since the couple came to Pittsburgh primarily for Dr. Klein's work and considering his age, the defendant did contemplate retirement. In consideration of those circumstances, the defendant had planned to retire to Florida because his sister lives there. Due to the investigation, the number of search warrants being executed and the fact that defendant could not work, Pittsburgh was not a friendly place to be for him and his minor daughter." Although Ferrante visited Kimberly in California and then his sister in Florida, the "defendant's whereabouts were never hidden from the commonwealth. Rather, throughout this process counsel kept in contact with the commonwealth, advising of the defendant's travel plans and even providing them with the defendant's passport as a show of good faith that he was not fleeing. The defense repeatedly asserted that it would make arrangements for a controlled turn-in (which counsel has done for many homicide defendants) if and when charges were brought. Instead, the commonwealth chose to issue a warrant and proceed with the 'dog and pony show' of having seventeen armed marshals arrive at defendant's sister's residence in her quiet, gated community, and then issue a nationwide BOLO."

Difenderfer told the court that his client was trying to provide for his children all along by giving Cianna all of her mother's estate and dividing his equally among his three kids. However, he noted that Ferrante had been unable to pay child support out of the money originally released by the court, and that there was not enough in that account to pay for everything necessary.

"At present, the amount released does not come close to the amount needed to defend this matter. Defense counsel anticipates hiring at least six expert witnesses, has already hired co-counsel, a private investigator (working almost full time) and has incurred thousands of dollars of expenses on computer specialists to decipher discovery material. Defendant has also needed to hire a family lawyer. In the vein of proving his innocence, the defendant must be able to properly defend these allegations and wishes to use his own money to do so. Due to the temporary restraining order, he is in the position of asking the court for an allowance of his own money to pay for his defense and child support."

On February 10, Manning held a hearing on the asset issue. Again, the prosecution asserted that there was potential for significant restitution in the case.

"Isn't that putting the cart way before the horse? There is no restitution nor is it ripe for restitution until there has been a conviction," Manning said.

"Except that the statute says that this can be done in anticipation of restitution as early as filing the criminal complaint," assistant district attorney John Fitzgerald responded.

"I've got the statute in front of me passed by the state legislature. I've got the Constitution here in front of me, too," the judge said. "Let me assure you statutes do not trump the Constitution and the defendant's right to effective assistance of counsel and the right to spend his own money to defend himself."

Fitzgerald asked permission to call to the stand John Gismondi, a civil attorney representing the Klein family in Autumn's estate matters, to testify about potential damages if a wrongful-death suit was filed against Ferrante. Difenderfer objected.

"As to whether or not my client has any liability is premature. It is offensive to me now that the commonwealth is concerned with the civil bar . . . and personal injury lawyers, and they want to protect assets for them. That is something that comes after, and that is something that is not appropriate in restitution."

Manning allowed Gismondi to testify, and the civil lawyer said that to determine damages, an actuary would look at Autumn's salary of more than $200,000 per year, her age of forty-one at death and possible retirement age of sixty-seven, and estimate what her lost earnings would be.

On cross-examination, Difenderfer went after Gismondi's potential earnings.

"If you recovered a million or two million, what would be your percentage of that figure?"

"In a case like this, it would typically be a third or 40 percent, depending on the circumstances," Gismondi answered.

"So if she gets, you're saying, a million . . . $400,000 would be yours, not the victim in this, correct?" Difenderfer asked.

"Not the estate, correct."

"So by preserving these assets, as well, they are helping you with your fee, correct?" Difenderfer continued.

"I can't . . . I mean, I think it's self-evident," Gismondi answered.

After Gismondi's testimony concluded, the attorneys made argument to Manning, noting that "$243,000 was unfrozen. Now, I don't know what Mr. Difenderfer's bills are. I don't know what Ms. Williams' are," Fitzgerald said.

"Nor is it any of your business," Manning interjected.

"Clear enough, but nobody has to pay $243,000 up front for these services that they are talking about. Your honor, the commonwealth is not begrudging them money for a defense," Fitzgerald said. "We're saying that if the court reviews this and says . . . if it's more than the $243,000 that was already unfrozen, they need to say that, and they need to present it to the court."

Manning told the parties he would take the issue under advisement. Two days later, he granted the defense request.

"The court is certain that defense counsel will act consistent with his ethical obligations as an attorney, and his obligation to this court as an officer of the court, in seeing that the only expenditures from the defendant's assets are for attorney fees and costs directly associated with the defense to the criminal charges," the judge wrote.

He forbade the dissipation of the defendant's assets in any other way, requiring that Ferrante's money to be used for the case be transferred into his attorney's escrow account.

A short time later, the defense also filed a motion asking for Ferrante's case to be heard by an out-of-county jury, citing "pervasive and prejudicial pre-trial publicity." Judge Manning granted that request as well, and it was determined that the case would be heard by a jury from Dauphin County, where Harrisburg, Pennsylvania's state capital, is located.

O N MAY 9, THE DEFENSE filed a massive pretrial motion spanning 107 pages accusing investigators on the case of running a "fishing expedition" and improperly seizing evidence without probable cause. Included in the motion were requests to suppress evidence seized from eighty-one of the search warrants that were issued. "Law enforcement officers went far beyond what they were permitted when they engaged in an expansive fishing expedition to acquire information in this investigation," the defense argued. The attorneys also accused prosecutors of failing to follow the rules of criminal procedure. "It is clear that, in this case, law enforcement officers prepared search warrants and affidavits but were only interested in searching as many places as possible in the hopes of finding incriminating evidence against Dr. Ferrante. However, the affidavits did not contain the requisite level of probable cause that contraband or evidence of a crime would be found in the places to be searched."

Nearly one hundred warrants were executed, and the defense was challenging almost all of them, including ones in which materials were seized from Ferrante's car, home, research lab, and computers, as well as bank records and Internet searches. In one example, the defense argued that when officers searched Ferrante's car, the warrant allowed only for the seizure of "any and all evidence of cyanide" or items capable of storing, transporting, or delivering cyanide. But nothing like that was found. Still, officers seized Ferrante's laptop computer—which is where they discovered the Google search about ECMO. Ferrante's lawyers also alleged that some of the affidavits filed by investigators in the case contained "untruthful and false information." As an example, the lawyers identified the affidavits seeking the couple's financial information. In them, the prosecution claimed that Autumn did not have health insurance and that the cost of fertility treatment was putting a strain on the family's finances. The defense called that "patently false" and said, "Law enforcement officers had knowledge that Dr. Ferrante and Dr. Klein [were] not only financially stable, but [also] wealthy by most standards. Moreover the allegation that Dr. Klein did not have health insurance was false. Law enforcement officers relied on a contrived story of financial woe to convince the issuing authority to sign the search warrant."

O N PAGE EIGHTY-ONE of the filing, buried within the defense's sixty-third motion to suppress, was mention of a safe seized from underneath Ferrante's desk in his office at Pitt. The safe, the defense said, had been seized during the initial search and contained a personal computer, two-terabyte hard drives, and three pairs of diamond earrings.

The motion alleged that no search warrant had been provided for those items and that they were illegally taken. "As no inventory has been submitted by the commonwealth for discovery, and there is no inventory return for the safe and its contents, Dr. Ferrante presumes that the commonwealth is not seeking to introduce any evidence obtained from the safe."

The defense requested its return.

That filing, detailing what was inside the safe, was exactly what the prosecution needed. Pellegrini had learned from detectives a short time before the motion was filed that the safe, seized months before on May 4, 2013, was still in the police department evidence room—and it had never been opened. They didn't know what was inside, and detectives wanted permission to open it. Pellegrini, who was frustrated when she learned about the safe's existence so many months after it had been seized, had to tell the investigators no. The search warrant they'd originally gotten was stale and no longer valid. Besides, she thought at the time, "what are the odds anything is in there?"

But with the defense motion referencing the computer, Pellegrini thought to herself, "Oh my God—that's going to be *the* computer."

The prosecution, which now included assistant district attorney Kevin Chernosky after Song left the office, feverishly got the warrant to open the safe on May 20 and executed it the next morning.

Armed with a pry bar, Detectives Provident, McGee, Graber, and J. J. Godlewski gathered in the large conference room used for media events. The heavy, gray Sentry safe was wheeled in from the property room on a dolly. Provident took his suit jacket off and went at it.

At first he began near where the locking mechanism was, banging on it to try to force the medium-sized safe open. Then the large man put his weight on it—so much so that the pry bar went all the way through the safe's seam and dented the MacBook Pro that was inside. As they sifted through the contents, the investigators found a lot of both foreign and American silver coins, baby teeth, a wooden alligator, and the diamond earrings referenced in Williams's motion. Graber left with the laptop, and on May 25, got a search warrant to review its contents. He then delivered it to the computer expert with the state police.

On August 22, Corporal John Roche delivered the report with the results to Graber. He began reviewing it the next morning, a Saturday, at home.

Immediately, Graber called Pellegrini.

"Hang on, I'm going to conference-in Diane and Law," he said.

Once everyone was on the line, he called the laptop—and the Google searches it contained—"the gift that keeps on giving."

Chernosky called it "manna from heaven."

"I couldn't believe it—the mother lode," Pellegrini said. "It was like looking into the mind of the killer."

Every day after that, as she continued her trial preparation, when she thought about what was on the laptop, Pellegrini smiled.

A S THE PROSECUTORS and detectives ground through trial preparation, something unexpected happened—they became close friends with the Klein family.

Whether it was because Lois and Bill were from out of town, that they had lost their only daughter, or simply that they were older and more vulnerable, those working for the prosecution took a special interest in them. Although they didn't attend every hearing, each time the family came to town in preparation for trial, they were given special treatment—being driven from their hotel to the courthouse by the detectives on the case and sharing dinners and breakfasts with them. McGee and his wife had the family over for dinner at their home, and

Provident invited Cianna to his home to go swimming with his own daughter, who was about her age. Another detective took Cianna to the zoo with her own son, and still others took the Kleins out to dinner.

Chernosky noticed that every time he met with the Kleins, they had some type of ladybug token with them—whether bracelets, pins, socks, or something else. He learned that ladybugs were Autumn's favorite. He ordered a pin and cufflinks of his own so he could wear them at trial—a type of physical connection to share with his victim.

When they came to town, the Kleins often wanted to go to a local mainstay, Eat'n Park, where Cianna would eat grape-jelly-and-cream-cheese sandwiches and drink chocolate milk. During one of those trips, Cianna was riding in the backseat of the detective car. She reached over the seat to Pellegrini, who was up front, took off the prosecutor's sunglasses, and put them on herself.

"I'm a supermodel," she said, posing, while Pellegrini snapped her picture.

The image remains on her desk.

By the summer of 2014, Pellegrini and Chernosky were in the midst of conducting their pretrial interviews—about eighty people in all. They had already agreed that Pellegrini would handle the medical evidence and experts, and Chernosky would question witnesses on the computer and cell-phone evidence, as well as the Google searches. Still, they did almost every interview together—in case something happened during trial, either of them could take the witness seamlessly. The two prosecutors and detectives made repeated trips to UPMC Presbyterian and the crime lab, and also traveled to Virginia and Boston together.

In August, Pellegrini, Chernosky, McGee, and Provident piled into a black, beaten-up 2002 Cadillac that had been seized by the police department—they called it their "Was-illac"—and drove nine and a half hours to Boston to reinterview Autumn's and Bob's colleagues there. They needed to figure out who they would call for trial and who they could eliminate from their witness list. Everyone took turns driving except for Pellegrini. She insisted on riding shotgun to avoid motion sickness, but did her part by serving as the navigator and feeding her colleagues an endless stream of red licorice and Pringles to keep them going at the wheel.

They took a short detour to visit a Maserati dealership—not Pellegrini's idea of a good time. She sat tight in the Was-illac while the men admired the cars on the lot.

On the way back to Pittsburgh, "Bad Moon Rising" by Creedence Clearwater Revival came on the radio. All four sang as they cruised along, replacing the line "There's a bad moon on the rise" with "Bob Ferrante's gonna get life."

PELLEGRINI LEARNED pretty early on in her preparation that the defense would be using forensic pathologist Dr. Cyril Wecht as one of the experts in its case. Wecht, who had previously served as coroner and medical examiner in Allegheny County, had earned himself an international reputation in his field. He had previously consulted on the Kennedy assassination, as well as the deaths of JonBenét Ramsey, Michael Jackson, and countless other celebrities.

But those in the legal community were split on their opinions of him. He was certainly brilliant, with an ability to capture his courtroom audience by using his charm. But Wecht also was verbose, self-important, and known to expound upon cases about which he had no actual knowledge for the sake of a good sound bite or to get his name in the story.

To do an effective cross-examination, Pellegrini wanted to get him off the stand quickly. Her ex-husband, who had been a longtime homicide investigator, remembered a cyanide poisoning from the 1970s, when Wecht was coroner. Working with another detective still on the county police force, they were able to figure out who the victim was, and Pellegrini had the medical examiner pull the file. She didn't know how the case would come into play, but she suspected Wecht might testify inconsistently between the autopsy reports on the old case and Autumn's. She was ready if he did.

ON SEPTEMBER 2, the prosecution filed a motion with the court asking for permission at trial to present evidence of prior bad acts by Ferrante. The filing, made under seal, asserted that a laboratory technician from Ferrante's lab would testify that Ferrante had asked her to bring him a lab mouse so that he could test the potency of 3-NP —the mitochondrial toxin investigators thought Ferrante might have used on Autumn prior to resorting to cyanide. The technician would further testify that she was summoned by Ferrante a short time later to retrieve the mouse's dead body.

Usually, Pellegrini wrote, 3-NP was used to induce cell death in research, but not normally on lab animals.

"Discovery materials pertaining to evidence of such other crimes, wrongs, or acts have been disclosed to the defendant. On August 22, 2014, investigators in this case discovered evidence on one of defendant's MacBook Pro laptop computers indicating that on January 31, 2013, between 2:26 p.m. and 2:33 p.m., the defendant conducted the following searches on Google's search engine:

- 'human toxicity 3 nitropropionic acid,'
- 'human toxicity 3 nitropropionic acid cardiomyopathy,'
- 'toxic dose human 3 nitropropionic acid cardiomyopathy' and
- 'toxic dose human 3 nitropropionic acid.'"

Therefore, Pellegrini wrote, testimony about Ferrante's injection of a lab mouse with 3-NP was probative of the defendant's opportunity, intent, preparation, plan, and knowledge in killing his wife.

In the defense response, Ferrante's attorneys said that what the prosecution wanted to admit was not evidence of a previous crime, wrong, or act under Pennsylvania law, and that instead it would "create a 'trial within a trial' on a nonprobative and purely speculative issue.

"The commonwealth in this case is alleging that defendant killed his wife with cyanide. Nowhere in this case does the commonwealth allege that defendant used 3-NP to poison Autumn Klein. In the voluminous discovery, there is no such evidence of that. Thus, the relationship between any alleged impropriety involving a mouse and 3-NP to a wholly distinct incident allegedly involving cyanide and a human is speculative and ambiguous. Alleged use of 3-NP on a mouse simply offers nothing probative about alleged homicidal misuse of cyanide on a human.

"Nowhere does the commonwealth state that it hypothesizes that defendant was testing 3-NP on a mouse for later use on his wife. Defendant, as an esteemed, highly educated, and experienced scientist, would hardly be guilty of the scientifically erroneous thinking that toxicity of a compound on a mouse would provide immediately relevant information about lethality and effects on a human."

The defense argued that Ferrante had, for years, worked with 3-NP and used chemicals on mice in his research, and that that one example, with one mouse, did not demonstrate any wrongdoing.

Manning reserved ruling on the issue until trial.

About a week later, Pellegrini filed another motion seeking permission from the judge to use a computer-generated animation at trial to explain to the jury the effects of cyanide on the human body. She noted in the motion that it was only for demonstrative purposes, and under Pennsylvania law it was permitted to illustrate the testimony of an expert witness.

"This animation will be narrated by Dr. Holstege to assist the jury in understanding this scientific material. Dr. Holstege will be able to use the animation to explain to the jury how the sounds of respiratory distress heard on the 911 call relate to cyanide poisoning." Pellegrini noted that the animation did not use any actual images of Autumn.

The defense, however, objected, saying that Pellegrini refused to provide the defense with the exact narration Holstege would use. Further, the attorneys argued that the potential prejudicial effect of the animation could outweigh its probative value. "Defendant asserts that it is unlikely that the proposed animation will fairly represent the existing evidence, is not adequately supported by concrete facts, and there is an unacceptable chance that it would mislead and confuse the jury."

Manning said the video was in.

The sides continued to argue over their expert reports and how discovery was exchanged until early October. But as the trial date loomed, both the prosecution and defense were simply trying to get the last-minute details handled—travel plans for some witnesses and making arrangements for two-way video testimony of those who could not make it to Pittsburgh.

Difenderfer had stopped working on all other cases in June and was spending dozens of hours each week with Ferrante at the jail. Although he didn't have the same manpower as the district attorney's office, Difenderfer proclaimed that he had the best worker in the world—his client.

PELLEGRINI, who had been working on nothing else for months, was ready for trial. But four days before jury selection was to start, she was assaulted in a domestic dispute. The man she had been seeing was accused of striking her head off of the dashboard of the car they were in and physically restraining her.

She was taken to the hospital for evaluation of a head injury and released.

The assault—and the man's arrest—quickly made it to the media, and the messy dispute erupted into speculation about whether she would be able—or permitted—to continue with Ferrante's prosecution.

Her bosses offered to let her step aside, but she declined.

"There are a lot of people counting on me."

Pellegrini returned to work as usual on Monday, preparing for jury selection the next day. But late Monday afternoon, Williams filed a motion asking for additional challenges for the defense during jury selection based on what happened to the prosecutor. She claimed that the extensive media coverage of Pellegrini's assault could jeopardize Ferrante's ability to have a fair jury.

"This publicity may cause prejudicial sympathy for ADA Pellegrini and undue bias to Dr. Ferrante," Williams wrote. She asked Manning to give her client five additional peremptory challenges during jury selection. Peremptory challenges allow a defendant to exclude any potential juror without giving a specific reason. Typically, each side gets seven in a homicide case.

Manning denied the request, and jury selection began as scheduled. Even though Ferrante's defense attorneys originally asked that the panel be chosen from elsewhere, they changed their minds about two months before trial. The twelve jurors, instead, were chosen out of fifty-four Allegheny County residents who were interviewed. Once four alternates were chosen, it was time to start the trial.

11 · · · · · · · · · · · · ·
the case begins

DAY ONE · *Thursday, October 23, 2014—Openings*

Everyone in the courtroom stood as eight men and four women filed into the jury box in Manning's third-floor courtroom—a high-ceilinged chamber brightened by a wall of windows behind the bench in the old stone Allegheny County Courthouse.

Chosen over two days, the jury included a receptionist, convenience-store manager, legislative assistant, power-plant operator, golf-course beverage manager, groundskeeper, and several who worked in information technology. Several jurors scanned the room as their vow was read, taking in the scene. Others looked nervous. The raised right hand of one shook violently throughout his pledge.

Judge Manning—tough, intelligent, quick-tempered, and with a hubris shown often on the bench—turned on the microphone in front of him and began his opening instructions to the jurors, telling them that what they were about to undertake was "one of the most solemn duties of citizenship."

Ferrante sat quietly at the defense table as the judge spoke to the jurors, his dark-blue suit jacket hanging loose. Next to him was Difenderfer. Manning went over with the jurors the structure of a trial, as well as the concept of burden of proof and the expected schedule. He explained that Ferrante faced a single, general charge of criminal homicide, which could include as many as three degrees of murder and two degrees of manslaughter.

First-degree murder, he told them, must include malice—the intent to kill, or "a wickedness of disposition, hardness of heart, cruelty or recklessness of consequences, and extreme indifference to the value of human life." An intention to kill, Manning continued, is a death committed by poison, by lying in wait, or any other willful and deliberate, premeditated act. Second-degree murder is a death that occurs during the commission of another felony. Third-degree murder, the court said, is any killing that is not first- or second-degree murder.

After concluding his instructions, and before opening statements,

Manning sent the jurors to lunch, telling them to enjoy it as it might be their last extended break for a while.

After the jurors filed out, Allegheny County Deputy Sheriff Mike Piscatelli removed the handcuffs from his desk drawer and moved to the defendant to restrain him for transport back to the court's bullpen. By now familiar with the process, Ferrante politely held up the tails of his suit jacket for the deputy to wrap the brown leather belt around his waist before attaching the defendant's manacled hands to the front. As Piscatelli guided the older man gently out of the courtroom, he saw Kimberly reach out for her dad's hand. Normally, strict security rules prohibit anyone from touching a defendant in custody. But the deputy, with a daughter of his own, felt for Ferrante. He allowed Kimberly to hug him quickly, and then led Ferrante the short distance down the hall to his holding cell.

When court resumed nearly two hours later, there was an air of anticipation. Pellegrini, wearing a black skirt suit and pearls, with her blonde hair partially pulled up, was instructing her interns where to set up and where to place the victim's family. The first two rows of the gallery directly behind the prosecution table were reserved for Autumn's loved ones. As Lois slowly made her way into the front row, Pellegrini turned to her, taking her hand, "You okay, baby? We're going to do it together."

The older woman responded confidently, "We are."

On the opposite side of the room, behind the defense table, the chairs reserved for Ferrante's family remained mostly empty. Only his adult son and daughter and his sister were there. Defense attorney Wendy Williams strode into the courtroom wearing a purple dress with gray heels, taking her place at the table next to Difenderfer.

Manning took the bench, a large elevated desk with files, law books, a laptop, and a container of pencils with two erasers on top in the shape of gavels. A glass of fresh ice water was within reach.

"There are two matters before we bring the jury in," he began.

First, he lifted the gag order, in place since a month after Ferrante's arrest, which had prohibited any of the parties from speaking about the case to the media.

Next, the judge turned to the motion presented by prosecutors earlier seeking to introduce evidence of Ferrante's alleged prior bad acts involving the 3-NP and lab mouse. Manning ruled that Pellegrini was not permitted to address the issue in her opening, and that he would reserve a final decision regarding its relevance until later at trial.

"Go get the jury," he instructed.

"MS. PELLEGRINI, do you wish to make an opening statement on behalf of the Commonwealth?"

"Yes, your honor."

"You may do so."

Although Pellegrini had given a lot of thought to her opening, she didn't start preparing it in writing until she arrived at the office around 6:45 a.m. that day. As she munched on a banana, light multigrain bread with peanut butter, and iced tea, she made herself a list of bullet points of the most important topics to cover with the jury.

Without notes or a lectern in front of her, she began.

"On April 17, 2013, Autumn Klein was an amazing woman. She was a brilliant neurologist, a beloved and respected colleague, friend and mother. A mother of a six-year-old daughter named Cianna, who was the light of her life. She was married to the defendant, a researcher in the field of ALS and Huntington's disease. Autumn Klein was what you want to call a shining star. Her career and her life had a bullet right to the sky."

Autumn was passionate about her field involving seizure disorders in pregnant women, but, the prosecutor continued, she was no longer that way about her husband.

"She was unhappy with her marriage. She was married to a much older man. They had been married for a long time. Things just weren't working. She desperately wanted another child, not so much because she was so much in love with the defendant anymore but because she was an only child of older parents. She was always afraid that if something happened to her, Cianna would be all by herself."

Pellegrini briefly told the jurors about Autumn's friend and colleague in Boston, Dr. McElrath, with whom she had confided about the problems in her marriage and of whom Ferrante was jealous. Then the longtime prosecutor moved to the facts of the case: Autumn returned to the couple's home about 11:30 p.m. after making the short walk from the hospital. By 11:52 p.m., her husband was on the phone with 911. Pellegrini recounted Ferrante's words and supposed panic in the recording, as well as what she said was his attempt to misdirect the paramedics to have them take Autumn to UPMC Shadyside—a hospital farther from their home and not a level-one trauma center. But the paramedics knew Autumn needed to be treated immediately, and they took her to UPMC Presbyterian. At 12:21 a.m., she was wheeled into the emergency room.

The staff at the hospital, Pellegrini told the jury, worked heroically to save their colleague, quickly ruling out a stroke, aneurysm, or heart attack. Because Autumn's blood work kept coming back normal, no one was able to figure out how a woman who had left work an hour before, perfectly healthy, was almost dead. But Ferrante, the prosecutor said, kept offering his suggestions—his wife had been taking fertility drugs, she used creatine, she'd been having headaches and fainting episodes.

Pellegrini described to the jurors the extensive efforts made by the doctors trying to save their friend and colleague, and the hunch of one of them to test Autumn for cyanide. The blood test was sent out to the Quest Diagnostics lab in Virginia and returned at a fatal level. First, the results were recorded at 3.4 milligrams per liter, although they were later revised to 2.2.

"Anything over one, you're dead," the prosecutor explained.

But, by April 20—when that test was conducted at the lab—Autumn was already brain dead.

Pellegrini next focused on Ferrante's wish that his wife not have an autopsy. He told colleagues and friends and Autumn's doctors that he did not believe an autopsy would reveal anything.

"But he doesn't realize that under the medical examiner's rule, an unexplained death of someone that is otherwise healthy is ruled a medical examiner's case. He didn't have a choice."

Pellegrini recounted for the jury the timeline of events. After her organs were harvested, Autumn's body was sent for autopsy, and the next day, it was released to the funeral home, where it was cremated. Then, on April 23, one of the original ED doctors who treated Autumn returned to work after being off for the weekend. He wondered what happened to his patient, and when he looked in her chart, he was stunned.

Autumn had a fatal level of cyanide in her blood, Pellegrini said.

Dr. Farkas called the medical examiner's office, triggering the investigation.

Pellegrini quickly shifted topics to describe to the jurors the evidence they would hear in the case. "Pay attention to this, it is very important, because this defendant loves his computers. Love, loves, loves his computers. He Googles everything. You are going to hear in January of 2013, he starts Googling cyanide poisoning. Then he starts Googling an individual—that is Dr. McElrath—his background, the person he is jealous of."

In February, when Autumn went to a conference with Dr. McElrath in San Francisco, Ferrante texted his wife to say he was coming to see her, but never showed up. Then he Googled "Suicides Golden Gate Bridge." When Autumn returned from her trip, Pellegrini said, he Googled whether increased vaginal size indicates your spouse is having an affair.

Then the prosecutor moved on to the next piece of evidence—the cyanide. She told the jurors that, traditionally, in a research lab, it is the office manager who orders supplies—not the lead researcher.

"We find out the morning of the fifteenth—remember, she is poisoned on the night of the seventeenth—he walks in to one of the administrative assistants and says, 'I want the purest potassium cyanide, and I want it tomorrow."

Not only that, Pellegrini said, but evidence would also show that Ferrante was online in the early-morning hours that day looking at cyanide on the Sigma-Aldrich website. The prosecutor speculated that Ferrante did not want to order the cyanide using a purchasing agreement because there were no ongoing research projects in the lab that would use it, and that might be noticed as unusual. He also knew, she continued, that buying something outside of a grant might be noticed.

"You will hear he got it on the next day, and when the detectives ultimately find it in the lab in a refrigerator—after being notified by his lab manager that the seal was broken and 8 grams were missing from the 250-gram bottle—when that bottle was ultimately examined by our latent fingerprint section of the medical examiner's office, his fingerprint is right there on the bottle."

The day after Autumn was cremated, Pellegrini continued, Ferrante started to Google "detecting cyanide poisoning" and "dialysis removal of toxins."

In addition, Ferrante was receiving the e-mails sent to the post–cardiac arrest team of which his wife was a member. Autumn worked in that service at the hospital, but after her collapse, she became a patient of the team, and, Pellegrini said, Ferrante was reading the progress notes to learn what the physicians had found.

And right after Ferrante was interviewed for the first time by the police, he did another Google search, the prosecutor said, "Will ECMO or dialysis remove toxins or poisons?" Another website he visited, she continued, was "How will a coroner detect if someone is killed by cyanide?"

"That is before he was supposed to know how she died."

For several months, Pellegrini said, the detectives investigated whether Autumn was accidentally exposed to cyanide through her research, whether she was suicidal, or whether she was the victim of a homicide. Autumn's friends, family, and colleagues made it clear that the woman was not suicidal, the prosecutor continued.

"That piece of the puzzle just doesn't fit," Pellegrini said. "Then they found out he ordered it [the cyanide]. All of those things, the pieces of the puzzle come to one thing. That she was poisoned. He ordered it, and he gave it to her. She died.

"All along, this defendant, the evidence will show you, thinks he is smarter than everybody. I submit to you the evidence will show you that he was one blood test, one phone call from Farkas to the ME's [medical examiner's] office, from getting away with the perfect murder."

Pellegrini strode to the prosecution table and sat down. It took her just twenty-four minutes to outline the case she had been building for eighteen months.

"Mr. Difenderfer," Judge Manning invited.

The longtime defense attorney had spent hours the day before the trial writing an outline of his opening on a legal pad and pacing the green carpet of his office practicing. For Difenderfer, the most important part of a trial is having command of the facts of the case, which is why he'd spent hours being tutored on the effects and symptoms of cyanide poisoning.

Unlike the serious and all-business approach taken by Pellegrini, Difenderfer, wearing a dark-blue suit and yellow striped tie, strode to the lectern he'd requested and began his opening casually. He spoke with the jurors in a conversational tone—about how he isn't fond of technology and chooses a legal pad instead of a computer.

"I will tell you there are a lot of complicated things in this case. If you see these books and these papers and these envelopes and these computers, I don't even know what it means, but there are gigabytes of information in this case. Secondly, there are a number of scientific things in this case. We're going to be talking about criminal labs, we're going to be talking about toxicology. We're going to be talking about a lot of medical terms. Fortunately for you, I'm not that smart. I struggle to remember and to understand what these medical terms mean, and I get infuriated when I hear *syncopal* means *fainting*. Why don't you just say *fainting*, just as an example?

"What I first want to tell all of you is that the defense in this case, myself and this table, and Dr. Robert Ferrante, do not accept and will never accept that Autumn Klein died from orally ingesting [potassium] cyanide, and they can't prove it. They can't even come close."

He had made a minor—but noticeable—mistake. Throughout his opening, Difenderfer repeatedly called the poison "hydrogen" cyanide, even though the toxin in question was potassium cyanide.

"Secondly," he continued, "I want to scream to the top of my lungs that Autumn Klein's unbelievably unfortunate demise—that this man," pointing to his client, "this doctor, this father, this husband, had nothing to do with her hospitalization and cause of her hospitalization. I truly believe that when you ultimately take this case into your deliberations you are going to agree that the reason why we're here is because of a medical laboratory named Quest giving the wrong levels of blood in a test that got this whole thing in motion."

Difenderfer then turned to his client's background—trying to establish early for the jury that his client was a good man who raised his children by himself while at the same time earning his PhD.

"His family and his children, as you will learn, were always the most important thing to him. Trust me, Autumn was no exception." As for his career, the lawyer continued, "Dr. Ferrante and his lab and his research . . . was focusing on the cure and treatment for probably the worst disease that has afflicted us in the history of mankind, called ALS, Lou Gehrig's disease, a disease that when you are diagnosed your death sentence is within three to five years. The last thing that you can move is your eyeballs until you actually don't have the muscle to breathe, and you suffocate and die."

To do that research, the defense attorney explained, researchers had to damage the mitochondria in cells to replicate the disease process, and then use various therapies to see how the damage might be treated. The damage, Difenderfer continued, was caused by applying a toxin—like peroxide, 3-NP, or cyanide—to the cell.

After telling the jurors that it was his client who was recruited to work in Pittsburgh, and that Ferrante helped land Autumn's position for her, Difenderfer turned to the couple's personal life.

"Now, contrary to what will be said here by so many people, but it will be documented, Autumn's health wasn't the greatest. Ms. Pellegrini, oh, headaches, headaches. Autumn Klein was treating with a physician off the record for extreme headaches and migraines and for years was complaining of that.

"Autumn Klein had a beautiful daughter, Cianna, with the defendant but was into almost an obsession with having a second child in terms of going for IVF treatments and taking tremendous IVF drugs, and because of her failure, becoming extremely obsessed with it and becoming very depressed for not being able to have a child."

Because doctors found that Autumn's eggs had mitochondrial damage, they suggested she use a drug to try to repair them. Both Autumn and Ferrante had studied creatine and its effects, Difenderfer told the jurors, and they decided, and her doctor agreed, to use that supplement.

Ironically, he continued, one of the by-products of creatine "can give false positives for cyanide because of certain chemicals involved in it."

As for his client ordering cyanide, Difenderfer said, Ferrante had just started a research project involving turning skin cells of ALS patients into stem cells. Those cells would then be treated with a toxin.

"Back in January, the doctor started researching cyanide as a possible toxin and maybe a better toxin than the one they were using, which is 3-NP and peroxide. If I was on Google looking for cyanide, you might want to ask a question. If I go on Google and do searches, it's not about cyanide. This guy looking at cyanide is like me looking at the Pirates. This is what he does. He is a scientist. He looks at toxins. He is a scientist. There are thousands of Google searches that you will find that he was doing.

"Coincidentally, you are going to hear there was cyanide in the lab before April 15 when he ordered it. There was already cyanide there. If somebody was planning a murder, do you go to your trusty assistant and say, 'You know what, I want you to order the best cyanide there is,' and do you tell the trusty assistant, 'Don't go through normal channels, I want to bring more attention to this and make it a big deal, and I want it overnight.'"

Or, Difenderfer continued, was it that Ferrante was trying to obtain a grant for his new research project, and that when the "demanding scientist" comes up with something and wants something, "he wants it now."

The defense attorney said that the day of Autumn's collapse was like any other until she returned home that night. "She comes in. She has had fainting spells before," Difenderfer told the jury, noting that at five feet seven inches tall and less than 110 pounds, they believe she had an eating disorder. "She comes home to her husband, in the kitchen, and collapses. He calls 911 and sees her condition in desperation and very upset—as anybody would be—begging the paramedics, 'Please get here, please get here.' He is extremely upset with her.

"Intellectual honesty," Difenderfer told the jury, referring to Pellegrini's statement that Ferrante attempted to mislead the paramedics. His client told the 911 operator he thought his wife was having a stroke, and UPMC Shadyside is a stroke center. Ferrante's referring to "her folks" was him suggesting that Autumn's neurological colleagues were at that hospital, the attorney explained.

Difenderfer then turned to what he considered the heart of the case —the science of what cyanide does to a person, and the symptoms shown by the victim.

"We are saying that there are so many characteristics that somebody would have if poisoned with a lethal dose of cyanide that, plain and simple, Autumn Klein did not have. She had symptoms of cardiac dysrhythmia. That overlaps with a lot of diagnoses, but the ones specific for cyanide—[she] doesn't have them."

The paramedics, Difenderfer said, would tell the jury that their patient had normal breathing, a strong pulse, low blood pressure, and reactive pupils when they arrived at the couple's home. Cyanide, he continued, was the poison used by the Nazis and is a "rapid knockdown agent."

"It affects the body by starving it of oxygen. Blood turns bright red, and you are dead—dead!—in five minutes."

It took two and a half hours before Autumn went into cardiac arrest, and she survived for two and a half days, the lawyer continued. "Not consistent, not consistent, not consistent, with somebody who would have died from cyanide poisoning."

Further, he went on, Ferrante allowed his wife's organs to be donated.

"If I'm in a hurry to get somebody cremated, and I don't want anybody to test any of her blood or any of her organs, am I going to say, 'You know what, let's take this liver that is laced with cyanide and give it to somebody?' This thing of autopsy—this man has more experience in hospitals than most MDs. Absolutely, a case that is an undetermined death . . . goes to the medical examiner."

In addition, he said, Ferrante was not against having an autopsy. Instead, he thought he couldn't donate his wife's organs if he did. When he learned both were possible, that's what happened.

Turning, again, back to the science, Difenderfer listed for the jury the symptoms of cyanide poisoning that Autumn did not have—vomiting, a slowed heart rate, high blood pressure, cherry-red skin, stomach corrosion, or elevated thiocyanate levels.

So how did the cause of death become cyanide, Difenderfer asked. Because Quest Diagnostics said so.

The lab returned a result of 3.4 milligrams per liter, although the measurement was changed to 2.2. "The DA, the district attorney's office, [claims], 'Guys, it was just a mathematical error.' Baloney." Then the county crime lab did a test. "Their testing does not tell you what levels, whether it is fatal or whether it is background levels, normal levels." They test the CORE samples, which are negative, the lawyer continued. People received Autumn's liver and kidneys, and they were fine. So the crime lab sends another blood sample out for an additional test—this time to National Medical Services, a forensics lab. "They are the real deal. They are it—arguably the best in the country."

It took a week before the blood arrived at National Medical Services [NMS] for testing, and the lab reported that the level it registered was nonlethal, Difenderfer told the jury. NMS staff suggested to the Allegheny County Medical Examiner's Office to send another sample to the Mayo Clinic for further confirmation.

"Was that done by the medical examiner? No. This is a high-profile case. They forwent it, and they charged him.

"This prosecution house is 100 percent built on the pillar of Quest," he said, telling the jurors that he would go after the lab and its employees in cross-examination, and that none of the defense experts agree with the Quest results.

"There is no evidence how she ingested it. They say so. No evidence how she encountered cyanide, even if she did. And I will be arguing in my closing they are not going to be able to prove that she died from cyanide poisoning."

Forty-three minutes after issuing the first defense volley, Difenderfer returned to sit next to his client.

"Ms. Pellegrini," Manning asked, "are you prepared to call a witness?"

12 · · · · · · · · · · · · · · · · ·
the case against him

PELLEGRINI QUICKLY MOVED into her case, starting with the 911 call.

After the emergency operator took the stand long enough to verify that he was the person who took Ferrante's call on the night of Autumn's death, Mike Manko, from the DA's office, handed out headphones and transcripts to the jurors. The sound of exhibit number one began to play on courtroom speakers as well as through the headphones. Abruptly, the voices of the 911 operator and Ferrante filled the room, which became still as the realization hit that those in the courtroom were hearing some of the last sounds Autumn ever made. As he listened, Ferrante closed his eyes.

The call, placed at 11:52 p.m., started out with Ferrante's voice, high pitched and pleading. "Please, please, please," he squeaked over and over. The call taker kept asking him to repeat the address, and those listening in the courtroom felt the same frustration that was evident in Ferrante's voice.

Ferrante explained that he thought his wife was having a stroke because she was staring and unable to answer him. The dispatcher followed the protocol for potential stroke victims, asking Ferrante to tell Autumn to smile. When Ferrante replied that she could not, it sounded as if the man wasn't listening. He asked Ferrante whether the smile was equal on both sides, and whether the smile was normal.

"The whole face is flaccid except for these big, white eyes," Ferrante responded, as those in the courtroom futilely willed the dispatcher to get things moving.

Three minutes into the call, it got worse. Autumn began to moan —a terrible, haunting sound that continued throughout the rest of the recording.

The call taker told Ferrante to ask his wife to raise her arms above her head.

"Sweetie, raise your arms above your head, please, please, please, please," he said. "She's just humming. She's audibilizing."

"Is she able to talk at all?" the dispatcher asked.

"No, she's not saying a word. Now, now she's like having a seizure like she's . . . Jesus Christmas, sweetheart, please, no."

It was still only four minutes into the call.

"Okay, you said she's got, she's got, she's now grunting, like she's moaning?" the call taker asked.

"Yes, we're both docs over at UPMC. She's a neurologist just came back from work."

"You said she's got numbness on her one side, or—?" the dispatcher asked.

"No numbness, nothing, it's, it's just like flaccid."

Again, the dispatcher asked about the groaning.

"You can hear her," Ferrante replied. "Oh God, please get someone here quickly."

"They're already on their way. It's not delaying the call at all. They've already been en route, okay?"

But the paramedics wouldn't arrive for seven more minutes.

"Oh, God help me. God help me."

"Okay, like I said, I'm sending the paramedics to help you. Okay, I'm making sure help is on the way. Don't let her have anything to eat or drink. Okay, Bob? Just, I want you to let her rest in the most comfortable position and wait for help to arrive."

"Her, her, her folks are down at Shadyside. Maybe that would be the best place to take her," Ferrante said.

"Okay, let the paramedics know that when they arrive that you want to have her taken to Shadyside, okay?"

"I, I, I will," Ferrante replied.

The dispatcher told his caller to make sure any family pets were put away—the dog was in his cage, Ferrante said—and to gather up any medications Autumn might be taking.

"Is it just you and her in the house?" the call taker asked.

"It's just me in the house, and it's my little daughter upstairs. Six years old," he answered. "I've got to find somebody to help take care of her."

Ferrante told the dispatcher that it looked like his wife was about to throw up, that her breathing had changed—first becoming huge breaths, and then more shallow—and that her face was turning bright red.

By eight minutes into the call, Ferrante was again expressing his frustration at the lengthy delay in response from the paramedics—telling the dispatcher he'd go out to check that the outside light was on again.

"What do I do about my daughter?" he asked. "I've got, we don't know anybody here from neighbors."

"Okay, um, are you guys new to the area?"

"Yes, we just moved from Boston," Ferrante answered.

He told the dispatcher that his wife had never had a stroke, but there had been episodes of fainting. He also volunteered that Autumn was trying to get pregnant.

At eleven minutes in, the dispatcher asked if the front door of the home was unlocked.

"Yes, the front door is unlocked," Ferrante said with frustration. "Where the hell is somebody?"

A few seconds later, Ferrante can be heard directing the paramedics, who had finally arrived.

"Please, please, please, please, please, please, please, yes, come here. This way, this way. Please, please, please, please."

When the recording ended, relief washed across the courtroom that the sounds, described by the district attorney prior to trial as Autumn's "death screams," had finally subsided.

PELLEGRINI'S NEXT WITNESS was Gerald Moran, the security operations manager for UPMC. He told jurors that after Autumn died, he went back through the various surveillance-camera recordings to try to piece together her movements that day.

"It was a little difficult because I didn't know Klein at all. What I wound up having to do was I kind of started at the end and worked my way backwards. I found out what time she was brought in by the paramedics into the hospital, and I was able to obtain video footage and able to view her coming into the hospital so I could see what she looked like, what she was wearing. I backtracked from there, and we have an electronic card access system throughout the hospital so I was looking at the card access system to see where she was at and be able to see cameras near those locations of the card readers."

Moran then walked the jurors through the video footage being displayed on the large screen on the wall across from them. There was the ghostly sense of watching a dead woman's last waking hours as she went through her long workday. The short clips slid by:

- Autumn arriving at the UPMC Presbyterian driveway at 8:27 a.m., her long hair down and her sunglasses perched on the top of her head.
- Autumn riding the elevator in the Lillian Kaufmann Building up to her eighth-floor office.
- Boarding the elevator again at 12:09 p.m., riding down to the first floor, putting her earbuds in.
- Entering the main lobby of Magee Women's Hospital—less than a half mile away—at 12:22 p.m., then a minute later going into the secure obstetrical wing on the third floor, where she spent fifteen minutes before going back to the lobby.
- Returning to her office at 12:50 p.m., then nothing until 10:59 p.m., when she is seen entering an elevator again—this time with her hair pulled back in a ponytail.
- At 11:11 p.m., again putting her earbuds in, taking an escalator up in UPMC Presbyterian, where she remains for six minutes before riding back down and exiting the Presby driveway.
- At 11:18 p.m., she can be seen texting on her phone as she walks.

After eighteen minutes of questioning, Pellegrini offered Moran for cross-examination.

It was the first witness Difenderfer really got to confront, and he made the most of it, almost immediately calling the man's investigation into question.

"When, and at whose direction, did you start looking up, searching through these videos?" the attorney asked.

"I first started looking at it when I heard of the incident," Moran answered.

"Give me a ballpark, what date? May? April?"

"It would have been the following day," the witness replied.

"The following day of what?"

"The following day of her death," Moran said.

But, Difenderfer continued, why look for information about Autumn?

"There was concern out there and being that she was an employee of the hospital and then there was some rumor out there," Moran continued.

"Concern about what? What were you concerned about?" Difenderfer asked.

"I was concerned about the hospital and her and making sure everything was proper."

"What doctor, what person, what person brought to your attention, first of all, that Klein was even in the hospital? Did you know that? Did somebody tell you or were you aware that she was in the hospital prior to the twenty-first of April?" Difenderfer pressed.

"No," the witness answered.

"So if you don't even know that she was in the hospital, what in the heck drew a concern to you about her passing away on the twenty-first of April?"

"I can't recall who mentioned it. I don't know."

"Somebody mentioned this woman might have been poisoned with cyanide?" Difenderfer continued.

"Something of that nature."

"So it was rampant throughout the community. Obviously, people in the hospital knew about it?"

"Yes, they did."

Difenderfer had the clips replayed, focusing on the two, seven minutes apart, of Autumn using the escalator as she entered and left Presby shortly after 11:00 p.m.

"Obviously, the fastest way home is not as you are walking past the emergency room, not coming in here, going up this escalator and coming down six or seven minutes later going down the escalator?"

"Correct."

"This is the building where Dr. Ferrante's laboratory is, isn't it?"

"No, he is in the building that connects through Scaife Hall."

"You can get into it through here?"

"Eventually, yeah, if you had the card access."

"You get off the escalator, come around the fifth floor, and if you have access, you go into his office?"

"That's correct."

"That is where the cyanide was, isn't it?" Difenderfer pushed.

"That's correct."

Next up for the prosecution was Jerad Albaugh, the paramedic who responded to the couple's home the night of Autumn's collapse.

Now working as a firefighter and paramedic in North Carolina, Albaugh recalled to the jury that he was dispatched on a report of a stroke that night.

"The patient was laying on the ground feet closest to the fridge, head up here where the sink was. Like I said, she was unconscious. Both of her arms were out in what we call an anatomical position laying on her back."

Initially, Albaugh said he and his partner, Steve Mason, checked her breathing and pulse, which were adequate, as well as her glucose level. When he checked her blood pressure, he continued, it was adequate. They spoke with their patient's husband, he said, to get a description of what happened and saw the bag of creatine on the kitchen counter. When the paramedics returned to their patient, they saw that her heart rate and blood pressure had "started to tank."

Her breathing had changed, too, into a pattern of eight normal breaths followed by very fast breathing.

"That signifies something seriously neurological is going on—whether it is a hemorrhagic stroke or regular stroke or a head bleed. At this point, I know that it is time to go. It is time to go fast because she was somewhat normal with her normal breathing rate. This is within three to five minutes that we had been there, and it is time to go, time to go fast."

He said it was a "load and go"—a "life and death situation."

"We were leaving pretty fast. I told Steve to get me there as fast as possible, to call ahead."

As the first day of trial began to wind down, Pellegrini called the first of several medical professionals from UPMC Presbyterian, who would talk about the treatment Autumn received and the difficulty they had in making their diagnoses. The first of those was Dr. Andrew Farkas, the emergency department resident who was the first to encounter Autumn when she arrived.

Farkas recounted his initial impressions of the patient—vacant eyes, shallow breathing, and low blood pressure. Very quickly, he said, the staff recognized that she would need to be placed on a ventilator, and, because of the low blood pressure, they gave her repeated doses of epinephrine.

"It was apparent that she was very gravely ill based on her low blood pressure and the lack of response to any therapy. Our initial working diagnosis was that maybe it was something neurologic because we had heard about a headache beforehand. That was sort of our first inclination, although that still honestly wouldn't explain the low blood pressure, but it was the best thing that we had to go on."

Farkas told the jurors about Autumn's normal CT results and that the staff ran every test they could think of for "terrible things that kill people quickly." He described the bright-red blood he saw upon inserting the patient's central line, as well as the measures taken to bring her back when she went into cardiac arrest. The physician finished his direct examination by recounting when he learned about the positive cyanide result and why he called the medical examiner's office.

"It became a concern to me that no one would report that value to the appropriate authorities," he said.

On cross, Difenderfer asked Farkas if he thought the physicians who ordered the cyanide test would ignore the results and not report them.

"It is not that they would blow it off, but when a patient is in the hospital, there is a feedback loop. This was an unusual circumstance with a lab coming back on a patient so far after they were deceased. I don't think that they would willfully neglect that, but there was a chance that perhaps someone might not notice it for some time later."

Then Difenderfer turned to a matter that Farkas had not addressed in his questioning by Pellegrini.

"When you were interviewed by the police, do you remember telling them that Dr. Klein had a gray and ashen color?" Difenderfer asked.

"I do."

The increased oxygen levels in the blood that caused the venous blood to become bright red, the attorney asked, wouldn't that cause the patient's skin to be bright red?

"It would," Farkas answered. "I misspoke. Gray and ashen was not what I meant to say."

"Gray and ashen. Are you saying that you meant pink and bright red? You made a mistake?" Difenderfer asked disbelievingly.

"It was a sixty-minute interview. I was speaking as contemporaneously—" Farkas said before he was cut off by another question.

Difenderfer wrapped up, and the first day of the trial was done.

DAY TWO · *The Prosecution Resumes Its Case*

The prosecution started its day by calling to the stand a series of physicians who treated Autumn after her collapse: Dr. Thomas Martin, who supervised Farkas and worked on the patient during her cardiac arrest; Dr. Clifton Callaway, who recommended the cyanide test; Dr. Jon Rittenberger, who suggested an autopsy could be useful when it was clear the patient would not survive; Dr. Lori Shutter, who discovered Klein's faint pulse following CPR; and Dr. Maria Baldwin, who worked with Autumn and was the on-call doctor who read her friend's EEG.

Baldwin, who appeared to have been the closest friend and colleague called by prosecutors, said she talked to Autumn several times a day, and that they were friends who shared personal information, including Autumn's struggle with infertility.

"Did she ever appear suicidal to you?" Pellegrini asked.

"No."

"Depressed?"

"No."

Later, Baldwin told Difenderfer that she remembered her friend telling her about having headaches and having sought advice and treatment from another UPMC neurologist. She did not know, though, that Autumn had been using creatine for fertility.

Baldwin told the jury that she got an e-mail from Autumn at 10:06 p.m. on April 17 in which she apologized for having memory lapses and said she'd been "going in and out lately."

"Would it be a fair characterization with the patient load that she had . . . as well as her clinical work or laboratory work that she was under a great amount of stress?" Difenderfer asked.

"Yes."

Next Pellegrini called Dr. Robert Friedlander, Ferrante's colleague and friend who accompanied him to the hospital that night. Friedlander described how Ferrante and Autumn were recruited in 2011 and then explained for the jury the way his lab, which he shared with Ferrante, was set up.

"If you need specific items for a research project, do you order them yourself?" Pellegrini asked.

"No."

"Who orders them for you?"

"I usually tell somebody in the lab and they will tell the lab manager or I would tell the lab manager, but usually I don't order it myself."

Friedlander explained that the lab could only be accessed with a key card and that he did not believe Autumn had one. Then Pellegrini asked the neurosurgeon if he was familiar with Ferrante's ongoing research.

"I would know in general terms the work that is being done there, but I wouldn't oversee directly his grants or the very details of the components of his work. That was his lab."

"To your knowledge, in April of 2013, did the defendant have any research projects involving the use of cyanide?"

"Not to my knowledge."

The prosecutor then turned to creatine. Friedlander described it as an energy supplement that is also used in research to treat a variety of neurological conditions. Ferrante had done extensive studies with creatine and preferred a manufacturer in Germany because he thought what was sold there was of the highest quality.

The night of Autumn's collapse, when Friedlander drove Ferrante to the hospital, he recalled his friend telling him Autumn had been unable to conceive a second child and was taking creatine to try to repair the mitochondria in her eggs. He also recounted conversations he had with the defendant throughout Autumn's hospitalization, including three separate discussions they had about having an autopsy.

"He did not think that an autopsy would be very helpful," Friedlander said. "I'm not quite sure why. He just didn't think that it was going to be helpful in figuring out what happened."

Later, after Ferrante learned from investigators that Autumn had died from cyanide poisoning, Friedlander said he and his friend spoke about how she could have been exposed to it.

"I was trying to figure out how to make sense of this, and given some of our previous conversations pertaining to the fact that there could be some cyanide contaminants in creatine, I, myself, started looking online and found one link that didn't really lead me anywhere, but I was trying to find an explanation of what happened, and Bob and I talked about that."

"You didn't want to believe that anyone poisoned her, right?" Pellegrini asked.

"That's correct."

"Certainly not her husband?"

"Correct."

"Did the defendant ever tell you that he ordered cyanide in April?"

"No."

On cross-examination by Difenderfer, Friedlander acknowledged that Ferrante actually placed the cyanide order through the lab manager and that it was purchased with money from a $600,000 start-up fund that was part of Ferrante's recruitment package.

"The start-up money, he can use basically for any purpose that he wants in regard to his research?" Difenderfer asked.

"Yes."

"And it doesn't have to be assigned to a grant?"

"That's correct."

"And he could purchase things overnight if he wishes?"

"It is his discretion."

"Whether he wants something overnight on the P card [purchasing credit card] or ordered through other sources, it is his total discretion?"

"As long as it is legitimate research, it is his discretion," Friedlander answered.

The next witness called by assistant district attorney Chernosky was Pittsburgh homicide detective Harry Lutton.

He told the jurors about the search he led on May 3 at Ferrante's home looking for anything that could be used to store, clean up, distribute, or mix with cyanide, as well as any computers that could be used to search for information about cyanide.

Lutton described for the jurors the couple's large home and its layout, walking them through a number of photographs, as well as listing the items taken, including three computers, an external hard drive, salt and pepper shakers, cupcakes, hairbrushes, vacuums, and dustpans.

The next day, Lutton continued, they served a warrant on Ferrante's lab, looking for the same types of things.

"Upon entering his office and conducting your search, what, if anything, did you observe?" Chernosky asked.

"I actually went in and sat down to see what was on the desk before I started searching the office," Lutton answered. "Right here on this green book is actually an order, submittal form, for cyanide, for purchasing cyanide."

The detective also described the safe under the defendant's desk that was also taken.

On cross-examination, Difenderfer returned to the issue of the cyanide order.

"When you go into his office, right on top of his desk is the order for cyanide, correct?"

"Correct."

"Certainly not hidden, was it?" the attorney continued.

"No, it was not."

The prosecution concluded the day by calling a few additional detectives who testified that they searched Autumn's office, as well as the couple's vehicles, and seized two additional computers.

DAY THREE · *The Detectives Testify*

By Monday the prosecution was rolling along, and Detectives Bobby Shaw, Provident, and McGee were up to testify. They told the jurors about getting Ferrante's computers, retrieving items from his office safe, and recovering the large containers of creatine from his lab. They also told the jury that it was 1.4 miles to UPMC Shadyside, where Ferrante wanted paramedics to take Autumn, and just 0.4 miles to Presby.

Although the testimony wasn't terribly compelling, it laid the groundwork for the rest of the prosecution's case, which would focus on Google and Internet searches, as well as the cyanide purchase.

McGee also described his first conversation with Ferrante, five days after Autumn's death. Ferrante was at the dining room table, Kimberly sitting with him.

"I asked Mr. Ferrante if he knew how his wife died. At that time, he told me he believed it was either from a brain condition or a heart attack," McGee said. "I said, 'Well, it was learned that your wife died of a fatal dose of cyanide.' At that point, he looked at his daughter and said, 'Why would she do this to herself?' and then he looked back at me and said, 'Who would have done this to her?'"

On cross-examination by Williams, McGee described the various medications belonging to Autumn that police seized during the investigation. They included drugs to treat hypothyroidism and acne. The defense spent a lot of time grilling McGee about the fertility medications —the fact that Klein had ordered them from Canada and ultimately had given them to her friend when she stopped taking them in January.

Williams then turned her questions to the topic of suicide.

"Now, when you talked to Dr. Ferrante, and he said that his wife had said something about Pittsburgh, being a city with a lot of bridges, and you asked if she ever talked about killing herself, you were investigating this as a possible suicide, is that fair to say?"

"At the time we were speaking to Dr. Ferrante, I didn't know what we had. I didn't know if it was suicide or homicide. I was trying to cover all the bases at that point."

"Is that a yes?" Williams pushed.

"That is one of the things that we were looking into, yes, ma'am." However, McGee continued, no one he interviewed ever said they thought Autumn was suicidal.

After Williams concluded, Pellegrini had just one additional question: "Detective, when you told the defendant that his wife died as a result of a lethal level of cyanide, did he tell you that he ordered cyanide two days before?"

"No, ma'am."

The prosecution moved through its next two witnesses quickly. The first, Jonathan Lundy, was the University of Pittsburgh hazardous materials specialist who was asked to look for and recover any cyanide from Ferrante's lab. In total, during three trips to Scaife Hall, Lundy testified that he recovered four bottles of cyanide—including the 250-gram bottle purchased by Ferrante on April 15. That one, he said, was found in the back right corner of a refrigerator in the lab.

On cross-examination, Williams asked Lundy if he talked to anyone in the lab about using cyanide in their work.

"I did not, no," he answered.

"You were aware that they used it in their work?" she asked.

"It is commonly used in university research," he answered. "I wasn't aware if it was being used in this specific lab or not."

"Based on you going back and finding more and more, there could be cyanide in the lab today, is that fair to say?" Williams asked.

"That's fair to say."

After the day's lunch break, Pellegrini recalled Friedlander to the stand to ask him an important question about his conversations with Ferrante from the night of Klein's collapse that she'd forgotten the day before.

"What did he tell you about Autumn when she came home?"

"He mentioned that when Autumn came home, he prepared for her a drink with creatine mixed in it," Friedlander responded.

"What did she do with it?"

"I assumed she drank it," he continued.

"Objection," Difenderfer said.

"Sustained."

"Doctor, do you remember speaking to the police?" Pellegrini asked.

"Yes."

"Do you remember what you told them about what the defendant told you about Dr. Klein's actions when she came home?" Pellegrini asked.

"Dr. Ferrante prepared a drink for her. That he mixed creatine, and she drank it."

The prosecution next presented evidence from one of the state troopers who analyzed the electronics that belonged to Ferrante and Klein. Former trooper Donald Scott Lucas said that, overall, he analyzed thirty-five devices, including mobile phones, computers, external hard drives, and memory cards.

Included in his review, Lucas also went over the text messages recovered from the couple from the day Klein collapsed, including their conversation about her ovulating and Ferrante's suggestion to take creatine, as well as the last exchange that they had while she was walking out of the hospital on her way home late that night.

Lucas recounted for the jury the last text-message exchange between the couple at 11:17 that night. "Walking out of Presby now," Klein wrote. To which Ferrante responded, "Okay, be safe."

Lucas also told the jurors that he discovered notes in Klein's phone regarding her infertility treatment and the creatine regimen, which could be sprinkled on toast or mixed in fruit punch.

Lucas concluded by testifying about searches conducted on two MacBook Air computers he analyzed. On one, he said he found 380 search queries, including one at 5:32 p.m. on April 25, "Would ECMO or dialysis remove traces of toxins or poisons?" On May 1, Lucas found the computer user had also accessed Google support pages for "remove items from your Google Web History."

On cross-examination by Williams, Lucas agreed that he could not tell the jury that it was Ferrante who conducted those searches.

The prosecution concluded the third day of trial by calling to the stand two administrators in Ferrante's lab at the University of Pittsburgh—Michele Perpetua, the lab manager for the Department of Neurosurgery, and Patricia Quirin, an administrator there.

Perpetua testified that she was the one responsible for placing orders for the researchers in the lab, and that the requests, generally, were made by staff members.

"Did Dr. Friedlander ever come and order from you?" Pellegrini asked.

"No."

"Prior to April the 17th of 2013, had the defendant, Ferrante, ever come to you to order anything?"

"No, he did not," Perpetua answered.

"Now, how often were things ordered on an overnight basis?" Pellegrini continued.

"I would say maybe a couple of times a year."

"I'm going to direct your attention to April the 15th of 2013. So in the morning about eight o'clock, did something happen?"

"Dr. Ferrante came to me and asked if he wanted to purchase a chemical to receive it overnight, what would he have to do?" Perpetua answered.

"What did you tell him?"

Perpetua explained that she told Ferrante he would have to order it with a P card, a purchasing credit card, because through the university's typical order process, called Panther Express, it would take two to four days.

"Did he tell you what type of chemical that he wanted to order?" Pellegrini asked.

"I asked him what chemical he wanted. He said potassium cyanide."

"Did he tell you what type of potassium cyanide he wanted?" the prosecutor continued.

"He wanted the best and the purest."

After Ferrante looked at the various purities available through Sigma-Aldrich and chose the 250-gram size, he remarked to Perpetua, "Oh, it is that easy."

They placed the order with the P card, charging $163.94 to be delivered the next day.

On cross-examination by Williams, Perpetua said she was familiar with the use of cyanide in mitochondrial research like that conducted in the neurosurgery lab.

"And you had ordered cyanide before?" Williams asked.

"Yes, I did."

Perpetua explained that there was no special permission necessary to have the toxin shipped overnight, and that Ferrante was the kind of person who wanted "everything yesterday."

"If something was required for a study, he needed it, he wanted it right away," the witness said.

She went on to say that Ferrante did nothing to mask his purchase.

"Everything was done according to the regulation?" Williams asked.

"Yeah, it seemed like it was okay."

"The purchase went through. Nobody had any problem with it, correct?" the lawyer continued.

"Yes."

"Until after Autumn Klein died?"

"Correct," Perpetua said.

Quirin, the other administrator, testified that she was responsible for keeping control of the P card assigned to Ferrante, and that she kept it locked in her desk drawer. The morning of April 15, she said, he asked her to get the card to make the purchase with Perpetua.

She said, too, that Ferrante had never made any purchase requests through her. Quirin estimated that in about two years, Ferrante had used his P card about twenty-four times. Typically, she said, purchases for research were made with Panther Express. Any purchases, she said, were supposed to be associated with a grant number so that they could be tracked.

DAY FOUR · *Google Searches and Good-Bye Letters*

After concluding the rest of Quirin's testimony, prosecutors called Lois Klein to the stand.

A large woman with her hair pulled up in a bun atop her head, Lois walked to the front of the courtroom with the slow gait of a person in pain. She was bundled in a dark-brown sweater on top of a blue sweater, and stopped by the witness stand to state her name for the record. She tacked on a fact: She and her husband had been married for fifty years.

"Could you tell us a little bit about your relationship with your daughter?" Pellegrini asked.

"A wonderful relationship. She was a fantastic daughter. Any mother would have wanted her," Lois answered.

"You were proud of her?"

"Absolutely."

Pellegrini asked her to describe the kind of mother her daughter had been.

"Autumn was an absolutely wonderful mother. She was a loving, caring, concerned mother. She wanted the right things for Cianna. She didn't want her to eat bad food. She wanted her to learn to read and to—I mean, she is just a sharp little girl, and Autumn was just a wonderful mother."

Lois described for the jury receiving the call from Ferrante after Autumn collapsed. She and her husband had already been scheduled to go to Pittsburgh on April 18 to watch Cianna while Autumn and Ferrante went to Nemacolin Woodlands Resort for a conference. Instead, they rushed up as soon as they got the call.

"Did he tell you at that point what had happened?" Pellegrini asked.

"He said something about she came home from work, kissed him as usual, said 'I don't feel well' and fell to the floor," she answered.

The Kleins arrived in Pittsburgh from their home outside of Baltimore about 5:30 a.m. and went straight to their daughter's house. There was no one there, but about fifteen minutes later, Ferrante arrived.

"He came in the front door. He did not see me right away. I mean, he looked fine. No problems. When he saw me, all of a sudden, he was like faking, trying to make like he was teary-eyed and crying," she said.

Lois then told the jury that Ferrante told her nothing about her daughter's condition, what hospital she was in, or offer to take the older couple to see her. Instead, Lois said, her son-in-law wanted to wait until Kimberly and Michael arrived in Pittsburgh before they went to the hospital.

"Does he tell you what happened to your daughter?" Pellegrini asked.

"Not that I can recall."

Lois told the jury that they didn't get to UPMC Presbyterian until 4:00 p.m.—more than sixteen hours after Autumn's collapse.

Lois described her interactions with Ferrante at the hospital—that she felt she was being kept out of the discussions regarding her daughter's treatment and prognosis, and that she was frustrated with her son-in-law. She also said she disagreed with his feeling that no autopsy was needed.

"I remember saying that I wanted an autopsy," Lois said.

"Why?" Pellegrini asked.

"Because I wanted to know what happened to my daughter," she answered. "He said people really didn't want to know what the results of an autopsy were because they didn't want to know what their health issues would be ahead of them. They didn't want to worry about things like that."

Ferrante told her, Lois said, that doctors believed Autumn had either had a heart attack or an electrical brain surge.

During cross-examination, Difenderfer went hard after Lois, calling into question her testimony that she and her husband simply sat at their daughter's home the entire day after they arrived without asking to see her, going to see her, or even asking questions about her.

"So, you and him, for the first time that you see him, you haven't seen your daughter yet, you say that you guys just hug and nothing is talked about, 'Oh my God, I've got to get to the hospital. I want to see my daughter.' None of that is discussed?" Difenderfer asked.

"That's correct," Lois answered.

"You are further telling us in terms of asking what her condition was—strike that—you never asked him what her condition was?"

"No, I did not," the woman replied.

He continued along the same path for several more questions.

"You just sat in his house?"

"We sat in his house," she answered.

Lois remained on the stand for forty-eight minutes before concluding her testimony and returning to her seat in the front row of the gallery for the remainder of the trial.

Later in the morning, the prosecution called two witnesses who worked in Ferrante's lab, a research assistant and a research associate.

Amanda Mihalik split her working time between Friedlander and Ferrante and was responsible for caring for the Huntington's disease mouse colony. She told the jury that the week of Autumn's collapse, she thought Ferrante was acting unusually.

"He seemed to be a little different that week. He seemed to have a little more energy. It just kind of struck me as a little bizarre at that time. I guess the day before Autumn was taken to the hospital, or the day that Autumn was taken to the hospital, I helped Dr. Ferrante take creatine from our lab and put it in a ziplock bag."

"Did you make any observations with regard to the defendant consuming anything to eat or drink in the lab?" Chernosky asked her.

"Yes. On that Monday and Tuesday, I saw him mixing things in the lab in beakers, and then he was drinking it at the sink. I thought that was very odd. Because you are not supposed to drink anything from the lab. We have very strict rules about you are not allowed to take any food or drink in the lab, and then you are not allowed to eat things from the lab. It is a dangerous place."

When Ferrante asked Mihalik for help getting the tubs of creatine down for packaging, she said he told her that he intended to give it to his wife.

On cross-examination by Williams, Mihalik admitted that she had previously told the police she thought Ferrante was a demanding boss.

"Did you say that he is very smart and expects a lot from himself and coworkers?" Williams asked.

"Yes."

"Is it true that he had personality conflicts with people because of his intensity and his expectations?" the lawyer continued.

"He had a lot of personality conflicts with people in the lab," the witness answered.

"Now, you also described him as, correct, as a good and bad boss because he was difficult to work with at times but yet he was very loyal to his employees?" Williams asked.

"I would say that he made a good show of being loyal, but I always found him very difficult to work with and very difficult to please."

While Mihalik was on the stand, the defense scored a significant point when she confirmed that there had been a meeting among the lab staff in which Ferrante talked about using cyanide in the stem-cell project.

"Specifically in the meeting when you say cyanide was discussed, was it your understanding that cyanide would be used to bring about cell death?" Williams asked.

"It was one of several options discussed."

However, the next prosecution witness, Dr. Jinho Kim, Ferrante's research associate, disagreed with that statement. Kim testified that the first time Ferrante had mentioned cyanide to him was on April 16, when the potassium cyanide his boss had ordered the day before arrived.

The defendant told Kim that he ordered the cyanide for some future experiment.

"Prior to April 16th of 2013, did he mention any future experiments that would use cyanide?" Chernosky asked.

"No."

Ferrante asked Kim to store it for him, and the researcher put it under his workbench in the lab. He asked whether it should be locked up, he told the jury, and Ferrante said no.

The next day, on April 17, Kim said Ferrante asked him for glass vials, and he gave his boss two of them and a Sharpie permanent marker.

"He measured—I thought it was creatine. He measured into two bottles 1 gram. The other is 2 grams. He marked it with the marker," Kim said, noting that he took a piece of tape and put it over the marker lines to keep them from being erased.

The next time Kim saw the potassium cyanide, he testified, was after the police investigation had begun—in a lab refrigerator.

"Is that where you had put it?" Chernosky asked.

"No. I put it under my bench. The next time I saw it, it was in the refrigerator," the witness answered. When Kim realized it had been moved, he told the lab administrators, who ultimately called university police.

Chernosky finished his questions, and, after the lunch break, Williams pushed Kim hard to try to prove the defense point that cyanide can be used in research to cause cell death. Showing him an article, she asked, "Is that a scientific treatise on the use of cyanide to cause apoptosis on cells?" Waiting for him to answer as he reviewed the document, she grew impatient. "Dr. Kim, you can clearly see in that article it is discussing cyanide to cause apoptosis in cell research. All you have to do is read the title of it."

As he began to answer, Williams cut him off. "Yeah, I'm not asking about the conclusion. This is a learned treatise discussing where scientists use cyanide as a toxin on apoptosis on cells, yes or no? Are they using cyanide as a tool in that article on cells to do research?"

"They use it, but they are not successful," Kim responded.

"I'm not asking if it turned out good, but did they use it as a tool?" Williams pushed.

"Yes."

A few moments later, Williams asked Kim why he wasn't looking at her when he answered.

"You seem like you are afraid to answer. Is your job at stake here because you are here with a lawyer today? Are you afraid?" she asked.

"No."

Williams went on to question the researcher about comments he made to investigators that he saw Autumn on April 17 and she did not look well.

"She looked tired, and you asked her twice if she was okay?" Williams asked.

"Yes."

"You remembered even though they didn't interview you until May. You told them on the [seventeenth] she was very pale?"

"She was there the seventeenth. She was pale."

Switching topics, Williams asked Kim about the ongoing stem-cell project.

"Was it moving ahead quickly from January to April? Was there a lot of push and a lot of excitement to get the project moving and to get the proposal done and get it funded?" the attorney asked.

"Yes."

Kim also verified for the defense that Autumn had been involved in the stem-cell project, had been included in group e-mails about it, and was attending lab meetings.

As for the cyanide delivery, Williams asked Kim when he first saw the toxin.

"When the cyanide comes to the lab, Bob gets it, and he shows it to you, correct?" Williams asked.

"Yes."

"He is not trying to hide it or act like it didn't come or anything like that. He opens it and looks at it. Everything that comes into the lab, he opens it, and he looks at it. Is it pretty fair to say that he is pretty hands-on? He checks things out?" Williams asked.

"Yeah."

Williams spent several minutes talking to Kim about the way chemicals were stored in the lab, with him confirming that dangerous toxins —like cyanide and 3-NP—were not kept locked up and could be accessed by anyone.

He also acknowledged on cross that it was not unusual for him to help Ferrante mark glass vials and measure them.

On redirect, Chernosky went back to the articles Williams had pushed hard on.

"In causing cell death in the lab, would you say that cyanide is a regular practice?" the prosecutor asked.

"No, we didn't use it."

"Prior to that conversation with the defendant on April 16th where he handed you the bottle of cyanide, had you discussed using cyanide to cause cell death?"

"No."

With Kim's testimony concluded, prosecutors tried to present evidence of what they thought was Ferrante's flight from Florida to avoid arrest. But the defense objected, and Manning agreed the evidence wasn't relevant. Instead, Chernosky moved on to the witness who tracked all of the Google searches conducted by the defendant.

It only took Pennsylvania State Police Corporal John Roche thirty minutes to go through dozens of searches conducted and websites visited on the MacBook Air that investigators found locked away in Ferrante's safe under his desk.

The software program Internet Evidence Finder discovered 3,463 search queries on that single computer. The first noted was "malice aforethought definition," at 6:26 p.m. on January 1. Roche quickly moved onto others:

- "cyanide poisoning," at 3:58 p.m. on January 8
- "Human toxicity 3-Nitropropionic acid," at 9:26 a.m. on January 31
- "Toxic dose human 3-Nitropropionic acid cardiomyopathy," a few minutes later
- "Suicides Golden Gate Bridge," at 8:43 a.m. on February 15
- "Divorce Pittsburgh, Pa," at 7:43 a.m. on February 18
- "Does increased vaginal size suggest wife is having sex with another," at 1:16 p.m. on February 19
- "McElrath, Thomas Frederick," at 10:10 p.m. on February 23
- "Potential cyanide neuroscience project," at 9:36 p.m. on April 14
- "Hospitals near Nemacolin," at 9:29 a.m. on April 17
- "Medical examiner toxicology report," and several variations on

the afternoon of April 22, as well as "toxicology studies potassium cyanide"

- "Detecting cyanide poisoning," at 5:03 p.m. on April 22
- "Dialysis and removal of toxins," at 1:23 p.m. on April 23
- "Acute cardiopulmonary failure metabolic acidosis cause," at 7:46 a.m. on April 23
- "Creatine and cyanide," at 3:26 p.m. on April 26

As for the websites visited on the computer, Roche said, they included one titled "cyanide poisoning, causes, symptoms, treatments, when to seek medical care," at 4:11 p.m. on January 8; "Illinois man killed by cyanide poisoning after striking it rich in lottery," also on January 8; "how would you test for potassium cyanide," at 11:48 p.m. on April 22; and also on April 22, "How would a coroner detect when someone is killed by cyanide."

By the time Chernosky finished with his witness, there was not much for the defense to do. Williams asked Roche several questions about the process used to analyze the computers, who set the parameters for what was reviewed, and how Google's autocomplete function works. She also asked if Roche had been asked to review any of Autumn's computers.

"I was not, no," he answered.

"So you wouldn't know if she ever looked and typed in cyanide or suicide or anything like that?"

"I wouldn't know."

As for the specifics of the searches he already read, Williams did not ask about those. She did ask, however, why Roche didn't note for the jury that on April 15, Ferrante looked online at the material safety data sheet information from the company where he ordered the cyanide.

"So if Dr. Ferrante was looking at how to safely handle cyanide ordered from Sigma-Aldrich on that date, and that's their safety policy, that would be something that you could provide, you just weren't asked to?"

"It's just something that I wasn't asked to go back and verify if this was there or not," Roche answered.

With nothing more to extract from the witness, Williams concluded. Pellegrini next called Detective Jackelyn Weibel of the district attorney's office to the stand. Weibel described for the jurors the search of Ferrante's home on May 28, when she discovered the shredded letters the man had written. Using blown-up copies on poster board propped in front of the jury box, Weibel read each one of them—all dated May 10—the day of Autumn's memorial service in Baltimore.

She began with the one addressed to the entire family. As Weibel concluded the letter, Ferrante, his hands clasped under his chin with his glasses on the table, was crying quietly. The next letter was written to Ferrante's adult daughter, Kimberly. He reminisced about her as a colicky baby who sang off-key and had curly hair. He also noted her inquisitive nature, especially one day when she ran from their backyard to find him because she had seen an "incredibly odd toad."

"Do you remember it was a snake that had swallowed a toad and the head remained in the mouth of the snake as it was swallowing the rest of the body?" He told his daughter to keep close her memories of her grandfather, especially when he moved in with them. "How difficult it was when your mom left our home but there was loving family members, Auntie and Papa, that filled the void."

He recounted several fond memories—Kimberly's love of horses and Friday nights of TV watching and laundry. Then he praised Kimberly's personality.

"You are such a social being, as is Mike, and have many friends to keep in your heart. I am unclear where each of you learned that. I was never that way."

Then he joked about Kimberly's decision to not pursue neurology, but called her success "nothing short of remarkable, just stellar. I am so very proud of who you are and what you have become. Please do not change that for any reason. You have such a giving nature. I admire that about you. It is imperative that you remain focused and become the best at what you do, if not for anything else but in memory of me. I will accept nothing less from you. Please promise me that you will finish what you have started and not change course for any other life event. I wish you every success and happiness in the road you travel. I will miss being with you. Keep me in your heart and mind. I love you dearly, my sweet daughter. Remain strong, keep family and friends close and live true to yourself. Love, Dad."

The next letter was to Michael. Ferrante began by calling his son "a joy." "I could not have asked for any better baby boy and young adult man to emulate what having a son is all about. Every part of your life and who you are and what you did is incredible."

He called his son a handful with a mischievous smile who made Ferrante one of the most frequent parents at school. Like in Kimberly's letter, Ferrante praised his own father for stepping in to help him raise his children. "His gentle and caring handling of us all put the family back together and made us whole again." He then reminisced about Michael's childhood—skateboarding, playing football and baseball, making pizzas, and playing Nintendo's *Legend of Zelda* with the game's passageways drawn on a map in the basement. Next, Ferrante turned to Michael's years in college, his time abroad, and recent marriage. "You have amazed me, Michael, and I have only great respect and praise for you and who you have become. I am so proud to be your father. I can only wish that you have children of your own to understand how I feel. Please promise me that you will not change the course of your life. I wish you every success and happiness in the roads you will travel. I will miss being with you. Keep me in your heart and mind. I love you dearly, my sweet son. Remain strong, keep family and friends close and live true to yourself. Love, Dad."

The third letter Weibel read was to Ferrante's sister, Dianne. As he listened to his reminiscences, the defendant smiled. He began by noting that his sister always called him Robbie and helped shepherd him through life. "When there was no one else to guide me, you were always there. Do you remember the three Musketeers picture, Jim and his ruffled clothes mom dressed him in? You with the bowl haircut and me looking at you with a smile. It is somewhere in my archive files. I hope someone finds it for you. I remember you helping me with my homework when others could not. I can vividly recall you throwing your hairbrush at me from the top of the stairs at Theresa Road for stealing your hairdryer. I also remember all the wonderful comfort food that you cooked. I'm going to miss not being able to grow old with you. You are the matriarch now. Please continue to care for everyone as you did me. I love you dearly. Love, Robbie."

The last letter, saved for its emotional impact—and the one that garnered the most physical reaction from Ferrante—was the one he wrote to his then six-year-old daughter, Cianna. "My dearest Cianna, how much I love you. I am certain that Auntie Dianne, Kim and Mike have shared their experiences with me to you. I am also assured that they will provide this letter to you when you are of an age to better understand my love for you and my absence in your life. You came later in my life, and I enjoyed every precious minute with you. From the moment you were born, you were loved by all. Such a wonderful joy to behold." He explained that Cianna was born within an hour of her mom arriving at the hospital and how Autumn nursed her to ensure she got "the best possible start in the world." Ferrante recounted to his little girl that she went to day care at a neighbor's house in Canton, was best friends with the little girl across the street, and that their Portuguese water dog, Bart, loved to be near her when she spilled her cheddar-cheese fish on the floor. "There are perhaps thousands of pictures and movies of you on storage drives from the home that will help you understand how excited we were that you were in our lives. Your mom and I loved each other very much and you were oh so important to both of us. We lived our life around you."

He recounted their trips to New York City to visit Kimberly, and how Cianna called it "You Nork." The letter also explained the family's decision to move to Pittsburgh and how quickly Cianna acclimated to her new home and school. "There was no one that would not fall under your spell. You were the most charming little girl. . . . There was so much you loved about Pittsburgh, going on the incline at Mount Washington, Dave and Andy's ice cream, the Pittsburgh Pirate games, Schenley Park and the carousel. The Porch Restaurant, soccer at Schenley Circle, sliding down Flagstaff Hill across from the Phipps Conservatory in the winter with Adam and Maggie Friday, playing in the Schenley fountain, the Carnegie Library and Museum, coming to work with mom and I, having dinner at the medical school when your mom was on service. And so many more fun events. You made friends wherever you went, adults and kids." Ferrante wrote that his daughter enjoyed his silliness—including that he ate dessert before dinner—and that they often played ball with their new Portuguese water dog, Santicola, or Nico for short. He described Cianna's laugh as infectious and said she enjoyed helping with chores around the house. "You were the most inquisitive girl. You found it funny to pin stink bugs with me and watch them wiggle on the pin. You read early and constantly wrote about anything that you thought of or observed." In addition to sending Cianna to art classes, Ferrante noted that every Friday was movie night. "We would watch them over and over until you knew the dialogue by heart. We had such a good time watching movies together.

Your favorite thing to do was to sleep in our bed. When either mom or I were away at a meeting, you would be on the empty side. Often in the morning you would come in to snuggle with us. You are a voracious reader. At bedtime, you would read—we would read many stories to you, and you would read to us." He noted that he was the only one who said her name using the correct Italian pronunciation, and that he believed she liked that it was his special name for her. "I would always call you 'Pumpkin,' as well. Just before your mom passed away, all three of us had the most wonderful vacation together in Puerto Rico. There are pictures of that I hope you have seen. It was an incredible time for each of us spent together."

Next, the letter turned even more sentimental. "Sweetheart, I hope that your life has been one without further anguish. I can't imagine losing both loving parents at such a young age. I hope that you remember us in a loving way and not with anger or remorse. I trust that your family has tried to bring you comfort in most ways possible and they have shared the events of my mom—of your mom and me with you. I am deeply sorry that we left you and greatly regret that we are not there to help shepherd you through life's passage. Please forgive us if you can. I cannot imagine how hard it is not to be there with you or share the events of your life. Cianna, I love you with all of my heart and soul, as I am certain your mother did. I was proud to be your father. You beamed with joy from the moment you awoke until the minute you fell asleep at night. You are the light of my life and so deeply embedded into the fabric of our lives. I am certain that you, like your sister and brother before you, are becoming someone that has great presence, incredible intelligence, physical beauty and will succeed in whatever endeavors you choose to challenge yourself with. Of that I have no doubt. I am so very proud of you, who you are, and what you have become in the six short years that I was with you. It is important that you remain focused and become the best at what you do. I'm so proud to be your father. I wish you every success and happiness in the roads you travel. I will miss being with you. Keep me in your heart and your mind if you can. I love you dearly, my sweet daughter. Remain strong, keep family and friends close, and live true to yourself. Love, Dad."

As with the previous witness, there was not much for the defense to question. Instead, Difenderfer confirmed with Weibel that his client was cooperative with her search that day and that he took her and the other investigators to the home office where the shredder was located.

With those emotional letters, court broke for the day.

Autumn Klein and Karen Kiang. Courtesy of Karen Kiang.

Leslie Hand, Emmy Ludwig, and Autumn Klein during their sophomore year at Amherst. Courtesy of Emmy Ludwig.

Autumn Klein after completing a marathon. Courtesy of Karen Kiang.

Robert Ferrante and Autumn Klein on their wedding day. Courtesy of Karen Kiang.

Robert Ferrante's house in Canton, Massachusetts. Autumn Klein later moved in with him. Courtesy of the *Pittsburgh Post-Gazette*.

The Robert Ferrante / Autumn Klein house in the Schenley Farms neighborhood of Pittsburgh. Courtesy of the *Pittsburgh Post-Gazette.*

UPMC Presbyterian, the hospital where Autumn Klein practiced and was treated after her April 17, 2013, collapse. Courtesy of the *Pittsburgh Post-Gazette.*

Autumn Klein in surveillance video at UPMC Presbyterian, on April 17, 2013. Courtesy of the Allegheny County District Attorney's Office.

The dining room in the house shared by Robert Ferrante and Autumn Klein. Courtesy of the Allegheny County District Attorney's Office.

The kitchen where Autumn Klein collapsed on April 17, 2013. Courtesy of the Allegheny County District Attorney's Office.

Surveillance video showing Autumn Klein being wheeled into UPMC Presbyterian after she collapsed. Courtesy of the Allegheny County District Attorney's Office.

Robert Ferrante is escorted to a court hearing by Allegheny County sheriff's deputies. Courtesy of the *Pittsburgh Post-Gazette*.

Robert Ferrante and his attorneys, William Difenderfer and Wendy Williams, head to court. Courtesy of the *Pittsburgh Post-Gazette.*

Assistant district attorney Lisa Pellegrini walks with Greg Stein, legal research assistant, and assistant district attorney Kevin Chernosky (*right*), the night after the verdict. Courtesy of the *Pittsburgh Post-Gazette.*

Robert Ferrante's office in Scaife Hall at the University of Pittsburgh.
Courtesy of the Allegheny County District Attorney's Office.

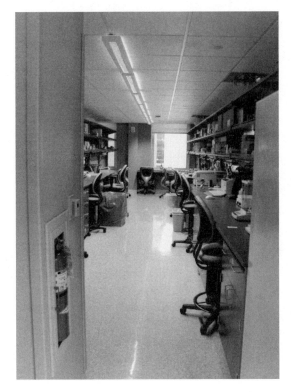

The lab where Robert
Ferrante worked in
Scaife Hall. Courtesy of
the Allegheny County
District Attorney's
Office.

The bottle of potassium cyanide prosecutors said Robert Ferrante ordered on April 15, 2013. Courtesy of the Allegheny County District Attorney's Office.

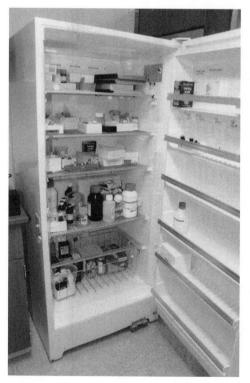

The refrigerator where prosecutors said they found the open bottle of potassium cyanide used to kill Autumn Klein. Courtesy of the Allegheny County District Attorney's Office.

Parsed Search Queries

Record	Search Term	Search Engine	Date/Time - (UTC-5:00) (MM/dd/yyyy)	Evidence Number
853	malice of forethought definition	Google	01/01/2013 06:26:28 PM	09-248(A)(N) #1 MACBOOK PRO SN-c02cm3h9dc7c
756	cyanide poisoning	Google	01/08/2013 03:58:57 PM	09-248(A)(N) #1 MACBOOK PRO SN-c02cm3h9dc7c
1080	human toxicity 3 nitropropionic acid	Google	01/31/2013 09:26:20 AM	09-248(A)(N) #1 MACBOOK PRO SN-c02cm3h9dc7c
1079	human toxicity 3 nitropropionic acid cardiomyopathy	Google	01/31/2013 09:29:59 AM	09-248(A)(N) #1 MACBOOK PRO SN-c02cm3h9dc7c
1078	toxic dose human 3 nitropropionic acid cardiomyopathy	Google	01/31/2013 09:32:00 AM	09-248(A)(N) #1 MACBOOK PRO SN-c02cm3h9dc7c
1077	toxic dose human 3 nitropropionic acid	Google	01/31/2013 09:32:26 AM	09-248(A)(N) #1 MACBOOK PRO SN-c02cm3h9dc7c
1168	suicides golden gate bridge	Google	02/15/2013 08:43:59 AM	09-248(A)(N) #1 MACBOOK PRO SN-c02cm3h9dc7c
2937	divorce pittsburgh pa	Google	02/18/2013 07:43:47 AM	09-248(A)(N) #1 MACBOOK PRO SN-c02cm3h9dc7c
2936	divorce in PA	Google	02/18/2013 07:45:58 AM	09-248(A)(N) #1 MACBOOK PRO SN-c02cm3h9dc7c
663	does increased vaginal size suggest wife is having sex with another	Google	02/19/2013 01:16:16 PM	09-248(A)(N) #1 MACBOOK PRO SN-c02cm3h9dc7c

A page of the Google searches prosecutors used as evidence at the trial against Robert Ferrante. Courtesy of the Allegheny County District Attorney's Office.

26125	http://answers.yahoo.com/question/index?qid=20100427150124AAO4UCP	How would a coroner detect when someone is killed by cyanide? - Yahoo! Answers	04/22/2013 09:07:58 PM
26274	http://www.cnn.com/2003/US/South/01/10/otsc.gupta.cyanide/	CNN.com - Dr. Sanjay Gupta: Cyanide poison hard to detect - Jan. 10, 2003	04/23/2013 03:50:41 AM
26275	http://wiki.answers.com/Q/How_can_you_detected_potassium_cyanide	How can you detected potassium cyanide	04/23/2013 03:49:37 AM
26276	http://www.madsci.org/posts/archives/2000-10/972325357.Ch.r.html	Re: How would you test for potassium cyanide?	04/23/2013 03:48:12 AM
26278	http://www.health.ny.gov/environmental/emergency/chemical_terrorism/cyanide_tech.htm	The Facts About Cyanides	04/23/2013 03:46:11 AM

Another page of websites prosecutors said were visited by Robert Ferrante. Courtesy of the Allegheny County District Attorney's Office.

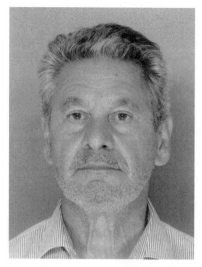

Robert Ferrante in his mug shot, taken July 30, 2013. Courtesy of the Allegheny County Jail.

Assistant district attorneys Kevin Chernosky and Lisa Pellegrini. Courtesy of the *Pittsburgh Post-Gazette*.

Attorney John Gismondi, who represents the parents of Autumn Klein in a civil action against Robert Ferrante. Courtesy of the *Pittsburgh Post-Gazette*.

13 · · · · · · · · · · · · · · · · ·
testing for cyanide

Wednesday morning the prosecution finally turned its attention to the issue most in contention by the defense—whether Autumn died from cyanide poisoning at all.

Pellegrini called to the stand Dr. Leslie Edinboro, the science director at Quest Diagnostics in Chantilly, Virginia. It was his lab that conducted the initial test showing that Autumn's blood tested positive for cyanide. Edinboro explained to the jury the process the lab uses to test for cyanide, which he described as a very simple molecule composed of just carbon and nitrogen. To do the test, technicians use a three-ringed Conway diffusion dish—the same as the Allegheny County crime lab—using a chemical reaction to draw the cyanide out of the blood sample in the middle ring and trapping it in the center. If there is cyanide present, when sodium hydroxide and other chemicals are added to it, it will turn red.

"If there is no cyanide in the sample, that solution doesn't turn red. It is very specific to cyanide," he said. "It is very simple, very elegant chemistry and very specific for cyanide."

"So what is the next step in the process, sir?" Pellegrini asked.

"So now we know that it is cyanide in there. Now we have to be able to show how much is in there because it is the amount of cyanide in the sample that is very important. Now, I don't know about you, but I drank a lot of cherry Kool-Aid as a kid. Cherry Kool-Aid is kind of like the same color as the solution. I could always tell when my mom was trying to stretch out the Kool-Aid when she put more water in it because it would be a lighter color. We kind of use that same principle to quantitate the amount of cyanide that is now in that red-colored substance."

A spectrophotometer, he explained, measures the lengths of the red wavelengths in the solution—known as the *absorbance*. "So the darker the sample, the more cyanide present, the higher the absorbance."

The technician then plots the numbers obtained on a graph. If the solution is so dark that the light from the spectrophotometer can't get through it, the solution must be further diluted until it can. The technician must also be running quality-control samples, as well, Edinboro continued, which include using samples with known cyanide values to ensure the test is working properly. Once the work is completed, a second technician checks the results to ensure the test was done properly.

During cross-examination, Difenderfer first zeroed in on the standard operating procedures (SOP) at the lab, including how long blood can be stored before testing it for cyanide and how often the equipment used to do that is calibrated. Then he asked for an explanation of the controls used at the lab to ensure test accuracy, as well as what, exactly, the test can determine.

"So somebody, who has certain types of vegetation or taking by-products of cyanide, these types of things can give a false reading?" Difenderfer asked.

"That's correct. The test measures all cyanide in all its forms."

"Not only in all of its forms but none of this testing tells you at all how it was introduced to the body?" the lawyer asked.

"Absolutely not."

"If I breathed in cyanide, like the gas chambers in Nazi Germany, you wouldn't be able to tell from this test?"

"We would not."

Although Edinboro was called by the prosecution only to explain the testing procedures, Difenderfer spent much time discussing Autumn's actual test—including the question of how the results were changed from what the technician originally found—a 2.2 reading—to a reading of 3.4.

"This test was submitted, and in terms of doing these tests, it was completed reportedly following your protocol, the results were submitted to the Quest here, and the results were submitted to the hospital?"

"That is correct," Edinboro answered.

"And those results and quantitative numbers, you learned, in that were wrong, correct?" Difenderfer continued.

"The report was wrong. The quantitative number was correct," Edinboro clarified.

"The 3.4 quantitative number was wrong?" the lawyer pushed.

"The quantitative result of the test was correct, the 2.2. What was reported, the 3.4, is wrong."

"What was reported to the hospital, what was reported to the media, and part of my client's affidavit subject to his arrest was the wrong amount stated—of 3.4?" Difenderfer continued.

"I'm not familiar with other than what was reported to the Pittsburgh business unit. That would have been 3.4."

Pellegrini jumped in on redirect to clarify, getting Edinboro to confirm that 2.2 milligrams per liter was the original number determined by the technician, and more importantly, that both levels were more than sufficient to kill Autumn. Was 2.2 a high lethal level? she asked.

"It would be," Edinboro answered.

"Whether it is 2.2 or 3.4, it is still a lethal level?"

"That's correct."

Next up was Sonia Obcemea, a lab tech who had worked for Quest for thirty-seven years. She estimated she had performed about one thousand cyanide tests.

Obcemea, who had emigrated from the Philippines, was firm in her answers, not intimidated by the courtroom or the lawyers' questions. She said her work on the sample in question began about 7:00 p.m. on April 20. She knew very quickly it was positive.

"Because the color is deep-red color, which means it is a very high level of presence of cyanide."

It was so dark that Obcemea had to dilute it twice to get a reading from the spectrophotometer. When she finally did, it was 2.2 milligrams per liter, "which is very, very high."

Obcemea wrote that number on her work sheet, showing her calculations, but it was later crossed out by the person checking her work, Ryan Bartolotti.

"Is it standard procedure to have someone else check your results?" Pellegrini asked.

"Right."

"They don't do retesting, they are just looking at your calculations?"

"Right."

"Looking back at your testing and your calculations, are you confident with the reported value of 2.2 milligrams per liter?"

"Yes."

"Why?"

"I am confident reporting that, performing thousands of cyanide [tests] when I'm there, I'm very confident that this is really a very high, toxic level of cyanide," Obcemea answered.

"In thirty-seven years and the thousand-plus tests that you have done, is this the first lethal level of cyanide that you ever found in a patient?"

"Yes."

The prosecutor then turned the witness over for cross.

"I want to apologize before I ask this question. I certainly don't want to pry, but it's a pretty significant case. Could you please tell me how old you are?" Difenderfer asked.

"How old is what? Say it again."

"What is your age?" he continued.

"My age is seventy-three years old."

After planting that seed, Difenderfer starting picking at her, asking multiple times and in multiple ways if she had followed the lab's standard operating procedure with Autumn's test.

"Ma'am, you'd agree with me, would you not, that your company's protocol is that you run on every test—before you run your test—the low, the high and the negative [control]?"

"Right," she answered.

"You didn't do that here, did you?"

"Well, because I put the high on the last part. My high control on the last part, because our standard procedure is to bracket the run between the control," Obcemea tried to explain.

Difenderfer brandished the operating procedure documents.

"Low, high and negative controls are run at the beginning of each run. A second low control is run at the end to bracket patient samples, correct?"

"Correct."

"That's in your protocol, correct?"

"Uh-hum," she answered.

"You didn't do that here, did you?"

"But it doesn't matter because the number that's going to be in there is, you know—"

Difenderfer cut her off: "Did you do that here?"

"I didn't do this here. Because it's a short run. This applies if you have a big run like a hundred or twenty."

"Where does it say that?" Difenderfer asked.

"It doesn't say here."

After a little more pounding, Difenderfer moved on to the change in the results made by Bartolotti.

"And did he come to you and tell you about this and ask why your test was wrong or why your sample was wrong and check with you?"

"No, he didn't. I didn't even know that he checked it. He changed my number."

"You're telling us that this is one of the few, if ever, a positive you guys saw in your experience?" Difenderfer asked.

"Yes."

"And you're saying that he makes—it's a substantial difference 3.4 to 2.2, correct?"

"Correct."

"Okay," the lawyer said.

"But the cyanide is really toxic," Obcemea said.

Difenderfer made the witness slog through every step of the testing process again, and then went back to the change in the test results and his incredulity over her assertion that no one ever told her the results were changed.

"When—were you ever asked or confronted about your testing in July of 2013? Did anybody come up to you and go, 'Hey, we went over your tests, and your results were wrong, we're making corrections,' did anybody go over that with you?"

"Nobody."

"Nobody even talked to you about it?"

"No."

Throughout, the big man with the big voice played it to the hilt, pacing back and forth, looking to the jury and then to the witness as he professed to be astonished at how this all went down.

After Pellegrini got Obcemea to reassert that it was the highest level she'd ever seen on redirect, Difenderfer took one last run on recross.

"Thirty-one years—thirty-seven years?"

"Correct."

"First time this ever happened, do you think you might have wanted to retest it to make sure you were right?" the lawyer asked.

"I'm positive that I'm right," Obcemea fired back.

Bartolotti was next. He had been working in a position as a mentor —one step below a supervisor—since 2012.

"It was my job to review her results before they were released to the client," he said. "Where I made the error when I did the checking of Sonia's work was I confused the axes."

"Why did you do that?" Pellegrini asked.

"I don't honestly know. So what I did then is instead of plotting the absorbances on the Y axis to get the concentration on the X axis, I plotted the absorbance on the X axis to then get the concentration on the Y axis giving me that higher value," he explained. "There was no changing of any—there's no additional work done with the sample. I used the data that Sonia generated."

"Now, did you retest the sample?" Pellegrini asked.

"I did not."

"Why not?"

"Because the data there is accurate."

"Okay. So whether it's 2.2 or 3.35, is it still a lethal limit?"

"According to what it says in our SOP, it is a toxic level."

Bartolotti said he didn't become aware of the error in his calculation until after the test results and work sheets were being gathered as part of the criminal investigation by his supervisor.

On cross, Difenderfer again hammered on the point that SOP regarding controls were not followed in the test.

"That's not optional, is it?" the attorney asked.

"No, it's my understanding."

"It's not an option, it should be done at every test?"

"It should be."

"Okay. It wasn't done here, though?"

"Okay."

"What's 'okay' mean? You're agreeing with me it was not done here?" Difenderfer continued. "Where is the low at the end?"

"There is none," Bartolotti answered.

"Do you go back to—Ms. Obcemea just testified, I'm not going to butcher her name, the young lady who just testified—"

"Sonia," Bartolotti finished.

"Did you go back to her and say, 'Whoa, let's double-check this, this is a high level, the first one I've ever seen, and to make sure that everything here jibes,' did you do that?" the lawyer continued.

"I did not."

"Did you ask her, 'How am I getting such a different number than you that is so much more than a 2.2? How is this huge discrepancy— how did this happen?' Did you go to her and try to resolve it and find out?" Difenderfer asked.

"I did not."

"So with this shocking lethal amount that might have killed somebody, you made your correction, and you filed it, and you sent it off to the medical place?"

"That's what I did."

The next witness, Michael Browne, explained to the jury how he discovered the mistake. The supervisor of clinical technology said that after he received a search warrant for the investigation, he got Autumn's blood-test results back on July 29, immediately noting the discrepancy as he reviewed the paperwork. The first thing that stood out to him, Browne said, was that the sample had to be diluted multiple times. He told the jury that was an "abnormality." When he tried to conduct his own calculations from the data, he got the same 2.2 milligrams per liter that Obcemea got. Browne immediately took the paperwork to Edinboro and was told to issue a corrected report.

"Did you have to rerun the cyanide test?" Pellegrini asked.

"No, ma'am. At this point, the sample had already been subpoenaed and was off-site. All of the end-run controls met criteria, so there was no need to repeat. It was just a recalculation of the data."

On cross-examination, Difenderfer questioned Browne extensively about whether the altered test results would have an impact on Quest's business.

"This is extremely significant for Quest now, isn't it?" he asked.

"Yes."

"Your lawyer is here for all of you guys, right?"

"Yes."

"Now, when we're looking at the hard file, those numbers and those calculations on that piece of paper, front page, or cover page that you call it, it's only as good as the technician, as the standards, as the accuracy of the test, as the accuracy of the machine, those numbers are only as good as the actual test was, correct?" Difenderfer asked.

"Yes."

"There's no way of going back and double-checking the results of 'did we do the right amount of drops in each one from each pipette of all the samples we used,' there's no way to go back and try to recalculate this and do this test, is there?"

"That is true."

After Browne finished, Pellegrini recalled Edinboro to testify that the spectrophotometers were recalibrated weekly.

Difenderfer used his cross, first, to point out the presence of a Quest attorney in the courtroom. When Edinboro said that was standard practice in any case in which there is a subpoena, Difenderfer snarled: "All right. I don't care about other cases, and I'm not asking you questions about other cases. The only thing I'm asking you questions about is this case here, do you understand that?"

"Correct."

Difenderfer then turned to the sheets used to document the weekly recalibration, suggesting that they were all written with the same ink and the same handwriting.

"Look at December 6, all the way to January 9, 2013, wow, look at those zeroes, look at this, look at the shade of this ink," Difenderfer said pointing at the calibration sheets. "Exact. So somebody on this eleven-twenty-seven, same person on this, same shade, same everything, same everything, same everything. Seriously?"

"Seriously, there are people in the laboratory whose jobs are to do the same job every week," Edinboro responded. "If that's their assigned duty, they're going to do the work, and that's how the form's going to look."

"Your testimony is these weren't prepared by somebody who sit down—sat down—and wrote these all out in response to my subpoena?" Difenderfer asked.

"That is absolutely correct."

IMMEDIATELY FOLLOWING the evidence from Quest, the prosecution turned to the cyanide test conducted by the medical examiner's office.

Alesia Smith, the toxicologist who performed it, used PowerPoint to walk the jury through the test she did on April 24. She explained that there were many samples of Autumn's blood—forty-nine in all—but that most were taken after she'd been on ECMO for three days, having her blood continuously cleansed. Only one vial had blood drawn within an hour of Autumn's arrival at the hospital.

It was during Smith's testimony that the issue of differing results from NMS Labs was brought up on cross-examination. NMS was the lab contacted by the medical examiner's office to conduct another quantitative test to measure the exact amount of cyanide in Autumn's blood. Smith told the jury that she helped prepare the specimen that was sent to NMS, and that she sent them the most valuable blood sample they had—2 milliliters of blood that had been drawn from Autumn within an hour of her admission to the hospital.

However, Smith said, NMS was unable to provide a result on the test and asked for an additional vial of blood, which she sent. The company did not explain why the test was not completed—including what happened to the additional 1.5 milliliters of blood that would have remained from the original sample sent to them, Smith said.

When NMS analyzed the second sample, it returned positive for the presence of cyanide, but the results showed the level was in the normal range—not fatal.

Smith explained to Difenderfer that she was not surprised by the NMS findings because they didn't test the second sample until eighteen days after the blood was drawn.

"Cyanide is not stable in the blood," Smith said later. "Timing is important. You have to get the test done as soon as possible."

"The Quest blood was drawn on the eighteenth and tested on the twenty-first, within forty-eight hours?" Pellegrini asked on redirect.

"Correct."

"Your blood was tested within six days?" Pellegrini continued.

"Correct."

DAY SIX · *Arguing about Cyanide*

Pellegrini next needed to explain the fiasco of the failed testing of Autumn's blood. To do that—with the technicians from NMS Labs—she needed to tread a fine line: to explain why the results were all over the map while convincing the jurors that there was absolutely no doubt Autumn died of cyanide poisoning. It would be tricky, particularly when she would have to treat her own witnesses hostilely.

Linay Williams was the first one called. She told the jury that she couldn't finish her test of 0.5 milliliters of Autumn's blood because her controls failed.

"So what does that mean?" Pellegrini asked.

"It means I don't know what the result is."

"Is the test invalid?"

"Yes."

Williams explained that she put in a request for the test to be repeated but that wasn't done. She was unsure what happened with the rest of the sample NMS had received. She further told the jury that her lab's spectrophotometer was not performing optimally at the time Klein's test was requested, which is why only the microdiffusion test was performed, despite the client's request to get a quantitative analysis.

Rebecca Reber, another NMS employee, testified that she was asked on May 6 to do a semiquantitative test on a blood sample for Autumn that would not give a specific value of cyanide in the specimen, but would provide a range.

"I determined that the sample was positive, and the color intensity was between my low control and my mid-control," she said.

That meant it was not a fatal level.

Difenderfer asked no questions.

Later in the trial, to further explain what happened with the NMS sample, Pellegrini called Jennifer Janssen, the assistant chief toxicologist at the Allegheny County Medical Examiner's Office. She reiterated that of all the blood tested, the sample taken at 12:48 a.m. on April 18, which was sent to NMS, was the most important for getting a true picture of what happened to Klein.

"What happens with regard to this 12:48 a.m. blood?" Pellegrini asked.

"The next communication that I received was from a customer-service representative who called me on 4/30. They indicated that they needed [an] additional specimen."

Janssen explained that she had sent 2 milliliters in that sample to the lab, and that the standard operating procedure at NMS said the quantitative test only required 0.5 milliliters. Therefore, she said, even after the first test failed, the lab should have had 1.5 milliliters left.

"Did they tell you what happened with that first test?" Pellegrini asked.

"No."

"Had they told you now on the thirtieth, had they told you, 'Hey, we don't do quantitative testing, and by the way, our first test was messed up,' what would you have done?" the prosecutor asked.

"At that time, a significant number of days had elapsed. Had I had the opportunity on 4/30 to send it to another lab, I would have."

"But at this point, you didn't know there was anything wrong?" Pellegrini continued.

"I did not."

"Do you have any idea why the retesting was not performed?"

"I do not."

"So that blood—we've got nothing from?" Pellegrini asked.

"That first sample that was collected within a half hour of her being admitted to the hospital, I do not have any kind of results on."

Janssen had no additional contact with NMS until May 7, when someone from the lab's customer service left her a voice mail saying the company was going to run only a semiquantitative test using the second sample sent on May 1 that would produce a range for the cyanide level, but not an actual amount. That sample, Janssen said, sat at the NMS lab for four days until it was tested.

"And the clock is ticking?" Pellegrini said.

"Correct."

By the time that sample was tested, Janssen told the jury, eighteen days had elapsed since the blood was drawn from Autumn, and because it was a hospital clinical sample, the tube had already been opened and tested for other purposes.

"Does that affect dissipation in the tube?" Pellegrini asked.

"Yes, it does. Cyanide is not stable in a test tube. With time, the concentration of cyanide will decline in a test tube depending on storage conditions. It is critical that once a tube is opened, cyanide could evaporate from that tube. So this particular tube had been used for previous testing where the Quest tube was not. It was drawn for the purpose of cyanide testing."

On May 7, Janssen said NMS contacted her, and a representative suggested that because the lab could not do the quantitative test that they send the blood sample they had left—1.5 milliliters of it—to the Mayo Clinic for a specific measurement. But when Janssen looked at the requirements of the Mayo Clinic for such a test, she saw that the facility required 3 milliliters of blood and that it be processed within fourteen days of it being drawn.

After discussing the situation with Allegheny County medical examiner Dr. Karl Williams, Janssen said they agreed to forgo the test.

Difenderfer hammered that point on cross.

"If it is refrigerated and stored properly, certainly there could be a tremendous value gained by testing that blood albeit after two weeks, correct?" he asked.

"There are a number of studies that have delineated what happens with cyanide when it is stored in a test tube," Janssen answered. "In this particular case, nineteen days had elapsed. That tube that NMS had at the time was opened by NMS and it was a hospital specimen collected for clinical testing."

The sample that NMS failed to get a result from, Difenderfer asked, should have been the best?

"I believe that was the most valuable specimen that we received due to the fact that it was collected so soon after she arrived at the hospital, and yes, I believe it would have had a high level of cyanide. I believe it would have been the highest level of the tubes that had been tested," particularly, she added, because it was before Klein received fluids or dialysis.

When NMS finally completed its semiquantitative study, Janssen said, the range was greater than 0.3 milligrams per liter, but less than 0.5.

"Toxicologically insignificant?" Difenderfer asked.

"It is on the high end of the normal range."

But it was the Quest sample, Janssen said on redirect, that proved to be most valuable. "It was drawn with the intention of performing cyanide [testing]. It was never opened until it was received at Quest. It is a sample that was collected, albeit the sample was collected fourteen hours later, it was shipped and tested within a very short period of time so that particular sample is the most valuable quantitative value that we have."

"In your opinion, does it make a difference whether the level is 3.4 or 2.2?" Pellegrini asked.

"It does not."

"Are they both lethal?" she continued.

"Yes." Although Difenderfer had done what he wanted to do—plant the seed among jurors that the testing was flawed—Pellegrini had scored the point she needed as well: revised results or not, Autumn had a fatal cyanide level in her blood.

AFTER TWO ALLEGHENY COUNTY crime lab technicians testified that they examined Autumn's medications, as well as the creatine collected from Ferrante's lab, and found no cyanide, Pellegrini called Autumn's cousin, Sharon, to testify. Sharon, very nervous and barely audible, said she spoke to Ferrante several times during her cousin's hospitalization and that he told her that "the best that they could figure was that she had like a brain surge and that that caused her heart to fail."

After just twelve minutes, Sharon stepped down. Then Chernosky called Lyle Graber, who was sitting on some of the much-anticipated evidence of the trial: the messages Autumn had sent to Bob suggesting marital strife in early 2013.

The detective read them out loud for the jury, his voice purposefully measured and flat, as he spoke the angry and anguished words written by Autumn, detailing the intimate details of her medical tribulations, her frustration at Ferrante's disinterest in her in vitro fertilization and his lack of emotion, and the increasingly tattered state of the marriage. As he read, jurors sat rapt, staring at the screen across the courtroom where the messages were blown up, larger than life.

Chernosky had Graber read the e-mail in which Autumn suggested that she and her husband needed to talk, and then asked him to read an e-mail to McElrath, the colleague with whom Ferrante suspected she was having an affair. The defense objected, and the judge didn't permit Graber to read the message in which Autumn asked to stay with him at a conference in May 2013. Graber also confirmed that he found automated e-mails sent to Autumn's account from the post–cardiac arrest team at the hospital after her collapse that had been forwarded to Ferrante's personal e-mail account.

DAY SEVEN · An E-mail and an Autopsy Report

The next morning, Graber continued on the stand, reading from an e-mail that Ferrante sent to his wife on April 16 at 12:52 p.m.—the day before her collapse.

"I'm sorry, sweetie. You seemed to be in such a great mood up until last evening. I guess I was not thinking. I thought it would be such a wonderful idea going to Boston together. We have not been back alone there. I thought it would be romantic to go to one of our old restaurants and see the sights. It seemed so easy, as well, to me to get the watch that you gave me repaired. I love the watch and wanted to get the battery replaced as soon as possible. Mother's Day is very special, and I see that more and more with my mom now passed. It is a special day for you and Cianna, as well. I just thought that having your mom here would be a joy to her, as well. There will not be many more opportunities. I'm obviously missing something here. I am sorry for that. I will take care of everything for your parents and your mom so you are not stressed over it. I will make sure that we, I, will not ruin your week off. I was unclear that you were taking the week off to get work done. I thought you said that you needed to take it or lose it. I did not know you were on-call again for two weeks after your week off. If you would like, I will not go to Boston, and I will stay home and take care of your parents that weekend. You are correct that we can't just tell your parents not to come up after I made such a big deal of it. It seems obvious to me now that you want to go to Boston alone. I won't go if that will make you less stressed, and I will make sure all is okay with your parents. My exuberance of going to Boston together and also having your mom celebrate Mother's Day with us was perhaps too much. You know me. I think of the fun and not the work behind it. Love you, F and A [forever and always], Bob."

During an uneventful cross-examination, Difenderfer asked Graber if he had done any search through Ferrante's e-mails corresponding to the Google search the defendant had done in January of "malice of forethought." The detective said he had not.

Then Pellegrini called McElrath.

He told the jury that he and Autumn had been colleagues for about eight years and had worked on research projects together.

"What were the areas of research?" the prosecutor asked.

"So her specialty was in neurology, or one of her specialties was treating epilepsy, people with seizure disorders. My specialty was treating women with high-risk pregnancies, and we collaborated on forming one of the first clinics which specialized in treating epileptics while they were pregnant. This is an issue because they need to be on medications and dosed and redosed, and with medications there are side effects for mothers and possibly developing babies. So we created this clinic that allowed patients to be seen in tandem rather than separate appointments."

McElrath confirmed that he had attended several conferences with

Autumn, including the one in San Francisco in February 2013. He also noted that he and Autumn were working on a project together that had received a grant from the National Institutes of Health. A meeting on it had been scheduled for early May 2013 in Boston. McElrath told Autumn she could stay at his home when she traveled for that meeting. He said that the invitation would have been open to Ferrante, too, though he had never spoken with him.

McElrath's testimony took just six minutes.

L UCKASEVIC, who had performed the autopsy, testified next, describing what an autopsy is and what he found in Autumn's.

"An autopsy, I like to say it is the final surgical procedure anyone will ever have," he told the jury. "It is a surgical procedure where we look at the internal organs both with a naked eye and underneath a microscope in relationship to the internal organs and how the body functions.

"My role as a forensic pathologist is to determine the cause and manner of death for individuals that die suddenly, violently, unexpectedly, or unnaturally in Allegheny County."

"What are the different manners of death?" Pellegrini asked.

"The five manners of death are natural, accidental, suicide, homicide, and the last one is undetermined or indeterminate." Autumn was autopsied, he said, because "we had a sudden, unexpected, unnatural death in a young individual with no obvious cause of death."

CORE had already harvested the liver, kidneys, adrenal glands, and pulmonic heart valve for donation before he received the body on April 21. Once he completed the autopsy—and sent specimens for toxicology testing—Luckasevic said he could not determine cause of death. His only two findings, he told the jury, were that Klein's lungs were filled with blood, which is normal upon death, and that there was a benign tumor in her uterus.

Because he could not make any conclusions, Luckasevic decided to send Klein's heart and brain out to special pathologists for further study, he testified, and then he released the body.

"Even though the autopsy results, the cause and manner, are pending, do you hold onto the body?" Pellegrini asked.

"Never. Rarely ever hold onto the body. It is routine for us after we do the autopsy, we have all the specimens that we needed to collect. I am confident that I have everything that I need to make the diagnosis.

If this is either a toxicology case, a brain disorder, or a heart disorder, I have what I need so the body is released."

After Farkas called the medical examiner's office on April 23, Luckasevic attempted to get Autumn's body back from the funeral home.

"What did you determine?" Pellegrini asked.

"She had been cremated."

When Luckasevic got the results back from the heart and brain evaluation, he testified, he found that neither organ caused Klein's death. The heart specialist at the Jesse Edwards Heart Registry found that Klein had a congenitally bicuspid aortic valve that was nonobstructed, common to about 2 percent of the population.

"In your opinion, was that contributory to her cause of death?" Pellegrini asked.

"Not at all."

And the neuropathologist's diagnosis was that Klein had global ischemic encephalopathy.

"What does that mean?" the prosecutor asked.

"That means the entire brain is dead due to lack of blood and oxygen."

"Knowing the Quest level, the lethal level from Quest, do you find that the global ischemic encephalopathy, do you find that significant?" Pellegrini asked.

"Yes, that is a very significant finding and consistent with a toxic ingestion of cyanide."

Like those prosecution witnesses who testified before him, Luckasevic said it did not matter if the Quest result was 2.2 or 3.4. That positive result, along with the test completed by the medical examiner's office, and even the NMS low-level finding, the pathologist said, led to his conclusion that Klein died from cyanide poisoning.

"What is the manner of death?" Pellegrini asked.

"Manner of death is homicide."

On cross-examination by Difenderfer, Luckasevic said that the blood test used to detect cyanide cannot identify how a person came into contact with the toxin—whether orally, through the skin, or through inhalation. But, the witness concluded, he considered, as part of his investigation, that Ferrante told Friedlander that when Autumn returned home just before her collapse she consumed a beverage with creatine in it and therefore would have orally ingested the poison.

"So based on all that you reviewed and examined, how did you determine the manner of death?" Pellegrini asked on redirect.

"The manner of death I determined [to be] homicide because someone gave Dr. Klein cyanide."

"Did you find any evidence in any of the records or anything else that this was an accident?" Pellegrini continued.

"No, I did not."

"Did you find any evidence in the record and all that you reviewed that this was a suicide?"

"No, I did not."

"Have you ever seen in your thirty-four hundred, I believe you said, autopsies that you performed a level of 2.2 in an autopsy?" the prosecutor asked.

"No, I have not."

Difenderfer tried to finish strong on cross by going after Quest.

"Doctor, where would you be without the 2.2? Where would you be without it?"

"I have my lab results for the forensic laboratory in Allegheny County," he answered.

"Qualitative?"

"Positive cyanide is a red flag, period," Luckasevic answered.

"What if the 2.2 is wrong?" Difenderfer pressed.

"What if?" Luckasevic responded.

"What if the 2.2 level from Quest is wrong? We know that the 3.4 in the affidavit that you put is wrong. What if the 2.2 is wrong, would that have an impact on your decision?" the lawyer asked.

"It sure would, but I still wouldn't have the cause of death."

"Whether she intentionally took it, whether she accidentally took it, whether she encountered it, cyanide could be encountered dermally, through your skin?" Difenderfer asked.

"Correct."

"So someone handling cyanide without the proper equipment could get lethal levels of cyanide through their skin?"

"It is possible," Luckasevic answered.

Difenderfer referred back to the missing seven minutes in the video surveillance when Autumn was leaving the hospital.

"If she was up in the office or lab handling it or doing whatever, all you can tell us is I'm relying on the level of Quest, and that is why I'm saying it, correct?"

"I'm relying on the whole. Again, I don't know how I can emphasize this anymore. I'm relying on everything."

After just over an hour on the stand, Luckasevic stepped down, replaced by a fingerprint analyst from the county crime lab.

Marla Priestly testified for several minutes from a lengthy Power-Point presentation in which she painstakingly walked through what a fingerprint is and how it is captured, despite two offers by Ferrante's defense attorneys to stipulate to her testimony. She ultimately confirmed for the jury that she examined the 250-gram bottle of potassium cyanide ordered by Ferrante on April 15 and found a print made by his left thumb.

After Priestly finished, Manning sent the jurors home early for the weekend. The prosecution's last witness, a cyanide expert, would be up Monday morning.

DAY EIGHT · *Expert Witnesses*

Dr. Christopher Holstege, the expert from the University of Virginia, spoke confidently and warmly as he described his background in toxicology, as well as his service as the medical director of the Blue Ridge Poison Center serving Virginia. In addition to his teaching and medical practice, he told the jurors, he had been enlisted by federal and international agencies to consult on several cases, including an investigation into the 2001 anthrax scare as to what went wrong to allow an attack from inside the United States; by the Ukrainian government to investigate a mysterious illness of Viktor Yushchenko, who was running for president there; and with the FBI in working with hostage negotiations involving Somali pirates and the kidnapping of Captain Richard Phillips.

In addition, Holstege had coauthored a book called *Criminal Poisoning*, as well as written a chapter in a toxicology book on cyanide. After spending several minutes on his credentials, Pellegrini asked the doctor to talk about cyanide and its history as a poison. Holstege described its use in World War II in Nazi Germany, as well as the mass suicide of the Jim Jones followers, who drank cyanide-laced Kool-Aid. In addition, he noted that cyanide was responsible for the Tylenol murders in 1982 when the acetaminophen inside the capsules was replaced by the deadly toxin.

"So it's got quite a history throughout time," he said. "Certainly as we do terroristic preparedness, it is certainly something that we worry about."

Pellegrini then played for the jury the eighty-five-second animation prepared by Holstege to demonstrate what happens inside the body when cyanide is ingested.

As the video began, it showed the cyanide being swallowed and working its way into the bloodstream. The red blood cells appeared as small flying discs, and the animation showed how the heart began pumping all the highly oxygenated blood through the body, before the heart turned blue and the patient died.

"So essentially, everything starts being deprived of oxygen: your brain, your heart, your lungs?" Pellegrini asked.

"So it is the inability of being able to utilize oxygen. In essence, it is like suffocating, isn't it? So my brain activity is going to be the first that is typically affected by cyanide. Again, it is about the dose. How much of it is affecting my mitochondria, the energy formation? How much energy do I have for my brain to function? It depends on where on the spectrum of the poisoning you are and how much is blocking that cytochrome system. It is all about dose and what clinical effects that you will see."

When the heart and cardiovascular structure are stressed because of cyanide poisoning, he continued, the body releases epinephrine to try to fight off that stress. "My heart rate is going to increase a bit because the body is giving the sensation that I'm not getting enough oxygen so I'm going to increase the blood flow, get more red blood cells going with oxygen. My respiratory rate is going to increase."

After that phase, he went on, the heart rate will start to slow because the body is losing energy. "As it slows, my blood pressure starts to drop."

"When your blood pressure drops and your heart rate slows, what happens to your body?" Pellegrini asked.

"At that point, as you can imagine, your blood flow is not nearly as good. I think there is some confusion that comes with cyanide as to what should your color be. Should it be bright red? Should it be the color of gray and ashen or cyanotic or a bluish color? The bright red comes because they can't extract oxygen well." The bluish or ashen color, he said, is because the body is not pumping the blood well.

How a person responds to cyanide depends on the toxicity of the poison, the dose given, and how quickly medical care is provided. "We know there is a spectrum of how people will present. Some people can get exposed to cyanide and drop immediately and die. Some people will get exposed to cyanide and become [unresponsive], not breathe well. They are not moving purposefully. They are moaning. They are brought in and put on life support. They struggle for a while."

As she listened to Holstege's clinical testimony about the process that killed her cousin, Sharon, who was sitting in the front row of the gallery, cried quietly.

Patients with cyanide poisoning are also given a lot of epinephrine to try to keep their blood pressure up, Holstege continued.

"So if someone that had received a large dose of cyanide and lived a couple tenths of a mile from a level-one trauma center and received extraordinary life-saving measures, would that affect their outcome?" Pellegrini asked.

"Yes, it could."

Diagnosing cyanide poisoning, Holstege said, is difficult because it can look like many different diagnoses. Among those that would be considered are an intracranial bleed, an aortic dissection in the heart, or another cardiac abnormality.

"So cyanide poisoning, however it may occur, suicide, homicide, or through a fire, that is not like the top of your list when you are looking at someone?" the prosecutor asked.

"A case like this, as a practicing emergency room physician, this is not the top of my list. There are many more things that I'm looking for that I'm worried about. The case is odd to me as an emergency room physician when it comes in looking like this. If I'm a toxicologist on a case and come later, usually when I get consults, the emergency department has already done the CAT scans and ruled out a number of things and then the question becomes what could potentially cause this? Could cyanide be on the list? Absolutely it could be on the list, as is toxic alcohol. So there are things that are very consistent for what we see in the literature for cyanide, again realizing if I'm the clinician I'm not expecting to see cyanide in this case."

"Why not?" Pellegrini asked.

"It is not prevalent. It is not out there. It is not common. If we're looking at cyanide and looking at this case and saying this was a case where someone was poisoned with cyanide, why would that be? Where would that come from? It is very rare. It is rare that we see cyanide cases. In homicides, we see poisoning's rare to begin with."

Poisonings, Holstege said, make up less than 1 percent of all homicides.

As for the notion of the creatine being tainted with cyanide, the expert said he'd never heard of such a thing.

Reviewing Autumn's medical records and lab tests, and noting that the blood drawn during the insertion of the central line came out of her veins a bright-red color, the expert said he believed cyanide poisoning was the cause of death.

Difenderfer began his cross-examination by discussing with Holstege the difference between toxicologists and pathologists before moving on to the witness's work, including the book chapter he wrote dedicated to cyanide. It was there that he tried to trip the witness up by contrasting the descriptions Holstege used there versus what happened to Autumn.

In the chapter, the expert had said that there can be an initial period of a slow heart rate in a cyanide patient.

"That is not the case here, is it?" Difenderfer asked.

"Initially she had a fast heart rate," Holstege answered.

"That is the opposite of what you said in your book?" the attorney continued.

"Correct."

"You don't have in parentheses or you don't qualify any of this in your book by saying initially you are going to see bradycardia and in parentheses the opposite may occur?"

"No," Holstege said, unaffected.

"Hypertension may occur," Difenderfer quoted from the book. "What is hypertension?"

"Increase in blood pressure," Holstege answered.

"She had low blood pressure initially, didn't she?"

"Correct," the witness answered.

"That is also contrary to what you are saying in your book, correct?" Difenderfer asked.

"Not necessarily contrary. Again, there is a spectrum of what you may see with poison."

The witness also agreed with the defense attorney that he wrote in the book chapter that with cyanide ingestion, it is expected that the patient would have signs of the corrosive product in the esophagus or gastrointestinal tract. Autumn didn't have this in either of those places.

Difenderfer also noted that Holstege had worked with the defense's own expert witness on a book, and that expert, Lewis Nelson, said he believed Klein could likely have died from a heart dysrhythmia.

"He has looked at the same documents, the same gases and everything that you looked at?" the attorney asked.

"Correct."

"And physicians and doctors can disagree, is that fair?"

"Yes," Holstege said.

Difenderfer then returned to the question of the patient's color.

"Nowhere in this clinical effects or findings or entire article as it relates to cyanide do you note anything about an ashen color, do you?" the lawyer continued.

"No."

"And in your report that you submitted that we received, nowhere in the report did you talk about an ashen color, did you?" Difenderfer asked.

"No."

"The district attorney brought this to your attention because she noted that during the testimony that one of the doctors, Dr. Farkas, noted that when he saw her when she was still conscious that her skin was gray and ashen in color. This is way before she passed. That is not consistent with what you are saying in your clinical effects, specifically the cherry-red color?" Difenderfer asked.

"Not consistent, but it is also reported in my other publications, yes," Holstege responded.

Later, turning to the lab results from Quest, the attorney asked if Holstege's opinion would be swayed if he learned that the lab technician didn't follow protocol, had committed errors in the calculations, and that the machines were not properly calibrated.

"I would be concerned."

On redirect, Pellegrini went back to the question of how Klein's organs could be successfully transplanted if she'd been poisoned with cyanide. Holstege explained that there are multiples reports in cyanide cases in which the patient is brain dead, but the organs recover.

As for the cherry-red color referenced by Difenderfer, the prosecutor asked Holstege to review the transcript of Ferrante's 911 call.

"Yes, her eyes are still opened. She is getting red in the face though, goddamn it," Holstege read.

And so, with that last witness, at 12:09 p.m., Pellegrini rested her case.

She had put the scenario of the jealous older husband and troubled wife before the jury. She had walked the jurors through the unusual cyanide purchase and made the argument that despite the inconsistencies in the results, the test evidence pointed to a fatal dose of cyanide. And most of all, she had hammered home the Google searches, which looked to be very, very difficult to explain away.

14 ∙∙∙∙∙∙∙∙∙∙∙∙∙∙
the case for him

SHOWTIME FOR THE DEFENSE arrived at 1:38 p.m. on November 3.

Difenderfer called Dr. Robert Middleberg, the first of his army of expert witnesses lined up to shoot holes in the cyanide testing and the idea that poisoning was the cause of death.

Middleberg, a forensic toxicologist, had the added distinction of being the medical director for NMS Labs, the company that had been asked to do the quantitative cyanide testing for the Allegheny County Medical Examiner's Office.

Difenderfer quickly asked him about the failed NMS test. Middleberg explained that when his technicians did the first cyanide test, their controls failed, and because of that, it was impossible to complete the original quantitative test that had been requested. He praised the lab employees for following the company's standard operating procedures by halting their work when the controls failed. Middleberg then went on to criticize the type of tests used by all three labs to measure the cyanide in Autumn's blood.

"These amount to what are called color tests. You put in reagents, you look for color reactions," he said. "Today, the standard in toxicology testing tends to be based on molecular identification of something. In other words, looking for a fingerprint of something, as opposed to a general reaction. And what we saw here is all the tests, whether it was NMS Labs or the Allegheny County Medical Examiner's Office or Quest, these are nonspecific tests that have some specificity for cyanide but also interact with other things. I feel very badly here because our laboratory was in the midst of validating one of these molecular identification tests for cyanide at the time that we were doing this testing, but we could not offer the testing because it wasn't validated."

"And that would have been able to give us a much more accurate, reliable sample, correct?" Difenderfer asked.

"I would say a better test."

Middleberg explained that Quest and the Allegheny County lab used different chemicals to develop the color reaction, and said that the NMS chemicals have less chance than the others of creating a false positive. He went on to say that despite the time difference between the Quest test and the NMS test, he would still have expected his lab's result to be higher.

"I think if there's a substantial amount of cyanide in the sample that we tested, it's unlikely that it would disappear." Middleberg said he was concerned by the dramatic difference between the Quest lethal level and the NMS background range findings.

"It would be my opinion that if there was, again, a significant exposure even in the sample we tested, we should have still found significant amounts of cyanide. Granted, could it have disappeared? Maybe. Could it have formed? Maybe we get a result because none was there and some formed, that's a possibility also. Do we have less interferences than Quest does, which is the same test as the medical examiner's office? Yes. It's for all these reasons with all these problems with cyanide that in a case like this where you get results that are conflicting at some level, and we will never by the end of the day figure out exactly what's what with it, where I would tell the individuals getting the results that you've got to put these in the context for which your case is. And perhaps you need to consider alternative explanations here other than cyanide because the analytical data has become somewhat equivocal."

Middleberg told the defense attorney that he would have recommended testing other samples—including tissue samples collected from Autumn at autopsy—and that with just the various blood tests alone, he could not say confidently that she died from cyanide poisoning.

Pellegrini immediately went after the perceived conflict of interest in her cross-examination.

"So the Allegheny County Crime Lab contracted with you to do cyanide testing in this case, right?" she asked.

"I believe so, yes, ma'am."

"And your lab got paid for that cyanide testing, right?"

"Yes, ma'am."

"And now you're testifying for the defense, right?"

"I prefer to look at I'm not testifying for defense or prosecution," the witness answered.

"Well, you're getting paid, aren't you?" Pellegrini pressed.

"Me, personally, no."

"NMS is getting paid, aren't they?"

"They're being compensated for my time."

After several more questions, Middleberg said his company would receive about $5,000 for his testimony. Pellegrini then turned to the issue of the test requested by Jennifer Janssen of the medical examiner's office.

"Did anybody tell her that, 'By the way, our spectrophotometer is not working and we can't do what you're asking for'?"

"I don't have a record of that, no," Middleberg answered.

On redirect, Difenderfer spent a lot of time on Middleberg's fees.

"Do you know of a lot of experts that travel across the country, get on planes, prepare reports as their status as physicians, PhDs, that do it for free?"

"No."

"Either way we look at this, would you ever jeopardize your intellectual integrity and misrepresent a thing for the benefit of either the defense or for the commonwealth?" Difenderfer asked.

"Never, never."

Next Difenderfer called Shaun Carstairs, an emergency room physician and toxicologist at the Naval Medical Center in San Diego. The witness went through a lengthy explanation of what cyanide does to the body—"you essentially get cellular asphyxiation, the cells are starved for oxygen and can't produce energy and ultimately in large enough amounts that can result in significant toxicity or even death"—and then a lengthy list of what he reviewed to write his report.

"So my general conclusion is that based upon the records that I had an opportunity to review, I can't—it's my opinion that it cannot really be definitively stated that Dr. Klein died as a result of cyanide poisoning. And there's a few reasons for that. Number one is that when she initially presented to the emergency department, she was noted by Dr. Farkas, one of the treating emergency physicians, to be conscious upon her arrival. That, in and of itself, is not consistent with cyanide poisoning. Cyanide is what we term a 'rapid knockdown agent,' and it acts very quickly. And in a patient with a purportedly toxic or fatal level of cyanide, I would certainly not expect the patient to be conscious upon arrival twenty minutes or so after purportedly ingesting or being exposed somehow to cyanide. So that's number one. Number two, with respect to the lab testing both by Quest and by NMS, there are a lot of disparities regarding which tests may be accurate, which tests may not be accurate. Obviously, the number one question I have is that initially Quest results were modified downward for unclear reasons to me. This leads me to question, really, the validity of their test, especially when a test sent to NMS Labs at a relatively similar time returned with a result that was significantly lower than that of Quest results, and which, in fact, were what's considered normal levels for an adult who's not poisoned with cyanide."

Furthermore, he said that Autumn's symptoms were not unique to cyanide poisoning.

"There's a lot of shared commonality with other conditions," he said, listing several, including abnormal heart rhythm, severe infection, and other toxins, including carbon monoxide.

Carstairs then went on to say that creatine has been found to have cyanogenic compounds in it. "So could that have explained a measurable level of cyanide in this case? I think it's certainly possible."

"Now, nobody is suggesting that the creatine injured or killed Dr. Klein in this case, correct?" Difenderfer asked.

"Correct."

"The purpose of addressing the creatine would be the levels and potential false positives, correct?"

"Well, it wouldn't necessarily be a false positive if there's, you know, if you get what I'm saying. Could explain the elevated levels of cyanide that were purported to have been measured."

Later, Carstairs said he thought that Klein's clinical presentation was just as likely to have been a cardiac dysrhythmia. "Certainly in light of the fact that the—I feel as a clinician that I can't trust the laboratory results that suggest an elevated level of cyanide. You know, a more likely explanation to me in the absence of that is somebody who's young and healthy with no obvious signs on autopsy would be a cardiac dysrhythmia, which you're not necessarily going to see any structural—any evidence of structural problems of the heart on autopsy. You might, but you don't have to.

"So in my opinion, it cannot be definitively stated by any means that Dr. Klein's death was a result of acute exposure to a toxic amount of cyanide." As the defense had hoped, the two specialists' testimony conveyed the idea that Autumn could have died of something other than cyanide poisoning. But would it be enough to erase the jurors' knowledge that her husband inexplicably ordered cyanide right before her death and that some of it was missing after?

The court day ended as Pellegrini was about to begin Carstairs's cross.

DAY NINE · *Cremation Questions*

On Tuesday morning, the prosecutor began immediately by questioning how much Carstairs was being paid for his work. He told the jury he was being paid $500 per hour and had put in between sixteen and twenty hours of work. Eventually, he retorted to her, "Your experts do not come here for free either."

Pellegrini wanted to know why Carstairs had chosen to throw out the Quest test results entirely.

"I cannot make any reasonable interpretation of that level," he said. "First, there is an incredible discrepancy between that and the NMS level. The second reason is because they amended their level, and after reviewing some of the other aspects of this case, I have serious reservations about the calculations that were done and quality control at Quest. First they said 3.4, and then they said it was 2.2."

"That is not correct," Pellegrini said. "They said it was 2.2. Sonia said it was 2.2, and someone changed her calculation."

"I don't know who Sonia is," Carstairs answered.

On redirect, Difenderfer asked if part of Carstairs's opinion was based on how long Autumn survived.

"Yes," Carstairs answered. "The fact that she survived for three days would be considered uncommon with cyanide poisoning, especially at the initial levels that Quest was reported to have measured."

The defense next called to the stand Dr. Lawrence Wechsler, the chair of neurology at the University of Pittsburgh. Wechsler, who met Ferrante in Boston in 1982 when he was doing his residency, was on the stand for less than ten minutes, testifying about his recruitment of Autumn.

"Were you asked to recruit Dr. Autumn Klein by somebody in particular?" asked Williams.

"Dr. Friedlander knew both of them from Boston, and he brought her name up to me and suggested that I look at her for potential recruitment."

Friedlander, he continued, thought that both Autumn and Ferrante were outstanding in their fields. Wechsler then went on to describe the night of Autumn's collapse. He said he arrived at the hospital just after midnight and stayed until about 5:00 a.m. Everyone's first thought was that Autumn had had a stroke. "There was a young woman that collapsed without any explanation, and a stroke is always the first thought in that situation." Wechsler described Ferrante at the hospital early that morning as noticeably upset and distraught.

Attempting to clarify what Ferrante meant on the 911 call referring to Klein's "folks at Shadyside," Williams asked the witness about that. Wechsler explained that the stroke service at UPMC Shadyside was the same as the one at Presbyterian. "It is the same stroke team," he said. Later, she asked him to review Autumn's curriculum vitae, which listed four papers or book chapters she had participated in involving creatine research.

"Clearly from her academic accomplishments she was very aware and worked closely with creatine?" Williams asked.

"Fair to say, yes."

The prosecution asked no questions, and Williams next called the owner of the funeral home that handled Autumn's cremation. Edward McCabe testified that he met with Ferrante and his daughter, Kimberly, on April 21 at 3:00 p.m.

"His wishes were to have his wife cremated and then to receive friends at the funeral home after the cremation. The cremation occurred on Tuesday, April 23."

"With respect to the cremation, was there any rush put on it or did Dr. Ferrante ask for it to be done in any hurry or anything like that?" Williams asked.

"No," McCabe answered.

"What did you tell the police when they asked if Dr. Ferrante was in a rush?"

"I had said that he had not indicated that he was in a great hurry for the cremation to occur."

Ferrante did, however, want to be notified when the funeral home picked up his wife's body, McCabe said on cross-examination.

The defense next called Dr. Laurie Knepper, a colleague of Autumn's with whom she cofounded the Women in Neurology Group. Knepper testified that Autumn contacted her by e-mail on February 25,

2013, to ask whether Knepper would be willing to examine her about symptoms she'd been having. Autumn asked whether they could keep it out of her medical records because she was going through in vitro fertilization and didn't want that information to become public at the hospital system. Knepper agreed, and Autumn visited her office after clinic hours. She had a "pretty classic presentation for migraines with aura," Knepper testified. The aura, the witness said, "starts as usually on one eye as scintillating, like [a] kind of shimmery object that partially obscures the vision. It can be wavy lines, it can be flashy lights. It can be this characteristic crescent, that's kind of things flying off of it. She was getting a lot of aura and then she was getting a headache."

Knepper said Autumn had been having migraines with aura all her life, but that she didn't recognize the aura until after she had Cianna. Often, the witness said, migraines are precipitated by hormonal changes. Despite Williams's questions to the contrary, Knepper characterized Autumn's near-fainting episodes as being more likely to be associated with migraines than with a heart problem. She also said that because Autumn's exam was completely normal, she did not send the woman for any tests.

The defense next called Dr. Sergei Baranov, a researcher in Friedlander's lab who worked on mitochondrial physiology. He told Williams that he used cyanide in his research, a common practice for decades in his field, and that he ordered cyanide in the lab in 2011—enough, he said, to last him for years.

On cross, Chernosky asked, "So from 2011 until April of 2013, did the defendant ever come to you and ask you to borrow cyanide?"

"No."

"To your knowledge, did he ever use it in his research?"

"I'm not aware of it. We never discussed the cyanide experiments."

The defense quickly moved through several more witnesses—including one who testified about protocol in using the university's P card system; another who said she saw Autumn in Ferrante's lab visiting often; and another who said she knew of a meeting scheduled in the lab that Autumn was going to attend involving the stem-cell project.

Next, the defense played for the jury the recorded testimony of another expert witness, Dr. Lewis Nelson. An emergency medicine physician at New York University who also runs the fellowship training program in medical toxicology, Nelson testified for just under an hour. Difenderfer immediately asked the million-dollar question.

"Do you have an opinion as to whether or not for certainty the individual by the name of Autumn Klein died from acute cyanide poisoning?"

"I do have an opinion."

"And could you please give that to us and the basis for your opinion, please?"

"Well, I don't think it can be said with certainty that she died of cyanide poisoning. I think there was some aspects of the case that are consistent with cyanide. I think there's some inconsistencies with cyanide as the cause of death, and I think there's some potential alternatives that potentially could explain the cause of death."

Nelson noted inconsistencies in Klein's vital signs—including blood pressure and pulse—during her course of treatment as well as in her presentation to the paramedics, and the report by Farkas that she was conscious in the emergency department.

"Typically, a lethal exposure will produce lethal effects. You should be unconscious, you should be quite sick by a few minutes, ten minutes, fifteen minutes. Forty minutes to still be awake sounds awfully long, particularly in the context of what we think her level would have been fourteen hours later."

Then, he continued, comparing the Quest level of 2.2 with the NMS level in the normal range is inconsistent.

"In terms of time delay and testing and storage with these vials of blood, if you will, assuming that they're packaged correctly, should there—could that have explained this large discrepancy between the two?" Difenderfer asked.

"Well, again, there are studies that have looked at this, and the numbers are somewhat all over the place, but in general, storage in a closed container, particularly under proper conditions, I think cyanide should be stable for the two weeks or three weeks that the blood was stored."

"So they should have been much closer in your opinion?" Difenderfer asked.

"They should have been the same, I mean, within, you know, a very small difference."

Nelson said that it was just as likely that Autumn's death was caused by a cardiac dysrhythmia as cyanide poisoning.

As Chernosky started cross-examination, he read from Nelson's expert report.

"In the last paragraph of the first page of your opinion, you say that her clinical course in the emergency department of the hospital is consistent with, but not diagnostic of, cyanide poisoning, is that correct?"

"Yes, that's correct."

"Isn't that just another way of saying that all the signs are there, but you don't want to call it cyanide poisoning?" Chernosky asked.

"No, I think what I'm saying is if you told me it was cyanide poisoning for sure, it wouldn't really be surprising to me. But there are enough inconsistencies and alternatives that I'm not convinced it's definitively cyanide poisoning."

"Dr. Nelson, what do you think that Autumn Klein died from?" Chernosky asked.

"I don't really know. I mean, I think that there's several things on the list. . . . I don't think treating this as cyanide poisoning would be incorrect. I think it's on the list of possible differential diagnoses."

After briefly calling a character witness to testify about Ferrante's reputation as a law-abiding and nonviolent person, the defense called a pathologist from Pitt to testify about the lack of security in the labs there.

Dr. Harry Blair testified that he worked in a lab on the seventh floor of Scaife Hall and said that items had been stolen from there.

"Does your lab, like all the labs, have doors with swipe cards?" Difenderfer asked.

"Oh, no. None of them have swipe cards. You just walk right in and during the day, they're mainly wide open. In theory, they're supposed to be kept locked, but nobody does that."

Blair told the jury that chemicals are kept out in the open on shelves in the lab. "We don't call attention to that, but that is the case." Furthermore, he said that it's not unusual to do Google searches on the chemicals and possible lethal levels.

On cross-examination by Pellegrini, Blair agreed he'd never been to Ferrante's lab and did not know what access was like there.

The last witness called by the defense on Tuesday was another neighbor of the couple, Michael Friday. He testified that the families had children of the same age who played together.

"They seemed like a loving couple to us," he said.

"Was there ever any overt display of affection, kissing and hugging, that you observed of the two?" Difenderfer asked.

"Shortly before this tragic event, the Ferrantes came to our house for Easter dinner, and they had just returned from a trip, I believe, to Puerto Rico. . . . We all noticed it when they walked into our foyer, they kissed. And we were, I don't know, it was just unusual. We don't—"

"You don't do that?" Difenderfer asked.

"It struck us. We don't do that."

Friday told the jury he never knew the couple to be hostile to each other.

"We never witnessed any of that," he said. "I think, to us, there was a lot of mutual respect and admiration."

On cross-examination, Friday said he'd visited Ferrante in jail about five weeks before the trial.

"And you said that you've been neighbors and good friends, right?" Pellegrini asked.

"Yes."

"Okay. Well, would it surprise you to know that on the 911 call the defendant said he didn't know anybody in the neighborhood?"

"Yeah, that would surprise me."

"And he was worried because he didn't know anybody to take care of his little girl?" Pellegrini continued.

"Well, he texted me that night, or left a voice mail, I don't remember which, I think it might have been a voice mail, which I did not hear."

Manning recessed court for the day following Michael Friday's testimony and told the jurors that he expected the case to conclude the next day, with closings and his instructions on Thursday.

DAY TEN · *Ferrantes for the Defense*

When court resumed on Wednesday morning, the attorneys met briefly with the judge to outline what was left of the case. As he prepared to call the day's first witness, Difenderfer said to Manning, almost in passing, "I'm going to spend, I think, the lunch hour colloquying my client, as well. I don't anticipate, but you know." He was referring to whether Ferrante would testify.

The Reverend Dr. F. Washington Jarvis, who had served as the headmaster at Roxbury Latin School in Boston, testified as a character witness for Ferrante. He told the jury that Ferrante's son, Michael, was his student, and he met the defendant in 1997.

"As you doubtless know, he was doing double duty as a parent. He was doing what a mother and father would normally do. Michael had no mother. His mother left when he was five years old. Bob—Dr. Ferrante—and his father, Michael's grandfather, really brought Michael and Kim up."

Moving on to the idea of character testimony, Jarvis said, "I think the opinion of virtually everybody I know was that he was law-abiding. Honest, completely, a person of sterling moral character."

Next the defense called what it considered to be its star witness: Dr. Cyril Wecht.

After detailing his education—he has both medical and law degrees—and his work history, Wecht listed for the jury the various documents, recordings, and medical reports he'd read in reviewing the case. He said he'd been hired initially by Ferrante's first attorney, Jerry Johnson, early on, and was earning $500 per hour, his usual rate. Wecht also noted that he'd appeared in hundreds of cases, including one just the day before in Fayette County in which he testified in a homicide on behalf of the district attorney's office there.

"In terms of your intellectual honesty and reputation, is that something that is very important to you?" Difenderfer asked.

"Yes, it is. To maintain your credibility in this business, you have to be able to explain and stand by your opinions. I have been doing this now for fifty-two years. So it is important, aside from any personal feelings, even just pragmatically, it is important, otherwise you don't have any credibility, and nobody is going to call you," Wecht said.

"This has evolved to where you've accomplished national recognition on a fair number of cases, is that fair?"

"I have been involved in cases that were highly controversial, cases that I have dealt with over the years. There [are] several of those."

After describing the concept of cause and manner of death, Wecht told the jurors that he believed that in Autumn's case, both are undetermined. Among the reasons he cited were the frequency of headaches, dizzy spells, and near fainting, as well as the disparity between the Quest and NMS cyanide test results. Wecht praised NMS as "the most prestigious forensic toxicology laboratory in the country," and said that "it is like the gold standard." Other concerns that he had included the findings of the heart exam done by the forensic cardiologist.

"That report came back, and it listed several things that are not normal for a forty-one-year-old person. They are just not normal findings."

He listed for the jury various spots of mild fibrous thickening around the heart valves, as well as abnormal arteries in the heart's conduction system. "This gives me pause because these findings collectively and a combination of them involving the conduction system could lead to a cardiac arrhythmia or dysrhythmia. Sometimes they produce sudden death. Other times it leads to collapse."

Although Wecht said he couldn't say Autumn's death was caused by a heart-rhythm disturbance with certainty, "all the characteristics are there."

Wecht also spent a great deal of time talking about creatine.

"In many of the reports that I have reviewed, there are references to Dr. Klein having used the creatine and some references suggesting that she had done it for a long time and in substantial quantities. Creatine can lead to the formation of cyanide." Later, he continued, "I don't believe that creatine would cause death. I don't believe it can produce enough cyanide to lead to death. I certainly don't believe that it would produce enough cyanide to produce a 2.2 level. I'm not sure. I can't tell you how much it might produce. It depends on how much she has taken, what degree or purity."

Wecht did say, though, that Autumn's consumption of creatine could have led to the positive cyanide test results obtained by NMS and the Allegheny County crime lab.

Wecht told the jury he thought more of Autumn's tissues should have been preserved for further testing, including organ samples, to try to resolve the inconsistent cyanide results.

"Because when considering whether or not to file charges such as these, you want to be really sure, don't you?" Difenderfer asked.

"I can speak as a coroner, yes. I am not going to send out a report from my office and call something a homicide where there are results from one of the most respected authorities in the country, and [the] homicide is based on laboratory results calling it a particular kind of poisoning, and I've got a report from the top lab in the country, how, what am I using them for?"

In a case with cyanide poisoning, Wecht told the jury, a pathologist would expect to find cherry-red skin. "In my opinion, gray and ashen implies deoxygenated blood, gray and ashen. So it is the opposite then of a super-oxygenated situation such as exists with cyanide poisoning because of the fact that the oxygen cannot be detached and picked up by the cells." He also noted that there were no signs of corrosion in Klein's esophagus or stomach.

Early on in her cross-examination, Pellegrini went back to Wecht's comments about preserving the organs for additional testing. "You did an interview where you talked about that it is regrettable that the body was cremated, right?"

"If I said that, yes. And yes, I would agree."

"Because it would have been nice to have the spleen, right?" Pellegrini continued.

"Yes, for further testing, but the organs can be saved. The body, the body itself can be cremated. It is the organs and tissues that would have been saved and portions thereof that we routinely do."

The prosecutor then went after Wecht's findings regarding the creatine.

"Now, you also list in your report as the manner of death on page seven, the large dose of creatine used for fertility enhancement might have precipitated dysrhythmia and cardiac arrest?"

"Yes."

"Could you cite where you saw in the record that she was taking large doses of creatine?"

"I don't recall specifically. I remember many places references to Dr. Klein taking creatine that I believe are attributable to her, to Dr. Ferrante, her husband. That is my recollection," Wecht answered.

"Well, the defendant's statement to the police was she was taking 5 milligrams in the morning and 5 milligrams at night, right?"

"Yes."

"So, in fact, that is kind of low, a low dosage?"

"I would agree that 5 milligrams—somewhere I know I had seen that she had been taking large doses. I cannot tell you specifically where."

Referring to Wecht's comments on Autumn's heart examination, Pellegrini asked whether it was normal to have fibrous thickening over the age of forty.

"Oh, yes, I would agree," he answered. "But I don't think many. I think you can find it. I certainly agree that, in and of itself, may not be fatal."

"Defense counsel asked you about CORE noting these black lesions on the heart. Do you remember that?"

"Yes."

"Are you aware that that notation was done by a tech with absolutely no medical training?" Pellegrini asked.

"What was done?"

"The CORE notations about black lesions—in the CORE records—that was done by a tech, not a medical doctor?"

"No, I don't remember who made the statement. I remember seeing pictures."

"But in the Jesse Edwards Registry, there are no issues with talking about the black lesions?"

"That's right."

"And this would have been the experts, right?"

"Yes."

Next Pellegrini asked about the lack of corrosion in Klein's stomach. Wecht said if the level of cyanide in the woman's blood was 2.2 like Quest found, he believed there would have been changes in her gastric lining. The prosecutor then presented Wecht with the autopsy report she'd dug up from 1979 when Wecht was the coroner. The patient died from cyanide poisoning, the report said, and there were no findings of any corrosion. Wecht responded that he was the supervisor at the time, and not the one who did the man's autopsy. He eventually conceded, though, that he would have signed off on the man's findings.

As for the Quest level of cyanide, Wecht said, "If that level were unequivocally correct and scientifically unchallengeable and there were no other findings of a likely conflicting nature that is what you had in the case, I would say that in the absence of any other explanation of death, that that would be the cause of death."

After nearly ninety minutes on the stand, Wecht stepped down—the defense confident he had bought their client reasonable doubt. He was replaced by the defendant's son, Michael.

Tall and dark-haired, Michael strode to the stand in a sharp gray suit accentuated by a bright-orange tie. As he sat, his father smiled at him from the defense table. With warm, dark-brown eyes, Michael spoke of his father lovingly.

"The older I get—I'm married, a baby on the way in January—I realize how much my father did for me growing up and being a single parent and getting his PhD."

"In terms of relationship and interactions, how would you categorize it?" Difenderfer asked.

"Extremely close. My dad is my hero."

As Michael testified, his sister, Kimberly, stood outside the courtroom doorway, peering in at her younger brother, awaiting her turn.

Michael described his arrival in Pittsburgh the day after Autumn's collapse and said he helped to take her parents back and forth to the hospital.

"When you arrived and saw them, did they appear at all upset to you, sir, about not being able to see their daughter or nobody taking them to see their daughter?" the defense attorney asked.

"They did not, and they did not mention it to me."

Pellegrini did not ask Michael any questions.

After the luncheon recess, the defense called Kimberly Ferrante, who told the jury she was completing a fellowship in female pelvic medicine at the University of San Diego.

She, too, described being raised by her single father.

"I had a very happy childhood. People always ask me why I didn't ever really contact or have contact with my mother—"

"Objection as to relevance, your honor," Pellegrini interrupted.

"Overruled," Manning said.

"I felt like I was in a very loved home. I felt very supported and just felt a lot of love," the witness finished.

Kimberly, who talked quickly, told the jury she first met Autumn when Autumn was in medical school working in the lab next to her father's. Kimberly was in high school and working in her dad's lab for the summer. It was Autumn who first took Kimberly on a tour of Amherst, where she went to college.

"She was a mentor for me. She told me not to go to medical school. But, you know, she would advise me about career decisions. She was kind of like an older sister."

Kimberly testified that Autumn was having a hard time advancing her career in Boston, and that because Ferrante had been so highly recruited in Pittsburgh, he had created a spot for his wife. She visited them in Pittsburgh a couple times a year, and Autumn visited Kimberly in San Diego twice when she was there for medical conferences. During one visit, Kimberly testified, Autumn was upset about not being able to have another child.

"She wanted me to freeze my eggs because she didn't want me to go through the pain that she was going through. So we talked about the pain of her not being able to have a second child. I also told my father I didn't think that she was going to jump off the Golden Gate Bridge, but there were those concerns. I actually went and found a therapist for her." Kimberly said she told her father Autumn was depressed and gave him the name of a therapist for her.

Kimberly then described her trip to Pittsburgh after Autumn's collapse.

The first time in the hospital room, she knew it was bad.

"You know, I looked—being a doctor—I looked at all her drips. I realized that she was not on any sedation. Usually, when someone has a tube down their throat, they need some sort of sedation if they have any brain activity at all because the tube is incredibly irritating. I knew it was an incredibly poor prognosis, which I then told my father."

"Now, at some point in time did you become aware of anything about toxicology screening or cyanide tests that were being done?" Williams asked.

"Yes, I knew that a tox screen was run and negative. I knew that a cyanide level was sent and pending." She said that she told her father about the pending cyanide test. Kimberly also said that everyone knew that there would be an autopsy, but that her father's concern was making sure that Autumn's organs could be donated.

During cross-examination, Pellegrini went hard after Kimberly on the issue of the cyanide test.

"What doctor told you about the cyanide test?"

"It wasn't a doctor. I overheard two nurses discussing [it] at the nurse's station."

"You were there when your dad was interviewed by the police, right?"

"I was," Kimberly answered.

"They told him that she died as a result of cyanide poisoning?"

"Yes."

"Did you say to the cops that [you] knew she had a cyanide test ordered, right?"

"I didn't say that to them, no."

"But you didn't think it important to say, 'My dad and I had known about this,'?" Pellegrini continued.

"I honestly didn't think it was important at that time."

"When is the first time that you told anybody that you knew about the cyanide test?" the prosecutor asked.

"When I told my father."

"No other than daddy?"

"I mean, my brother, you know, knew about it. I don't think I told many people because I didn't think it was important that I knew about the test."

Kimberly testified for twenty-one minutes, and as she stepped down from the witness stand, there was a feeling in the courtroom that the defense case was rapidly winding down. The trial, which was initially expected to last several weeks, instead was nearing an end.

Then Difenderfer stood up.

"The defense calls Dr. Robert Ferrante."

15 ·
ferrante takes the stand

A MURMUR AROSE in the courtroom as reporters scurried to the hall-way to notify their editors that the defendant was about to testify. While Pellegrini and Chernosky always assumed Ferrante would tes-tify, court watchers were surprised.

Within a few minutes, every available seat in the courtroom was filled by attorneys, staffers, and others closely watching the case as Twitter lit up and courthouse word-of-mouth spread with the news that Ferrante was on the stand.

Dressed in a dark-blue suit and tie, Ferrante settled in to the chair on the witness stand, while several of the jurors leaned forward in the box —wanting to get themselves as close to the action as possible. Several looked skeptical as to what was about to happen.

Difenderfer began his direct by walking his client through his bio with quick questions. Quincy, Massachusetts, childhood, school, first marriage in 1971. Ferrante's voice, when he answered, was much deeper than expected given the high-pitched pleading the jurors had heard in the 911 call.

Referring to his client's first wife, Difenderfer asked, "Did you have two children with her?"

"I did."

"At some point in time did you have a marital breakdown with her and subsequent divorce?"

"I did."

After the divorce, Ferrante said that although they had shared cus-tody, his wife didn't want to participate in raising the kids.

"At that time did your wife, unfortunately, have a diagnosis of men-tal illness?" Difenderfer asked.

"She did."

There was no elaboration, and none sought by Difenderfer, who moved on to Ferrante's research to try to find therapies for people with diseases like Alzheimer's and Lou Gehrig's.

Difenderfer asked his client to describe the mechanics of his studies, telling him to keep it simple.

Turning to face the jury, Ferrante took the tone and manner of a schoolteacher explaining a complicated lesson. Before he got too far in —explaining to the jurors that mitochondria in cells are like the gas for a car, necessary for function—Difenderfer jumped in, abruptly asking about when Ferrante met his second wife.

It was 1995, while Autumn was in the middle years of her dual PhD and MD program at Boston University. She had been assigned to another researcher at his lab, who asked Ferrante to instruct her.

"So you two became romantically involved?" Difenderfer asked.

"Not immediately, but we worked very close together, and then within a few years, yes, we became romantically involved." They married in 2001.

After their 2001 marriage, Ferrante continued, his wife began working at Brigham and Women's Hospital.

"My wife and I were like peas in a pod. We were almost exactly alike. Other than the years between us, we thought alike, did everything alike," Ferrante recalled, sounding wistful.

Ferrante told the jury that over the years Autumn had trouble getting ahead in Boston.

"She was having difficulty. She was becoming marginalized by the system. Harvard is typical of that. What they try to do is just create lots of competition for people so they get the best people there all the time. Being sent forty miles out to be engaged in some of the peripheral hospitals, and they hired a number of people to directly compete with her, and it became difficult [for] both her research and clinical practice."

Ferrante, who had previously been characterized as the trailing spouse, said it was the other way around. He said that when Friedlander recruited him, he made his hiring in Pittsburgh contingent on Autumn getting a job there as well.

"Would 'a very talented and upcoming doctor' describe Autumn?" Difenderfer asked.

"My wife?"

"Yes."

"Yes, Autumn was a very bright person," Ferrante said.

However, he made clear under Difenderfer's questioning that he was the one who brought his $3 million lab to Pittsburgh, as well as nine research grants and three staff members. He was the one offered $600,000 over four years in startup funds and moved to a brand-new, state-of-the-art facility.

Difenderfer switched back to Ferrante's lab work, bringing up 3-nitropropionic acid, the toxin used in research to mimic the effects of diseases on lab animals so the researchers could test therapies on them.

Ferrante testified about administering the proper dose.

"I was probably one of the first people to use it and develop it as a mechanism for research," the witness explained. "Mitochondrial dysfunction is important in cells. One mechanism to do that would be to use 3-NP. It is actually a mitochondrial toxin. It is specific to mitochondria. So we could give small amounts of toxins to cells or animals and produce a clinical effect in the animals and damage effect to the cells," Ferrante said, again turning to look at the jury as he explained the process. "What we would do then is not to use a dose sufficient enough to kill the animal or to kill the cells but just enough to make them very sick. What we would then do is apply therapies like creatine or many other kinds of therapies to determine whether or not the animal would survive or the cells would survive."

Finally Difenderfer got to the matter at hand: the homicide charge against his client.

Would Ferrante ever hesitate to order something for the lab overnight, he asked.

"No."

"Was that a common practice?"

"For me, yes. I want everything yesterday."

And he wanted cyanide, he testified, because he had a major funder for an exciting new direction in his research, one in which he needed a new toxin to replace 3-NP, which wasn't working well.

In the fall of 2012, he had begun working with a local ALS patient, Neil Alexander, who wanted to be on the forefront of research for the disease. Alexander, who had founded the Live Like Lou foundation along with his wife, Suzanne, agreed to give Ferrante and his lab $100,000—and potentially up to $200,000—to start a project that would allow researchers to turn the skin cells of ALS patients into stem cells, replicating brain cells.

Ferrante's team would apply toxins to them to replicate the damage caused by ALS and then treat them with various therapies to try to find individualized treatment for the patients.

"In terms of one to ten, one being really dull, and ten being really excited, this project was on what number?" Difenderfer asked.

"Eleven, eleven," Ferrante answered. "It was just remarkable."

But he needed a new toxin.

"We had other toxins in the laboratory but one of the ones that we would primarily use would be this 3-NP. We had great difficulty with it. In the fall or late summer of 2012 it wasn't working well for some reason," he said. "We could not understand that. I had gone online and researched cyanide, found it to be a much better type of toxin to use in these kinds of experiments for a number of reasons."

So in January 2013, he began doing research on cyanide—which explained, he said, the Google searches he'd done.

"I wanted to know more about cyanide. It was the first time that I was going to be using it within our laboratory."

Difenderfer asked about the cyanide already present in the lab. Of course, Ferrante said, he knew there was cyanide in the lab. None of it was locked up.

"For some reason other than research, would it have been difficult for you to take some of the cyanide that existed there and take it out of the lab?" Difenderfer asked.

"No," his client answered.

At that time, in early 2013, Difenderfer asked, "Was there any difficulty that you were having with your marriage?"

"Yes," Ferrante answered. "My wife was very concerned about having another child. She was very concerned about it."

He and Autumn had tried to conceive a second child beginning in late 2009 and tried for three years, he said, including completing four rounds of in vitro fertilization.

"It had a significant effect, impact, on her for a number of reasons. She saw pregnant women all the time, and it disturbed her to see pregnant women. She got very depressed. She got very depressed at Christmas and did not want her family there, did not want my family there."

Autumn even signed up at the women's hospital in Pittsburgh to cuddle newborn babies from 1:00 a.m. to 2:00 a.m.

In early 2013, Ferrante testified, he saw flirtatious e-mails his wife had written to her colleague, Dr. McElrath, in Boston, that concerned him.

Difenderfer broke into his own line of questioning to ask about a prenuptial agreement. Ferrante confirmed that the couple had one.

"Did you keep your money from your prior marriage and monies that you accumulated over the years, did you keep a substantial [sum] of those monies in your own name?"

"Yes."

"Did Autumn have monies in her own name?"

"Yes."

"And she had a very promising career?"

"Yes, sir."

"In terms of your finances, were you financially comfortable?"

"Yes, sir."

What about the e-mail Autumn sent just after Valentine's Day saying the two needed to have a discussion, Difenderfer asked. "What was that about?"

"Me not being very supportive of having another child, which initially I thought I had been by going to all the clinics and just really trying to have a child. I guess, in reality, I really wasn't as supportive because I had essentially given up. We had been trying to have another child for three years."

"At your sit-down meeting and talk, was it clear to you that she still wanted another child?" Difenderfer asked.

"Oh, absolutely, yes."

"Did that trouble you in terms of her obsession with this?"

"Somewhat. But I had already had three beautiful, wonderful children, and she had only had one with me, and she wanted to have another with me."

Ferrante told the jury that he had participated in the IVF treatments by being the sperm donor, but that he never helped his wife with her injections or even knew what medications she was taking.

"She took care of her own care," he said.

Ferrante said he raised his concerns about her flirtation with McElrath during that discussion.

"Did you guys talk it out?" Difenderfer asked.

"We did."

After that, Ferrante testified, the marriage was rejuvenated. The family took a trip to Puerto Rico in late March, and he rated the couple's relationship after that as an eight on a scale of one to ten.

After that, too, the couple began talking to the IVF specialist again.

"My wife had a mitochondrial dysfunction in her eggs. We needed to figure out a way for her to recover from that in order to have another child."

The specialist had recommended something called coenzyme Q-10, which helps rebuild mitochondria, but Ferrante suggested she take creatine, which he had studied extensively in his research.

Autumn's specialist agreed, he said, and she began to take the supplement to see whether she could tolerate it. She started on a low dose, and when it was clear she wasn't having any problems, they began to escalate her level—up to 10 grams per day.

"She had her own little baggy," Ferrante said. "Her own little baggy that she would have creatine in."

Initially, he continued, she sprinkled the supplement on her toast.

Around that same time, Ferrante said, he was still working on his ALS stem-cell project.

"At some point, do you decide to order cyanide?" Difenderfer asked.

"I do. I ordered cyanide to use as a toxin in the stem-cell experiments. It was vital that we move those experiments along very rapidly. We already produced the stem cell, as well as myself, we needed control people that did not have ALS, and many of the physicians and other people were giving their own skin cells to do the same thing, to create a comparison from someone that didn't have ALS to someone that did. Everything was at the ready, and we had a deadline to put the grant in."

"If you had intention to kill your wife with cyanide salts, potassium cyanide, was that already in the lab?" Difenderfer asked.

"Yes."

"Did you do anything to covertly order this cyanide?"

"I did not. In fact, I advertised it to everybody."

Ferrante explained to the jury that he asked the lab manager to order the cyanide and have it shipped overnight. He also said that there had been a lab meeting three weeks earlier in which the team had discussed his plan to use cyanide on the stem cells—even though only one of the staffers who testified remembered such a conversation.

Difenderfer then asked his client to walk the jury through April 17— the day of Autumn's collapse. Much like the rest of his testimony, Ferrante's tone remained steady and unaffected—even as he described his wife's collapse and ultimate death.

"In the morning, it was a day like any other day, rushing around try-ing to get our daughter dressed to get her out. I went off to work, and Autumn was driving Cianna to school. Her car wouldn't start, so she used my car. She asked me to look at her car. There were lots of [mes-sages] all day long back and forth."

"That day, were you guys fighting or having any problems?" the at-torney asked.

"No, sir. I came back from work late in the day, around four o'clock, to go pick up Cianna from school. That was my routine. We first played in the yard, then prepared dinner. I gave her a bath, put her in jammies, and put her to bed and read lots of stories.

"Typically, when one of us are not home, our daughter sleeps in our bed. So Cianna was asleep. I did my work in bed and waited for my wife to come home."

Autumn was on call, which meant she wouldn't get home until late that night.

Ferrante explained that he and Autumn exchanged several messages throughout the day, including that she was ovulating and had a mi-graine that afternoon. He suggested that she take the creatine.

About 11:30 that night, Ferrante said he sent Autumn a message ask-ing where she was.

"'Hon, you are not home yet. I'm getting worried about you,'" he recalled.

"Did you mix up any of the creatine that night?" Difenderfer asked.

"No."

"At some point, did you hear her come home?" the attorney con-tinued.

"We have this bell on the back door. I was upstairs with my daughter in the bed doing my work. I heard the ding-a-ling of the bell that rings when you open the door."

"When that happens, do you go downstairs?" Difenderfer asked.

"I did not. I expected her to come up and say, 'Hi, hon.' After a few minutes that she did not come up, I went downstairs to greet her."

Difenderfer gave no hint of discomfort about the fact that his client had just put himself upstairs instead of in the kitchen, where previ-ous accounts had placed him at his wife's arrival, but those who'd paid close attention took note of the inconsistency.

"I was there in the kitchen and said, 'Hi, hon. Love you,' She gave me a peck on the cheek and fell to the floor on her knees. She said, 'I feel like this happened the last time I was in church.'

"I kept saying to her, 'Hon, are you okay?' She kept moving her hand this way," he demonstrated as if she was brushing him away, "as if 'I'm fine. I'm fine.' That is typical of my wife. She is very stoic. I kept asking her that and asking her that. She fell to her side. Now she was completely supine on the floor near the stove. I kept on asking her the same thing. I recognized this is not good and called 911."

Referencing earlier testimony, Difenderfer asked, "There is discussion about you directing the 911 person to take her to Shadyside, 'Her folks are there, her folks are there.'"

Ferrante didn't seize the chance to offer the planned explanation—that by "folks" he meant colleagues, not Autumn's parents—in a way the jury could grasp.

"I felt my wife was having a stroke because we previously [had] spoken about the bad things that could happen with IVF drugs, and one of them is strokes. With women when you are taking IVF, that is one of the complications. There are many others."

"What is your understanding of the staff at Shadyside?" Difenderfer asked, trying to steer Ferrante to the point of his question.

"It is a level-one center."

"In terms of 'folks'?" the attorney pressed.

"That is neurology folks, neurology people," Ferrante responded, finally making the connection.

"'Folks' is an expression that you use commonly?"

"All the time."

When the paramedics arrived, the lawyer continued, was there any pressure to dissuade them from taking Autumn to Presbyterian?

"No."

Difenderfer then broached the next thorny topic—Ferrante's decision to cremate Autumn. He asked whether the couple had discussed what they wanted to have done with their bodies after death.

"What was the choice of you two?" Difenderfer asked.

"Cremation," Ferrante answered, noting that both of his parents had been cremated.

"Had you also had discussions in a way whether or not that you would have your organs harvested?"

"Autumn always wanted to be an organ donor. Had it on her license in Boston and here."

"There was discussion in this case about your inquiring with a lot of people, and we saw a letter that you wrote to Dr. Friedlander, where you were debating autopsy versus organ donation, is that fair?"

"I don't know if I was debating. I was agonizing. I asked everybody multiple times."

"Sir, was it your understanding if you have an autopsy you jeopardize the harvesting?" Difenderfer asked.

"Yes, sir."

Ultimately, Ferrante explained, he learned that there could be both organ donation and an autopsy.

"At some point, did you learn or hear from your daughter that there was a tox screen and a cyanide screen?" the lawyer asked.

"Yes, sir."

"When you heard that, knowing yourself, did you inquire?"

"No, not immediately," his client answered. "I was just in disbelief. Just because of everything else that was going on, I wasn't really focused on it at that particular moment."

But, later on, Difenderfer continued, Ferrante had done online searches about the medical examiner detecting cyanide.

"I knew her organs had been donated. It was still unbelievable to me that her organs could be donated if there was cyanide. I knew the ME had done his exam and had not heard back, no results. Typical of myself, when something really bothers me, I just Google and look up everything about it, how it could have happened, why it could have happened, et cetera."

Again, abruptly, Difenderfer changed topics.

"Now, doctor, the cyanide that you purchased through the University of Pittsburgh, was it purchased for the purpose of you plotting or attempting to kill your wife?" Difenderfer asked.

"Absolutely not."

"The night of the seventeenth, had you acquired cyanide or went to the lab and removed cyanide and somehow, some way, orchestrated it to be ingested by your wife?"

"Absolutely not."

"Would you on the 17th of April or any time, would you ever physically harm your wife?"

"Never."

And then, concluding, Difenderfer asked one last set of questions referring to his client's computer.

"There was a search there how to get rid of Google searches later on in May. Did you have any knowledge of that?"

"No, sir. None."

"Did you do that?" Difenderfer pressed.

"I did not, sir."

Pausing to check with his cocounsel to see if he missed anything, Difenderfer concluded his questions.

"Thank you, doctor."

His client had been on the stand for an hour and seventeen minutes. Ferrante had a nineteen-minute break before having to face the prosecution.

PELLEGRINI, ALWAYS PROTECTIVE of her victims and icy toward her defendants, pounced immediately, putting one of the exhibits Difenderfer had just used up on the courtroom screen.

"What date is up here? The date it was printed, what date is that?" she demanded, pointing to the image of an abstract from a research paper about cyanide that the defense said Ferrante would have reviewed in prepping for his project.

"That is May 26, 2013," Ferrante answered.

A month and six days after his wife's death.

Pellegrini moved on.

"Now, 3-NP, that is a neurotoxin as well?" she asked.

"Yes, ma'am."

"And if someone had been exposed to 3-NP, what would be the symptoms, the signs and symptoms?"

"So, 3-NP was characterized and found in China. It was a fungal contaminant of sugarcane. A lot of young people and elderly people are fond of sugar. As a treatment, the findings were similar to Huntington's disease where there was a very specific brain lesion in the brain and that is why we began to use it, because it mimicked Huntington's disease."

"Would some of the symptoms be looking tired, headaches, fainting?" Pellegrini asked.

"Not to the best of my knowledge, no, ma'am."

"Do you remember Googling 'human toxicity and 3-NP?'" the prosecutor continued.

"Absolutely," Ferrante answered pleasantly.

"Four times in January?" she asked.

"Yes, ma'am, as well as others associated with that," he answered.

Pellegrini dropped it, satisfied she'd planted the idea that Ferrante could have been using another toxin on his wife in the months leading up to her death. She moved on, jumping from subject to subject.

First, "You told this jury that Autumn was a really great researcher, right, really great doctor?"

"Yes," the witness answered.

"She was an absolute gold-medal find for UPMC and Pitt?"

"I would agree with that to some degree," Ferrante answered. "Yeah."

Then, "There was a major age difference between the two of you, right?"

"Yes. Twenty-three years."

Then, "Now you stated that it was really important for you to use cyanide in these stem-cell research projects, right?"

"It was important to identify a better functioning toxin in the stem-cell projects," he answered.

"You were here when Dr. Kim testified and said there were no pending research projects using cyanide?" Pellegrini asked.

"Well, Dr. Kim was at the lab meeting, and it is inexplicable why he would have said that."

Next, she focused on the cyanide order. How often had he gone to the lab manager to order supplies? Ferrante said about a half dozen times.

"You heard Michele and she said this was the only time that you [had] gone to her and ordered something directly. You heard her? Weren't you in the room?" Pellegrini asked.

"Yes," Ferrante responded. He tried to explain that it was the first time he sat down with the woman to place an order.

"This was the only time that you come to her to order anything, let alone anything overnight. Did you hear that testimony?" Pellegrini pounded.

"I did."

"Are you saying that is incorrect?" the woman continued.

"What I'm saying is that this was the only time that I sat in front of her, looked up a particular product, identified what it was, identified its cost, and identified and specifically sat with her and worked with her until the product was ordered, but there were other times when I asked her to please, if she would get something ordered, talk to Jinho, talk to one of the other technicians to get that done."

Ferrante said that the day the cyanide arrived, he and Dr. Kim unpacked the bottle together.

"Do you know how the cyanide got from under Dr. Kim's bench into the refrigerator?" Pellegrini asked.

"I have no idea."

"By the way, what happened to the 8.3 grams that are missing from that bottle?"

"I have no idea."

"Wasn't [it] some of your research that you needed it overnight for?"

"It was," Ferrante continued.

"But you have no idea what happened to the 8.3 grams that are missing?"

"I do not," he replied.

Pellegrini changed course again, questioning the witness about his marriage and the couple's bank accounts. Ferrante acknowledged that he had a lot of money in his separate accounts from assets accumulated earlier in his life, and he noted, too, there was a prenuptial agreement.

Even with the prenup, Pellegrini asked, a divorce would still be costly?

"I don't know, ma'am. I have no idea," the witness said steadfastly. "If it were like the latter, I would do what I needed to do, take care of my child or children."

Then, Pellegrini asked him: "You potentially could have lost custody of Cianna, too, right?"

Ferrante seemed to not know how to answer.

"I'm unclear," he responded.

Then Pellegrini asked about the defendant's Google searches about divorce in Pennsylvania.

"I had been through a divorce previously. I know how painful divorce is," he answered. "I didn't want that to happen to my now younger daughter and my current wife."

While his first divorce was a "no-cost, split-down-the-middle" break-up, Ferrante said it was still difficult.

Pellegrini again shifted gears, turning to the e-mails Autumn had sent Dr. McElrath.

"You started suspecting she is having an affair, right?"

"No, ma'am," Ferrante answered. "I did not think she was having an affair."

"Well, you talked about flirtatious e-mails?"

"Yes," he answered.

"Why would you be worried about flirty e-mails if you didn't think she was going to have an affair?" Pellegrini pressed.

"I guess the issue is you can flirt with somebody without having an all-out affair with somebody."

"Well, it made you jealous, didn't it?" she continued.

"Yes, ma'am."

Later, after questioning Ferrante about his wife's plans to take creatine, Pellegrini asked the witness whether he had gone into his wife's e-mails and read messages there.

Without hesitation, he said he had.

"Did you get into her e-mail after she died?" Pellegrini asked.

"Oh, yes, ma'am."

"Did you get in there to look at her medical treatment?"

"Yes, ma'am."

"Did you forward e-mails to yourself?" Pellegrini continued.

"I did. I wanted to know everything and anything I could about her. She was my wife."

Pellegrini went on to question the witness about his access to Autumn's text messages and the electronics that he handed over to his attorneys before turning to the newly learned information from Ferrante's daughter's testimony that she knew the hospital was testing for cyanide.

"Did you talk to [the doctors] and say, 'Why are you ordering a cyanide level?'" Pellegrini asked.

"I did not."

"Weren't you perplexed?" she continued.

"I was very perplexed, but until someone told me what was going on, I remained trying to look up all kinds of other issues associated with my wife's illness."

Ferrante also had done a Google search to find out what hospitals were near the secluded resort the couple was planning to go to the weekend after Autumn's collapse. He explained that search as him having been worried about his wife's previous fainting episodes.

What about the Google searches that Ferrante conducted about detecting cyanide at autopsy?

"Did you call the medical examiner's office to find out what the results were of the cyanide test?" Pellegrini asked.

"No, ma'am. It was at the hospital that the test was requested," he answered.

"So what doctor did you call to find out what the results were?" she continued.

"I did not," he replied.

"But here you are looking at the toxicology report. So why would you be looking at that if the test was done at UPMC?" Pellegrini asked.

"So when my wife's organs were donated, I was very concerned. I called CORE that same morning, and I asked if anything was wrong. They told me no, that her liver and kidneys were donated. That got me very concerned. I knew that her body had gone to the medical examiner, and I had not heard back anything from them. On that same day, that next day, I started Googling all kinds of things about cyanide."

"And you didn't think it was important to tell the CORE people, 'Hey, we better look into this before you take my wife's organs'?"

Ferrante did not have a direct answer.

Pellegrini then put the Google searches on the screen.

Using the laser pointer, she asked, "We have nine searches here 'detecting cyanide poisoning,' right?"

"Yes, ma'am."

"Did you know about the results then?" the prosecutor continued.

"No, ma'am."

"But you are Googling 'detecting cyanide poisoning'?"

"Trying to find out what is going on and how someone would look at that."

Then Pellegrini repeated the Google search, "Would ECMO or dialysis remove toxins or poisons?"

"Yes, ma'am. That is when I knew that it had been suggested that she passed from cyanide. It was still unbelievable to me, and even to this day still unbelievable."

Pellegrini then quickly jumped from Ferrante hearing the tinkling of the bell on the back door, to having his wife's body cremated, to the types of cyanide there are, back to the bell.

"You said that you don't go downstairs right away?" the prosecutor asked.

"I did not that evening," he answered.

"You told Dr. Friedlander that she drank creatine when she came home?" Pellegrini continued.

"I told Dr. Friedlander that she took 5 grams in the morning and 5 grams at night when she came home."

"Do you remember Dr. Friedlander testifying?" the prosecutor asked.

"I do, ma'am."

"He testified that . . . she drank creatine when she came home that night from the hospital?"

"Yes, ma'am. I assumed that she did."

The two went back and forth for a few more minutes about why Ferrante failed to mention to the ED doctors that his wife complained when she collapsed that she felt like she had been at church when she fainted, and about the length of time that elapsed between her collapse and his 911 call.

Pellegrini finished her cross-examination by asking if Ferrante's fellow researchers at Pitt ended up using cyanide in the stem-cell project after his arrest.

"I don't know what happened, ma'am. I was completely gone, and no one was communicating with me," he answered.

Satisfied that she had sufficiently called into question Ferrante's actions during his wife's treatment at the hospital, as well as his need to order cyanide in the first place, Pellegrini sat down.

D IFENDERFER PICKED UP where she left off.

"After the hospitalization, within days, you are being confronted with police. You are locked out of your office, et cetera?"

"Yes, sir. All of my projects were stripped and given to Dr. Friedlander at that time."

Difenderfer then showed Ferrante another list of Google searches he conducted. Among the terms he looked up were "catecholamine storm," which was among the suggestions raised by her doctors for his wife's collapse.

"At any time, did you believe that she had a lethal dose of cyanide in her?"

"No, sir."

"When you found out that they were testing, did you ever think that it was going to be positive for any cyanide-lethal level?"

"No, sir."

"Do you believe that today?"

"I still do not."

Taking one last shot at recross, Pellegrini repeated some of the websites Ferrante visited in the days after his wife's death. They included one, "How would a coroner detect if someone is killed by cyanide."

When Ferrante denied visiting that website, Pellegrini reminded him that a state trooper testified that the computer user clicked on that link.

"If he said that, yes, ma'am."

Pellegrini was done.

She strode back to the prosecution table, and Difenderfer told the court, "No further questions."

"You may step down," Judge Manning instructed the witness.

After two hours and seventeen minutes on the stand, Ferrante wearily walked back to his seat.

It was 4:20 p.m.

After the jury had been led out, Difenderfer announced that the defense had no further witnesses.

Pellegrini, who had two experts in reserve that she wanted to call to rebut testimony by Wecht and Middleberg, was immediately shut down by the court.

"You had the opportunity to call anyone that you chose in your case until it gets to the point where it becomes cumulative," Judge Manning said. "It is not proper rebuttal."

When the jury returned, the defense officially rested.

"That closes the testimony in this case. What remains is for the closing arguments of counsel and the court's instruction on the law," Judge Manning said.

"Because of the serious nature of this matter, it is my intent to sequester you as a jury. You are not to separate once you begin to deliberate. We will provide you with housing and food. If you make it to dinner tomorrow, you will have a good meal," he continued. "The way it will work is this, bring with you tomorrow a change of clothes as you see fit and toiletries and medicine that you might need. We provide everything else for you."

Alternates, the judge said, would be kept separate from the rest of the panel unless one was needed.

With that, the judge sent the group of six women and ten men home with the same instructions they'd had all along.

"Don't discuss the case with anyone and particularly [don't] allow any information from any source to come to your attention. We'll resume closing arguments of counsel at nine thirty tomorrow morning."

16 · · · · · · · · · ·
the verdict

During the course of the trial, Difenderfer believed his multifaceted approach had done a good job of explaining away much of the evidence against his client: the Google searches, the marital strife, the cyanide purchase. He also was confident that the defense had convinced the jurors that there was reasonable doubt that Autumn had even died from cyanide poisoning.

And finally, at 9:50 a.m. on Thursday, November 6, he was down to his last chance to convince the jury that his client had done nothing wrong.

The smooth and polished defense lawyer stood up from the counsel table, pausing to unbutton his suit jacket. He slowly moved around the table and warmly clasped Ferrante's shoulder before walking toward the jurors. He stopped just a few feet in front of the wooden box.

After fifty witnesses for the prosecution and nineteen for the defense, this was it, and Difenderfer told them so.

He began by thanking the panel for being so attentive throughout the lengthy, often complicated testimony. And then he told them not to allow themselves to be misled by the commonwealth.

"This case is about whether or not my client intentionally murdered his wife," Difenderfer said. "It's not about the tragedy of the death of Autumn Klein. It is a horrible tragedy. We realize it, and we appreciate it."

But, he continued, "We don't decide cases on emotion or on fear or what we want to believe."

Instead, Difenderfer told them, verdicts must be based on logic and the law.

Reiterating what he told the panel in his opening, the defense attorney spoke about the burden of proof and what it means to find someone guilty beyond a reasonable doubt.

In civil court, Difenderfer explained, the burden is a mere preponderance of the evidence—a slight tipping of the balance, he said, using his hands to portray the scales of justice. In family court, he continued, the burden is higher—clear and convincing evidence.

But in criminal law—where a person's life is on the line—the burden is beyond a reasonable doubt. A reasonable doubt, Difenderfer explained, is a doubt that causes a person to "pause or hesitate" in deciding a matter of utmost importance.

"The cost of a conviction in this building actually destroys lives, and it's irreparable harm," he told them. "Here, it's devastation."

It was nine minutes before Difenderfer spoke a single word about his client. And when he did, he implored the jury to think about who Ferrante was—a neuroresearcher and family man.

"There wasn't one blemish in the history of my client, not one bit of any kind of violence or anything in his history other than a man who is brilliant, and because of his brilliance is on the front line of attempting to solve one of the most crippling diseases and one of the worst diseases that you can get, Lou Gehrig's disease.

"If you get diagnosed with it, it is a death sentence."

Difenderfer then turned to Ferrante's relationship with his wife.

"She was the love of his life," he said. "She still is."

The defense attorney explained to the jury that it was Ferrante who wanted to promote his wife's career, and that his agreeing to come to Pittsburgh was for her—"putting his wife first."

"This couple had a great marriage, but they encountered some difficulties."

Ferrante's concerns about his wife and her relationship with Dr. McElrath, as well as suggestive text messages and e-mails, would be enough to prompt a reaction from any spouse, Difenderfer said.

But just as quickly as he hit upon the couple's marriage, the defense attorney turned his attention and focused on the cyanide instead. Ferrante was in the middle of his stem-cell project, planning to apply for grants from the National Institutes of Health in June or July.

"My God, cyanide is common in this type of thing. Common. It is unequivocally scientifically sound introducing cyanide especially into the project that they were commencing with the stem cells," Difenderfer said.

The courtroom, packed with reporters and attorneys, was rapt.

And then the defense attorney flashed back again to the couple's relationship, referencing Autumn's e-mail to her husband in which she told him they needed to talk.

"If I got a letter like that from my wife, I would be a little concerned, too," the attorney said. "Please keep in mind, there is a prenuptial. If there is any divorce, the economic issues are resolved by contract. They both had plenty of money, and they both had wonderful careers."

But, he continued, it was clear the couple had the talk.

"What do we know? They went to Puerto Rico as a couple, with their daughter. It sounds like they are getting along," Difenderfer said.

If they weren't, he continued, why would Autumn, even in her last waking hours, continue to talk about wanting to get pregnant by her husband?

"If you are going to leave somebody, are you going to go, 'Hey, listen, before we break up, I want to have your kid again?' Does that make sense? It doesn't. It doesn't."

The defense attorney abruptly returned to the issue of the cyanide and Ferrante's stem-cell project.

Difenderfer then played out a preposterous scenario for the jury of how his brilliant client made sure everyone in the lab knew he was ordering the cyanide and then used it to kill his wife the day after he received it.

"Does he order it somehow privately? The whole lab knows that he is bringing it in. Is that something you do? Please," Difenderfer said with disdain.

Throughout his closing, the defense attorney skimmed a number of issues that figured prominently throughout the trial. That his client's fingerprint was found on the bottle of potassium cyanide was no surprise. His client said on the stand he opened the package when it arrived.

"Dr. Ferrante made it very clear, 'We sat down, I opened the box, I pulled out the bottle, I handled it, I put it back.'"

He told the jurors that both Ferrante and Autumn were familiar with creatine use for its mitochondrial benefits, and that she was using it to help her eggs become healthier.

As for the 911 call, Difenderfer characterized his client as "absolutely frantic and absolutely concerned for his wife's health."

To the prosecution's contention that Ferrante tried to divert the paramedics to Shadyside hospital, the defense attorney said there was simply no evidence of that.

"The prosecution in this case has taken headlines, and then they want to fill in the gaps just by saying so," Difenderfer said, referring to a theme he used throughout his closing. "We need evidence in cases such as this—not misinterpretation."

An ED doctor who described Ferrante as acting oddly the night his wife collapsed, Difenderfer continued, "is not evidence. He was grieving. He was a mess."

Then Difenderfer turned to the Google searches. He explained them away by saying that each time Ferrante did one, there was a reason.

"'What's going on with my wife?' He Googles it."

During Autumn's hospitalization, Ferrante also did searches for "catecholamine storm" and "channelopathy."

When Ferrante heard from his daughter that a cyanide test was ordered, "he Google-searched it. His nature is to look it up and to learn everything that he can about it."

Difenderfer next spoke to the jury about the prosecution's contention that his client tried to avoid an autopsy and hurried his wife to cremation.

"There's an issue here of autopsy versus organ donation. It was her absolute wish to have her organs harvested to give the gift of life to other people."

At first, Ferrante did not know that both organ donation and autopsy could occur concurrently, and when he learned they could, that's what happened, Difenderfer said. As for the cremation, "There is not one thing, not one piece of evidence of any kind of rush."

The last major issue addressed by Difenderfer was the question of how Autumn died and the various cyanide results.

First, Difenderfer again praised NMS Labs as the "gold standard" in the industry, noting for the jury that the prosecution was unable to call into question any of the procedures used there—unlike what he showed in terms of the calibration of equipment at Quest Diagnostics.

The lab technicians at Quest failed to follow their own protocol in running the test and then for no apparent reason edited the results. At NMS Labs, they followed procedure and ultimately obtained results that were of a nonlethal level.

The prosecution could not criticize NMS results, Difenderfer continued, "because it was perfect and pristine."

Then the defense attorney criticized detectives working the case as well as the staff at the Allegheny County Medical Examiner's Office for not making the tests to determine cyanide level a higher priority.

"This could be it on a murder prosecution, first-degree murder prosecution," he said. "They have all the resources in the world. All the money needed on these cases. There is no phone call made to NMS of, 'Hey, we got something really important here.'"

Instead, he continued, they sent a vial of blood with a form. It arrived on a Friday and got tested a few days later.

In addition to walking the key sample through the process, they should have sent additional blood samples for testing as well.

Turning to the expert testimony regarding cyanide, Difenderfer singled out prosecution witness Dr. Holstege. In his book about poisonings, the Virginia physician said that cyanide would cause a slow heart rate and low blood pressure. But, as Dr. Holstege conceded in his testimony, Autumn had the opposite.

"He has no more expertise in this than our experts," Difenderfer said. "Many symptoms you have in this case fit the symptoms of other diagnoses.

"We don't guess. We don't speculate. It must be absolutely positively is what has to happen here. Don't go jumping to conclusions because it may not be what you think.

"That is the danger."

Difenderfer attacked Pellegrini's cross-examination of Dr. Cyril Wecht—calling it insulting of her to suggest that he and the other experts were hired guns.

But, he continued, she didn't have any testimony of substance from Dr. Wecht to challenge.

"He's right, that's why. He's right."

As he neared the end of his one hour and twenty minute closing, Difenderfer appeared to run out of steam. He walked back to the defense table, whispered loudly, "Is there anything I forgot?," and, getting his answer, returned to the lectern.

"When you are deliberating, all of you, individually, I want you to ask yourself: 'What if Dr. Wecht is right? What if he's right?' There is no way this case has shown that he is not maybe right," Difenderfer said. "What if Holstege is wrong? What if? Are you positive? Can't be."

Ferrante, he continued, will never accept that his wife died from cyanide poisoning, and there is no evidence of how she would have ingested it.

In conclusion, Difenderfer asked the jurors to listen to their "internal gut. Is it right? Let that be your compass. You want to make sure as you are alone you know, in your heart, you did the right thing."

M ANNING ORDERED a short break, and immediately Pellegrini removed her suit jacket in the hot courtroom and ordered everyone around her and Chernosky to leave them alone.

They had worked on the closings the night before—both of them writing up notes on what was important—and were back in the office at 6:15 a.m. to put together their argument.

They knew that their boss, district attorney Stephen A. Zappala Jr., wanted them to highlight Ferrante's Google searches again, so Chernosky was responsible for putting those together in a PowerPoint presentation. But they also had to make sure they hit all of the important pieces of evidence from the ten-day trial.

As they conferred early that morning, Chernosky read to Pellegrini from his notes, and she'd interrupt and say, "Write that down just the way you said it."

But as they sat in the courtroom, moments away from the biggest closing of her career, Pellegrini said, "I don't know how to start."

"You'll be fine," Chernosky reassured her. "Listen to me for a sec. Agree with everything he said. You have to answer the questions he posed at the end."

When court resumed, her cocounsel's words stuck with her—along with the phrase he had shared about the improbability of Ferrante's situation.

Pellegrini, her blonde hair pulled back, approached the panel.

"Let's address what the defense said last. What if their experts are right? What if she didn't die of cyanide poisoning? Well, then, he is the unluckiest man in the world."

Then Pellegrini ticked off, one by one, the pieces of evidence against Ferrante.

"His marriage was on the rocks. He was awfully jealous of Tom McElrath. She dies two days after he orders cyanide overnight—something he has never done before personally."

The cyanide bottle was moved in the lab. It was missing 8.3 grams. It had his thumbprint on it.

"His daughter, Kim, conveniently hears two nurses talking about cyanide poisoning, and he's furiously Googling it, and he happens to Google, specifically, the kind of cyanide he ordered."

Throughout her closing, Pellegrini's tone rose and fell with the moment—coming off like someone talking to her friends, though occasionally taking on such a sarcastic bent that even her supporters squirmed with discomfort.

During one of those, Pellegrini reenacted for the jury Ferrante's response when he was told his wife died from cyanide. Slapping her cheeks at the same time, she spoke mockingly, "'Who would do this to her? Oh, why would she do this to herself?'"

She noted, too, that not a single person in Ferrante's lab said that cyanide was urgently needed for the ongoing stem-cell project on the day it was ordered.

"It all has to be just one coincidence, and he's the unluckiest man on earth," Pellegrini said, dropping her voice to a whisper, "Or else, he's guilty."

Speaking to the jury almost in confidence, Pellegrini said, "I will tell you this: He is brilliant. He was well-respected. People liked him. That is what makes this crime so diabolical. Because he is a master manipulator."

Her words prompted someone from Autumn's family in the gallery to quietly agree.

Pellegrini urged the jurors to judge the demeanor and credibility of the witnesses who testified.

"You saw him up there yesterday, right? Flat, rehearsed. He had an answer for everything. Did you notice that?"

Until, she continued, she asked him tough questions.

"Where did he look? Right over at the table," she said pointing to defense counsel.

"What happened to the glass [Autumn drank from that night in the kitchen]?"

"'Well, I don't know,' he answered. 'I was upstairs.' I thought you told people that she walked in the door and gave you a kiss? I don't know which story you are going to believe up here.

"What happened to the 8.3 grams missing in the bottle, the bottle that you needed overnighted because you were going to treat those stem cells? 'I don't know. I don't know.'

"Did you listen to him when he was describing his wife's collapse?" Pellegrini continued. "Did you see a tear? Did he act like a grieving husband? I submit to you not one bit—because he is a master manipulator.

"He thinks he can manipulate everyone."

Pellegrini then turned to the dozens of Google searches found on Ferrante's computer and the contention by the defense that he was doing research for his stem-cell project.

"Come on, is he going to research sites? No! What he is going to is Wikipedia about cyanide poisoning. Does that sound like research to you?"

The prosecutor called Ferrante the "master of control," alleging that he conveniently had an answer for everything. Except, she continued, for how to control his wife, that "young, beautiful, shining star."

Abruptly, Pellegrini switched gears, turning to Autumn's move to Pittsburgh and what she described as Ferrante's motive: jealousy.

"By the way, how dare they disparage her career—really? Did you hear her colleagues? She was world renowned. She didn't need his coattails anymore. He didn't like that, though. He was ready to retire. She is in the prime of her life."

Although it had certainly been hinted at by both sides throughout the trial, Pellegrini continued, the idea of Autumn having an affair came from Ferrante.

"I never, ever said that she was having an affair. You know where all of that stuff came from? In that brilliant brain. What did he tell you yesterday? 'I'm jealous of Tom McElrath. I'm jealous.' Motive. Motive."

Then, Pellegrini directed her intern at the prosecution table to begin a PowerPoint display.

"We rarely get a road map into what people are thinking. This is the road map into his diabolical mind. A road map of how to kill your wife."

The presentation started with a list of the online searches investigators found on the laptop locked in the lab safe.

Pointing at the screen that listed "human toxicity 3-nitropropionic acid," Pellegrini said, "Toxic dose of 3-NP and cardiac myopathy. What does he tell you? We don't use 3-NP on humans. You know, he is looking up human toxicity and neurotoxicity that you don't use on human beings, you use it on cells to kill the cells."

Then to another, "does increased vaginal size suggest wife is having sex with another."

"Who Googles this? Really? Really?" Pellegrini asked. "This is somebody who is pathologically jealous. Really?" she said again, her voice rising. "It's disgusting."

Then the prosecutor asked a question that many watching the trial had pondered: Why wouldn't Ferrante wait until the couple's upcoming weekend away at a rural retreat to kill his wife?

Pellegrini said she had wondered about that since she initially received the case. She finally realized, though, when she saw the text messages between the couple suggesting Dr. Klein take creatine for her ovulation that Ferrante decided to seize the moment: disguising the cyanide in the powdered supplement.

"He saw that opportunity, and he took it. But what he didn't count on was Autumn's will to live and the heroic efforts of the doctors. If he had poisoned her at Nemacolin, she would have been dead before paramedics even arrived," Pellegrini said. "He was just too smart because if he had done it at Nemacolin, he would have gotten away with the perfect murder."

Pellegrini went on to question whether Autumn was even taking a creatine regimen, noting that the only person who ever said so was Ferrante.

Then the longtime homicide prosecutor attacked the entirety of the defense-trial tactics. Ferrante's attorneys shifted from theory to theory, she said, trying to see what might stick with the jury. First they tried contaminated creatine, then moved on to potential false positives in the blood tests. Then, she continued, they argued Autumn was suicidal. Finally, it was that she died from a heart ailment.

"This whole defense is about collateral journeys. Look here. Look there. Look everywhere but right there," she said, pointing at the defendant. "It is creatine. It is heart dysrhythmia. It is this. It is that. Pick one! Pick one!"

In addressing the defense experts, Pellegrini argued that their suggestion of a potential heart disturbance was simply wrong.

"Pick the one thing you can't prove that looks an awful lot like cyanide," she said. And in doing so, those same experts had to completely ignore the positive test results from Quest.

"But for all the defense experts to be right, they want you to ignore that. Throw it out. I don't care if it's 2.2 or 7.9. It's lethal. You're dead!"

Of the NMS results, she continued, that lab failed to complete the tests that were requested and didn't alert the medical examiner's office for days.

"Once again—look here, look there. Look everywhere but where it matters."

Pellegrini further attacked Ferrante for not wanting an autopsy and hurrying the cremation. "Don't you want to know what happened? The implications for your child?

"This is not some dumb-dumb," she told the jury. "You know what? He's getting rid of the body."

Making a personal attack, Pellegrini criticized the defense for allowing Kimberly, who claimed Autumn had been depressed in the months leading up to her death, to testify on her father's behalf.

"It is shameful this defendant threw his daughter under the bus"—the prosecutor's words for the first time eliciting a response from Ferrante, who shook his head in disgust. "She loves her dad, and I submit to you she will say anything to help her daddy. They had to have an answer for everything."

Pellegrini continued working her way through the PowerPoint road map, highlighting Ferrante's Google searches in the days after his wife's death. "How would a coroner detect whether someone is killed by cyanide?," "potassium cyanide detection blood urine," "detecting potassium cyanide poisoning," "remove all google web history," "Would ECMO or dialysis remove traces of toxins and poisons?"

"Look at this," Pellegrini told the jurors, pointing at the screen. "Look at the dates. It is Monday. The day she is being cremated. Look at this. The same day he is interviewed. What is he doing?"

Nearing the end of her closing, the prosecutor explained the requirements of first-degree murder: premeditation and a specific intent to kill. Poison, Pellegrini continued, is part of the definition.

"Ladies and gentlemen of the jury, you don't poison somebody unless you want to kill them. He picked a murder weapon that would destroy her cells and lead her to a painful, awful death. I submit to you it wasn't ten minutes like he told the 911 operator. She drank that creatine. She fell to the ground. He got rid of that glass. He called 911.

"I submit to you he gave her that poison to drink, called 911, and stood over her and watched her suffer. You heard how awful that was. Could you imagine? He never counted on how hard she would fight for that little girl. He thought she'd never make it to the hospital."

Again, Pellegrini turned to her intern, who began a new, rudimentary PowerPoint presentation of puzzle pieces joining together. She went through each piece, one by one.

The cyanide order. The Google searches. The 911 call. Ferrante's conduct at the hospital. His wish that no autopsy be conducted.

"When you put all of those pieces of the puzzle together, they only lead you to one conclusion: This defendant premeditated the murder of his wife. . . . He wanted her dead, dead, dead because 'if I can't have you, nobody will.'" First-degree murder, she concluded, is "the only verdict."

After fifty minutes, Pellegrini returned to her table.

There was a sense of relief in the room now that both attorneys had finished, leaving only the court's final instructions to the jury. Judge Manning called for a short break. As Pellegrini made her way through the crowded gallery to speak to the Klein family, Michael, who had been in the front row behind his father, spoke directly to her—insulting her closing.

"You should have let Chernosky do it."

Pellegrini paused a beat and then gave the same high-pitched "Really?" that she had repeated over and over to the jury, before hissing, "How low class," and making her way out of the courtroom.

Besides the prosecution's cross-examination of the Ferrantes on the stand, it was the only interaction between the sides throughout the trial.

During the next forty minutes, Manning spoke to the jurors about their duties. He told them that the only choice they had to make was whether Ferrante was guilty of first-degree murder. Unlike in other homicide cases in which the jury might get to decide from among first-, second-, or third-degree murder, as well as voluntary manslaughter, in the Ferrante case, the defense attorneys had agreed to take a chance. It was all or nothing.

At 1:00 p.m. on Thursday, November 6, the jury on the Ferrante case left the courtroom and climbed the steep twenty steps up to their room to begin deliberations.

It was a cold, stark place with a dark-brown cement floor, frosted-over and painted-shut windows that not even a fresh coat of white paint on the walls and a few new ceiling tiles could soften.

The fifteen-by-twelve-foot space was stuffy and confining, with mismatched chairs around an old, brown Formica conference table. The walls were sparsely decorated with only three old courtroom scenes, including one that was water stained.

The panel had already chosen the foreman before closing arguments started. Four people were interested, and so they made their selection randomly—picking the winner's name, juror number seven, Brian Maitz, out of a hat.

When they first returned to the room after receiving their final instructions, the jurors agreed that they should do a preliminary poll. They used a number system, one for guilty, two for not guilty, and three for undecided.

In that first poll, three people wrote number one on their slips of paper, two wrote number two, and seven wrote number three.

Most of the group agreed that it was a starting place, but juror number one was outraged. She didn't understand how anyone could believe Ferrante was not guilty. The rest of the panel had agreed the best way to begin their deliberations was to simply walk through the case —witness by witness.

Number one refused to participate, making the already-stressful situation even worse.

Juror number six, Lance DeWeese, who had been pacing around the room, was frustrated. He finally addressed juror number one directly about what he called the "elephant in the room.

"Whether you want to be here or not, it's how some people make a decision."

Because of the hostility in the room, the jurors agreed that when they wanted to speak, they had to raise their hands.

And so they began.

Almost immediately, they were stuck. Because they had listened to the 911 call so early in the trial, much of the nuance of it had been lost to them. Without having the information to know why it might be relevant that Autumn's face turned red during the call, or who suggested initially that she might be having a stroke, the jurors knew they needed to review the transcript again.

They thought that they would be permitted to have a copy of it because they used it when the recording was played initially on the first day of trial. They sent a written note to the court asking for it.

But when Manning reconvened the panel in the courtroom, he instructed the group that the physical transcript was not evidence, and that they could not leave the courtroom with it. What he could do, though, was have the 911 call played again—again with the jurors reading along.

As the haunting moans of the victim bounced off the courtroom walls for a second time, juror number one kept her head down, repeatedly wiped her eyes, and flipped each page angrily.

When the call ended, the jurors left the courtroom again. But it was less than an hour before they returned with another question. They requested a transcript of the testimony of Dr. Jinho Kim, Ferrante's lab associate, who had been difficult to understand with his thick Korean accent.

Manning refused the request, telling the panel that they must instead rely on their collective memory and notes about what the researcher said.

The jurors again retreated upstairs and gathered around the table, which had bottles of ibuprofen and antacid within reach, along with homemade cookies made by a juror's wife and premixed packages of coffee and hot chocolate.

By 6:00 p.m. Thursday, the group had started to discuss the various cyanide test results from both Quest and NMS Labs. They got stuck on the clinical aspects of the tests and finally decided they were tired and hungry. Knowing they were going to be sequestered in a hotel under police guard, they agreed to call it a night and left for dinner just after seven.

After breakfast on the seventeenth floor of the Doubletree Hotel Downtown the next morning, the jurors divided up between two shuttle buses to make the three-minute return trip to the courthouse. At 9:00 a.m. Friday, they started where they left off the night before—discussing the cyanide test results—most of them agreeing that the 2.2 milligrams per liter lethal result from Quest was valid. The voting started to shift—it was seven guilty, two not guilty, and three who remained undecided.

They kept working.

As they moved their way through the evidence, DeWeese requested a large whiteboard and dry-erase markers. They used them to list the Google searches, in order, in an attempt to complete a full timeline along with the e-mails and text messages from Autumn and the date that Ferrante ordered the cyanide.

The foreman took notes in a small, spiral tablet, copying down from the whiteboard when it needed to be erased so they had more room to continue.

The emotions in the room remained tense as everyone on the jury recognized the responsibility that they had. The smokers, who had repeatedly asked to go outside, were instead allowed to go to an adjoining jury room where there was an air-purification system when they needed a break.

As the eight men and four women continued their discussions, Autumn's parents tried to keep themselves busy out of the eyes of the media. Bill, who was using a wheelchair to move throughout the long halls, and Lois sat at a table outside the Gold Room, reading magazines, eating leftover Halloween candy, and talking to their loved ones.

Although the jury had returned to the courtroom with two questions Thursday afternoon, throughout the entire day on Friday, they asked nothing. For those watching the trial, their silence was impenetrable. Did it mean they were stuck? That they were making progress? That they were simply working methodically through the evidence?

None of the attorneys would speculate, though, knowing that in a jury trial, anything could happen.

Late Friday afternoon, Pellegrini joined Lois and Chris Chambers, the victim advocate working with the family, as they waited. The women laughed like old friends.

In the meantime, the jurors had started working their way through the defense witnesses. They kept returning to the timing of the cyanide order, the e-mails about the couple's relationship, and the online searches.

A new poll put the split at nine guilty and three who were undecided.

Those who were still not sure explained to the group why they were conflicted. One was stuck on the idea that the dialysis should have cleaned Klein's blood, and another just couldn't believe that, given Ferrante's character, he would kill his wife.

"It's happened for thousands of years," DeWeese argued. "This is nothing new."

He recounted the biblical story of King David, who had Bathsheba's husband killed so he could make the woman his own.

The jurors, who had been working for more than six hours straight on Friday, agreed they needed some air, particularly given the stuffiness in the room. They asked to go for a walk outside.

As they strolled around the courtyard, the jurors felt like they were on display, looking up at the stone walls of the castle-like building into the third- and fourth-floor windows as reporters and attorneys and Autumn's relatives looked down at them.

When they returned, there was another poll. It was eleven to one.

For the next hour and a half, the lone juror who was still undecided sat in front of the whiteboard, talking through each step in the timeline of the case. The others in the group sat around quietly, interjecting when necessary, as he thought aloud about the case.

As that juror continued through his process, Michele Kearney, the court tipstaff, knocked on the door.

"Now's not a good time," DeWeese said. But Kearney said, "The judge wants—"

DeWeese, who had opened the door, cut her off. "Now is not a good time."

He closed the door.

A few minutes later, juror number eight, the lone undecided juror, said, "I believe he's guilty. Let's flip the light switch."

For the last time, the twelve people—from all over Allegheny County, who had been thrust together not knowing what they were getting into—sat around the table, voting one last time. There was no discussion or commentary. Somberly, each person repeated, "Guilty."

Just before 6:30 p.m., the red jury light in the courtroom went off. There was a complete lack of urgency because speculation from media and court staff was that the jury wanted to break for dinner.

But then, every member of Autumn's family, who had spent eleven days watching the horrible details of the case spill out, walked into the room. Next, Ferrante's family walked in. Then, additional sheriff's deputies.

There was a verdict.

Reporters snuck out of the room to alert their copy desks and to Tweet the news before the tipstaff announced for the last time in the Ferrante case, "All rise!" as the jury filed into the room.

In the front row behind the prosecution team, each member of the Klein family grasped the hand of the person next to him or her, tears already falling.

As the foreman read the verdict, guilty of first-degree murder, Lois's body began to quake—heaving sobs of sadness, joy, and relief.

17 · · · · · · · · · · ·
the aftermath

JUST AFTER 11:00 A.M. on February 4, 2015, Ferrante walked into the courtroom just like he had done dozens of times before.

This time, though, sheriff's deputies did not remove the brown leather belt around his waist they used to guide him—or the handcuffs that ensured his cooperation.

He was already guilty, and there was no longer any reason to treat him otherwise.

The courtroom, which had often been packed for the trial, was barely half full. Autumn's parents and their victim advocate, Chris, sat in the front row of the gallery, behind the lead detectives in the case. Behind them sat one of the jurors who helped decide Ferrante's fate.

On the defense side of the room, no one showed up to support Ferrante. Neither of his adult children, Kimberly and Michael, who testified for him at trial, attended, nor did his sister.

The defense had told them not to bother.

Ferrante, who had lost a significant amount of weight in the three months since his trial, looked small. With close-cropped hair, he wore a dark-blue blazer, yellow tie, and charcoal pants. He had been stunned the evening of the verdict, sure that he would be acquitted, not only by what he heard in the trial, but also from what he'd been told by watching deputies.

Now, though, he remained dignified, standing straight with his chin up, as he stood before Manning, prepared to accept his punishment.

Although the sentence for first-degree murder is mandatory under Pennsylvania law, Ferrante, who'd been placed on suicide watch near the end of his trial, knew that there would be victim-impact statements before the judge condemned him to spend the rest of his life in prison.

Manning addressed the prosecution first: Were there any witnesses?

Pellegrini said she had just one, Autumn's mother, Lois. But first, she said, she had a letter to read from the victim's cousin and best friend, Sharon, who could not attend the hearing.

In her one-page letter, Sharon described the "sometimes unbearable pain" she had felt since Autumn's death—that she no longer had the person with whom she'd shared all of the important moments and issues in her life.

But she talked, too, about the impact on Cianna and her own young son.

"Now I watch her little girl grow up without her amazing mother. And I have to explain to my little boy why his favorite Auntie is gone. Such big, nasty life things for such young minds to comprehend . . . when I can't even comprehend or make sense of them as an adult and as a mother. So, to honor Autumn, I will do my best to take their little hands and walk this awful journey alongside them. I will do what Autumn and I had planned and help raise them to be kind and strong and close."

After Autumn's death, Sharon wrote, she withdrew from volunteering at her son's school, her community group, and her church. She also questioned her own security.

"This tragic murder strikes to the core of my belief that the world can be a safe place, since her life was taken in her own home, downstairs from where her own daughter was sleeping. How do you believe in love and the safety of trusting when the one closest to you takes your life in such a violent and diabolic manner? These beliefs were shattered when Autumn was murdered."

As he stood between his attorneys, Ferrante offered no expression or comment to Sharon's letter.

In another letter that was submitted to the court but went unread at the hearing, Sharon's husband, Jeff, focused on the impact of the homicide on his wife.

"They were intimate witnesses to each other's lives," he wrote. "Autumn balanced my wife's life in ways I cannot fathom. It has been almost two years since she was murdered, and it is clear to me that my wife will never have that kind of balance again."

Then, Pellegrini called her only witness.

Lois walked to the front of the courtroom, her hand clasped in the prosecutor's. The older woman was given the opportunity to sit in the witness chair, but she refused, instead choosing to stand just a few feet away from the man whom her daughter once loved.

Pellegrini had already offered to read the victim-impact statement to the court because Lois worried her nerves would stop her from getting all the way through. She was right—as Lois introduced herself to the judge, her voice broke even as she spelled her last name.

"The loss of Autumn was never expected and has been extremely hard on both William and I," she read out loud. "She was our only child, and the light of our lives has now been extinguished. We used to enjoy visiting with her and the family. Now instead, we are raising her child, Cianna."

Lois described Cianna as a bright and lovely little girl enrolled in a Lego club and karate class and art program. Last year, she took dance classes and swimming. She was a good speller and above the national average in math as well.

Autumn was a terrific mom, Lois stated, no matter how busy she was with work.

"There is no longer peace in our lives. Every day something is different," she continued. "He has certainly ruined our lives."

Lois also addressed the more practical ramifications of their daughter's death: The Kleins had lost some of their retirement income fighting for Cianna's custody in court, and without Autumn, they lost some of their mental and medical support. A trip they expected to take to Ireland and Scotland to celebrate their fiftieth anniversary in 2014 with their daughter and her family was canceled.

"All she ever wanted to do was to be able to help people. People all over the world are now losers."

Her letter concluded, Lois turned around and returned to her seat.

With the prosecution's evidence closed, Difenderfer told the court he had nothing to present—no witnesses, no argument.

Manning then asked Ferrante whether he had a statement to make on his behalf.

"I have none, your honor," the defendant answered.

Ferrante listened silently as the judge quoted early twentieth-century author W. H. Auden, who wrote that society must stand in for the murder victim to demand "atonement and grant forgiveness."

"You are here today for the demand of atonement," the judge said.

"Robert Ferrante, it is the sentence of this court that you undergo imprisonment for the period of your natural life and stand committed and be committed to the custody of the Department of Corrections for confinement."

After spending several more days at the Allegheny County Jail, on February 12 Ferrante was sent to the State Correctional Institution at Camp Hill, a processing center for new inmates. There he went through a battery of classification tests, including psychological, educational, medical, and dental before a treatment plan was devised to determine which prison would best suit him. Then, on June 1, 2015, Ferrante was transferred aboard a full prison bus to the State Correctional Institution at Houtzdale, a 2,300-bed facility in rural central Pennsylvania.

The prison, which was built in 1995, is classified as medium-security and houses 2,505 inmates in two-man, eight-by-ten cells. Just five weeks before Ferrante's arrival, there was a riot resulting in injury to five officers. Visitation for the inmates was canceled until just before Ferrante's arrival.

A typical day begins with a standing inmate count at 6:15 a.m., followed fifteen minutes later by a breakfast that might include cold cereal, pancakes, or cheesy grits—though made with American cheese and not Parmesan as Ferrante used to make them.

The inmates, who wear cocoa-brown pants and a button-down shirt, sit four to a table, with their stools bolted down. Following breakfast, they can either work, go outside to the rec yard, or attend programs or classes for which they've signed up. Lunch is served at 11:00 a.m., again followed by one of those options, and dinner is at 4:30 p.m.

Almost immediately upon being transferred to Houtzdale, Ferrante was targeted by other inmates, who shook him down for money. He quickly learned that he needed someone to protect him, and he now pays another inmate regularly for that service. He has not been physically harmed.

"You learn to realize that you just need to follow the straight and narrow path here, and you're fine," Ferrante said.

He believes the prison system accomplishes its mission.

"It's designed to help individuals not want to come back here," he said. "There's a sort of strictness to it all, but it's necessary to keep unwanted behaviors from erupting."

"He has incredible coping skills," said his new appellate attorney, Chris Rand Eyster. "He is able to maintain his personality, which is unusual in prison."

Early on at Houtzdale, Ferrante had a job cleaning other inmates' toilets but shortly after was assigned to serve as a tutor in the education department. Now, he spends his days—from 8:00 a.m. to 3:30 p.m.— helping other inmates in a variety of areas, such as earning a GED or diploma and learning social interaction and financial responsibility skills.

"They do extremely well," he said. "Many of them come in here and have a very low education level and have never been exposed to a lot of different things. It's wonderful to see them. They're like grammar-school kids. Many of them have a grade equivalency of fourth or third grade.

"It's rewarding."

Ferrante spends his down time writing letters, drawing, and reading whatever materials his family sends. He has no access to the journals that once played such a large role in his professional life and said he cares little about his legacy as a medical researcher.

"My seminal scientific medical findings and those identified by my colleagues and me are only useful in whether they provide further knowledge and expand our understanding of biology and medicine," he said. "My findings are not lost, they are within the medical literature. I am not important. The work I was performing will be done by others. I welcome their success."

In the evenings, Ferrante spends time exercising in the gym or the yard—lifting weights, using a stationary bike, or doing aerobics. He also goes to scripture readings and religious services. On his block, the inmates talk and play cards, chess, and pinochle. They also have a television.

The last standing count of the day is around 9:15 p.m., followed by lights out.

Ferrante has a roommate and acquaintances in the prison. He doesn't characterize anyone as his friend.

Among the most difficult parts of incarceration, Ferrante said, are waking up each morning and realizing all over again where he is, the sensory deprivation, and the lack of interaction with his loved ones.

"We were a very, very close family and did so much together," he said. "I cope by knowing in my heart and mind that I did not do what I have been accused of."

Ferrante still dreams of Autumn—that she is alive, and they are together.

"I have been unable to fully grieve for her and am unclear if I ever will be able to. I love her and miss her so much," he said. "I miss touching and holding hands, kissing her, laughing and dancing, caring for Cianna, cooking together, talking about medical issues. Just our lives together."

He called Autumn the "love of his life" and his "soul mate."

Ferrante does not deny that the two of them were having difficulty in their marriage, but, he said, they never argued or fought, and it did not mean they were no longer in love.

"Autumn and I never stopped telling each other how much we loved each other during all this time in Pittsburgh and in Boston. We texted and e-mailed each other all the time and ended with an 'I love you.' Yes, people can still be in love but upset about marital issues," he said. "This was about our inability to have another child. And yes, I took the brunt of it."

But he continued, when Autumn began the creatine regimen—giving her a renewed hope that she could become pregnant—and they took their vacation to Puerto Rico, their relationship surged.

"I remain in disbelief of her death, my circumstances, and the absence of my young daughter's presence in my life, along with my adult children and new granddaughter."

If there was one thing Ferrante could change in the months leading up to Autumn's death, he said he would have taken her fainting spells and other medical concerns more seriously.

"I really kick myself. Months prior to Autumn passing, I would have been more forceful in making sure, medically, that she was okay."

Ferrante is angry at how the custody situation with Cianna has played out and fears that she feels abandoned by him. He misses doing homework with her, pushing her on the swing, playing tag, having water fights, reading bedtime stories, eating ice cream, and flying kites.

Of Autumn and Cianna, he said, "They were life. My life."

Shortly after the sentencing, Cianna began writing letters to her father, but Ferrante wasn't allowed to have them. Under the rules of the Pennsylvania Department of Corrections, inmates are not permitted to have homemade art in their cells. In her letters, Cianna colored on them, drawing stars and the sun. In one, she asked her dad if he thought she could have the big TV from their home so that she could watch movies and have a sleepover with friends.

Although Ferrante isn't allowed to keep the letters, Eyster can share them with him, and so when he makes the two-and-a-half-hour drive to visit with his client, he takes the letters with him. Ferrante reads them in one fell swoop during the visit. When Eyster returns, he gets letters from Ferrante for Cianna. Those letters get filtered through the Kleins' family lawyer and a counselor to ensure they are appropriate.

In one dated July 1, 2015, Ferrante wished his daughter a Happy Fourth of July and asked whether she would be watching fireworks and attending a "birthday party for our nation." He also drew for her a horse—colored brown with a red halter—explaining to Cianna that when she was little she enjoyed a book about an Indian girl who liked horses so much she turned into one. He told Cianna, too, that Kimberly liked horses when she was a child. In the neatly written letter, Ferrante talked about the weather—it had rained eleven inches in June, "an all-time record," and asked about the family dog. He encouraged Cianna to keep reading and punctuated the letter with three smiley faces colored green.

The letters, typically just one page, often include drawings. In one just before Thanksgiving, Ferrante drew a colorful turkey. In another two weeks later, a very good Charlie Brown. "My dearest Cianna, happy Thanksgiving to you from Pilgrim Charlie Brown and me. I hope you are well and that you are enjoying yourself. Do you still play soccer? Are you going to art classes? Dance or music lessons? I want to let you know that I love and miss you very much. I think of you all the time and wish you the greatest happiness in the world. You are a wonderful girl. Have a terrific week in school. Remember to read as much as possible. It will help you to learn about things. I love and miss you and will write again next week. Love, Daddy xxxooo."

They are tender and sweet and sad.

Since his incarceration, Ferrante writes letters constantly to his adult children and has been able to visit with them as well. Kimberly got special dispensation to have an extended visit with him over the summer, and was able to spend six and a half hours with him. All they did was talk. "It was like being on the front porch," he said.

They were permitted to hug both at the beginning and end of the visit while being watched by a corrections officer.

Ferrante spends as much time as possible in the law library working on his appeals. He sent Eyster a letter outlining for him how he thought the testimony at trial from Lois, Sharon, and Autumn's friend

Dr. Maria Baldwin was inappropriate because it was only designed to elicit an emotional response from the jury. He cited the court precedent that it violated and encouraged Eyster to pursue it.

But Ferrante's lawyers need no encouragement to continue to fight. Difenderfer made his first attempt at an appeal even before his client was sentenced.

He argued that the conviction should be overturned, claiming that the prosecution's case was purely circumstantial and that there was no evidence proving Ferrante was the person who administered cyanide to Autumn. More than that, Difenderfer claimed, there was not proof beyond a reasonable doubt that she even died from cyanide poisoning.

"We believe the verdict was absolutely contrary to the evidence," he said.

But Pellegrini argued that the unanimous jury verdict showed otherwise. Under the law, Manning said, he was required to consider the evidence in the light most favorable to the verdict winner—the prosecution.

Therefore, he said, motion denied.

That result was expected, and so Eyster began the first steps of appealing the conviction through the state superior court. Among the issues he believes could succeed are the overbreadth of the prosecution's search warrants and the weight and sufficiency of the evidence at trial.

He also will argue that the science in the case was not properly considered by the jury—if Quest and the medical examiner's office came up with a positive cyanide result but the NMS test result was negative, then good science says that neither result is definitive.

That, Eyster said, is reasonable doubt.

And if there was reasonable doubt, then Ferrante should have been found not guilty.

But Eyster's strongest issue might be one that never came up at trial.

A subsidiary of Quest Diagnostics, Nichols Institute, entered into a settlement with the federal government in 2009 to pay a $40 million criminal fine and $262 million in civil penalties. The fines were assessed because, the Department of Justice said, Nichols was aware that, beginning in May 2000, a test used to measure parathyroid hormone levels provided inaccurate and elevated results for patients. Still, the company continued to market the test.

Eyster argues that the prosecution failed to turn that information over to the defense prior to trial, and that it is a violation because it could have been exculpatory. Had the jurors known about the previous issue with Quest, they may have more heavily scrutinized the lab's results on Autumn's cyanide test.

The defense is also hopeful about another avenue for appeal—trying to prove that the creatine Autumn was using to help with fertility created a false positive on the cyanide tests conducted by Quest and the Allegheny County crime lab. Shortly after the trial, Ferrante and his lawyers were contacted by a researcher in Boston who was working with the defense on another creatine-related poisoning case in Virginia. She promised them that she could prove that the tests conducted on Autumn's blood showed a false positive. After doing additional research and speaking with a number of experts, Eyster plans to conduct experiments to prove a false positive can occur and then request a hearing on the issue of newly discovered evidence.

"I think there's more than hope. There's a big difference between optimism and realism," Ferrante said. "Now all of my colleagues are fully on board with regard to how this particular false positive occurred. It's just a matter of demonstrating it scientifically. I hope that it's recognized by the courts that there's potentially great error that may have occurred.

"It didn't come forward well during the trial."

The longer Ferrante has been incarcerated, the more dissatisfied he seems with how his case was presented to the jury. He believes much of the exculpatory evidence was not presented, and he can quickly list eleven reasons that his wife did not die from cyanide poisoning.

"Much of what happened in my defense was not articulated well in the courtroom, despite my developing cross-examinations to every witness and issue—especially surrounding both the medical and scientific evidence," he said. "The evidence at trial, when carefully reviewed in its entirety, is so contradictory that it is incapable of supporting a guilty verdict and insufficient as a matter of law alone, despite common sense. The commonwealth failed to show the element of causation and that I caused Autumn's death."

J UST A WEEK AFTER Ferrante was found guilty, the Klein family filed a wrongful-death lawsuit against him to attempt to collect any money left from the $2.5 million in assets he had prior to the trial to pay for Cianna's needs.

At the same time, prosecutors, who had initially planned to go after Ferrante for restitution, filed a request with the court demanding that there be an accounting of his assets. They cited what they considered to be his suspicious transfers of assets, including moving money and changing bank accounts and Autumn's car registration in the weeks shortly after her death.

The transfers, prosecutors said, demonstrated that Ferrante "places no significance on the financial debt he owes to the estate" or to Cianna.

In his response, Ferrante denied doing anything improper with the money, instead suggesting that he be allowed to create a trust fund for Cianna that would provide for her health care, education, home buying, and professional or business pursuits. It suggested a graduated disbursement system based on her age.

The motion also asked that his son, Michael, serve as the trustee—an idea that infuriated the Kleins.

"This seems to be an attempt by him to continue to try to exert control from his jail cell," said Gismondi, the Kleins' civil attorney.

It was expected that the defense and prosecution would address Ferrante's remaining money at the sentencing hearing—it is believed that his criminal defense had cost more than $1 million—but instead of a public airing, both sides agreed that they were working toward a settlement that would bring to an end the civil lawsuit.

There was also a concession from the defense to allow the Kleins to go into the home on Lytton Avenue once shared by their daughter and her husband. Prior to trial, they had only been allowed inside once, for less than thirty minutes, under guard by police escort and their victim advocate. Lois had been particularly upset by that because she wanted to get some of Autumn's things. She also wanted to retrieve a cut-glass punch bowl she had once driven all the way from Baltimore to give to her daughter in Boston.

A real estate company listed the home for sale just before Ferrante's sentencing, and it sold four months later for $685,000.

Although the parties were able to work out some of the outstanding issues they'd faced for more than a year, the question of Cianna's custody remains and is not likely to be settled quickly. In the meantime, Kimberly and Michael have made another request to have the previous no-contact order lifted so that they can at least visit with their half-sister. It has not yet been lifted, but they both have spoken to Cianna on the phone.

Despite his feelings about the court system that allowed Cianna to be taken from him and his family, Ferrante said he continues to pray for the Klein family every day.

"I pray that their care of Cianna remains exemplary and that she is well and happy and safe in their care."

THE DAY AFTER Ferrante was sentenced, the University of Pittsburgh announced the new Live Like Lou Center for ALS Research, which is dedicated to finding treatment and a cure for the degenerative disease Ferrante had studied for much of his career.

The Alexanders, the founders of Live Like Lou and former supporters of Ferrante's research, were thrilled to move on with their work even after they had been so sorely disappointed by the man they trusted.

"He let down a lot more people than his family. He let down a whole community," Suzanne said. "He hindered important outcomes. He stalled our research. He hurt the reputation of an organization when they needed him most."

Still, the Alexanders regrouped after Ferrante's arrest and, using the spirit they had sustained since Neil's June 2011 diagnosis, rebounded.

The new $10-million center housed at Pitt's Brain Institute recruited an expert in the neurobiology of ALS to run it. Among its goals are to develop a nonhuman primate model of the disease, explore brain-computer interface technology to foster patient independence, award annual innovator grants, and create a prototype of a "smart house" to test neurotechnologies and neuroprostheses in a real-life home setting.

"We're doing this for the next guy, for the next father, the next husband, who looks down and realizes the muscles in his left arm have been twitching uncontrollably," Neil said. "We're doing it for when the doctor walks into the examining room and says, 'I'm really sorry, we think you have ALS,' and when that father and husband says, 'Okay, what do we do now?' so that that doctor actually has something to say."

Seven weeks after the announcement, Neil died from complications of ALS.

WHILE THE Live Like Lou Center for ALS Research will continue on, there are others impacted by Autumn's death and Ferrante's trial who have not found it so easy.

Helen Ewing, juror number three, who was the only one to return for the sentencing, said months after the verdict that she still thinks about it frequently. Attending the penalty hearing, she hoped, would provide her a sort of closure.

"I felt like I needed that," she said. "But I don't think I'm going to stop thinking about it."

It wasn't that she questioned the jurors' decision—"I don't doubt the weight of the evidence we had at trial. The circumstantial evidence was sufficient to be beyond a reasonable doubt"—it was the idea that a man of Ferrante's character and background could have killed his own wife.

"He seemed very relatable to me," Ewing said, "so I found it so hard to accept a person like that could do that.

"What is anyone capable of?"

FOR THE PEOPLE who knew Autumn—who loved her—one of the worst parts of her death is knowing that Cianna will miss out on knowing so much of the important stuff of her mother's life.

Not just that she was a well-regarded doctor and pioneer in her field, or that she liked to do needlepoint and bake. But also that she had the best laugh in the world—one that would rise up from the depths of her body like pure delight. That she had long, ET-like fingers, and a tongue that could touch her own nose. That her favorite color was purple, and one of her favorite books was Wally Lamb's *I Know This Much Is True*.

And that she loved being Cianna's mother more than anything else in life.

Dr. Roos, the journal editor who met Autumn at Massachusetts General Hospital when Autumn was chief neurology resident, recalls fondly repeated conversations the two women had for years about balancing motherhood and their professional pursuits.

"She was one of the most loving, gentle, kind human beings I've known in my lifetime," Roos said. "She had an incredible sense of what she wanted in life. She's all of us who have families and careers and what our priorities are."

Besides the loss to Cianna, Roos said that Autumn's death will impact an entire generation of women who could have been her patients. Autumn worked tirelessly to dispel the myth that women with epilepsy should not have children. She studied other issues too, such as migraines in pregnancy and headaches in women caused by epidurals. She wrote a manuscript of best practices for neurologists to use to help guide them through those problems.

"There are only a handful of people in the country who have Autumn's skills," said Mike Abney, a former business manager at Magee-Womens Hospital of UPMC who managed Autumn's team of EEG technicians. "One of the tragic things about losing Autumn is the opportunity cost to the patients, particularly women with epilepsy, that she would have seen over the next twenty years of her practice."

After Autumn's death, a former patient set up a Facebook page to post remembrances and updates on the trial.

Several patients cried when talking about her—not only for their own loss of a trusted physician, but also for the greater loss to women everywhere.

"She was one of those doctors who didn't look at her watch. She wasn't rushed," said Leigh Monahan.

Monahan was diagnosed at age seventeen with epilepsy. During her first pregnancy, she had a terrible time with her neurologist, who was constantly upping her dosage of medication to ensure she wasn't having seizures. When Monahan switched doctors for her second pregnancy, Autumn lowered the dosage of her antiseizure meds, and the pregnancy was easy. She remembered Autumn calling her at the end of the day, telling her about blood test results and checking in on her.

"I felt like she wanted to get to know me as a person."

Sharon is not surprised by the patient stories.

"Autumn had this insatiable thirst for getting to know people and their stories," she said. "I lost my other half. But sometimes, I feel more loss for her patients. I feel that so deeply."

CIANNA, WHO TURNED NINE in January 2016, told Lois that Lois needed to say no to her more frequently.

"Mommy would tell me no more often," the little girl said.

Since her mother died, Cianna has not talked about her parents a lot. She says she misses her mommy on occasion, and said after the trial that she missed her father, whom she hadn't seen since July 2013, when he was arrested.

One day, just before the trial, in their Maryland kitchen, Lois said to Cianna, "It must have been strange going to bed with Mommy there and you woke up the next morning, and Mommy was gone."

Cianna didn't really answer, and dashed out of the room as kids do. But then she turned around and stuck her head back in.

"I think I know what happened to Mommy," Cianna said. "I think Daddy killed Mommy."

Lois explained to Cianna that her dad was in jail because "people thought he committed an adult crime," and that twelve people would decide whether he did it, and when they did, she would tell Cianna what they said.

Cianna did not attend the trial, and her grandparents had been back in Maryland for about a week after the verdict before Cianna asked what the twelve people said.

"I said, 'They think Daddy's guilty, and Daddy's going to have to go to prison,'" Lois told her. "And she said, 'Oh,' and away she went."

AFTER THE TRIAL ENDED, Pellegrini and Chernosky knew that they would eventually want to give the Klein family a transcript of the trial so that Cianna could read it when she gets older. They also wanted to make sure the little girl would have all the photographs they'd found of her and her mom on Autumn's phone. Chernosky spent his down time during the summer of 2015 putting all those items together on a flash drive.

The pictures dated back to August 2011: Cianna wearing scrubs at the hospital; posing with a soccer ball and her team; at the Schenley Park fountain; at Michael's wedding; playing in the snow; cuddling with her dog; cooking with Autumn in the kitchen in chef's hats; getting her hair and nails done; riding a merry-go-round with Bob in a red T-shirt, shorts, and sandals; and sitting at Autumn's computer with EEGs on the screen.

There were videos, too, of Cianna singing Christmas carols in the car and another of Autumn teaching Cianna how to read. Wearing green pajamas with white polka dots, Cianna holds the Sandra Boynton book *Hippos Go Berserk*.

"Why do you want to learn how to read?" Autumn asks.

"I want to read because I want to learn," Cianna answers.

"Great," Autumn cheers.

"Two hippos on the phone," Cianna reads. Then, impatiently, "What does this say, Mom? Mommy, what does this say?"

"Can," Autumn answers.

Among the most recent images on the phone were pictures of Cianna digging in the sand at the beach in Puerto Rico the month before Autumn died.

Chernosky had everything packed and ready to be shipped when he learned he was scheduled to travel to Baltimore for work in late August. He decided that instead of shipping the package, he would deliver it in person.

The Kleins made arrangements to meet him at Cianna's school on a Friday morning. He was already standing outside when Lois pulled up and dropped off Cianna. The then eight-year-old ran straight up to Chernosky with a wide smile, her backpack bouncing against her. He leaned over to give her a hug, and she said, "Okay, I have to go," and ran inside the building. Lois and Bill then introduced the prosecutor to the head of the school, and the group went inside to a conference room. Cianna joined them a short time later, and she and Chernosky spent about twenty minutes getting caught up.

She talked about math and what she was learning in the third grade and that she'd received five letters from her dad.

They also took pictures, which Chernosky had promised to do for Pellegrini.

After Cianna returned to class, Chernosky joined Lois and Bill for breakfast at a Towson diner. Lois asked about everyone in Pittsburgh, and noted she'd gotten a letter from Detective McGee a few days earlier.

"It occurred to me that no one has ever asked you if you still want to have contact with us," Chernosky said to them. He had wondered whether hearing from the team that prosecuted their daughter's killer might be preventing them from moving forward. "So I'm asking you now."

Without missing a beat, Lois responded, "We love you guys. I wouldn't change it for the world."

EVEN THOUGH IT IS HARD for the Kleins, who are now eighty-one and seventy-nine, to raise a young child, it's fun to have her in the house, too.

"She keeps you moving," Lois said.

Cianna stays in her mom's old bedroom, kicks the soccer ball around the backyard, and lives an active life.

Not too long after the trial, she said to her grandmother, "Life is an adventure."

"Yes, it is," Lois replied.

The irony is not lost on the woman who worried about her daughter's safety in school and in the world, but not at the hands of her own husband.

"I prayed to God to give me one child and let me raise her right," Lois said. "I never believed anybody would take her away from me."

Among the worst parts for her is that her daughter does not get to enjoy her accomplishments.

"What she worked so hard for, she'll never see," Lois said.

But as Autumn's good friend, Karen Kiang, said at the memorial service on May 10, 2013, her influence will continue.

"Even in your passing, you are still teaching, teaching all of us that our lives hang but on a fine, gossamer thread—teaching us to make sure our loved ones know how much they are loved. May we all find peace and consolation knowing that you have touched so many lives in your short time here."

sources

Newspapers

"Irretrievably Broken." *Pittsburgh Post-Gazette*. February 1–5, 2015.
http://newsinteractive.post-gazette.com/longform/stories/ferrante/1/.

Online Sources

Allegheny County Real Estate Portal. http://www2.county.allegheny.pa.us
/realestate/GeneralInfo.aspx?ParcelID=0027L00176000000%20%20%20%20
&SearchType=2&CurrPage=1&CurrRow=0&SearchName=&SearchStreet
=lytton&SearchNum=219&SearchMuni=&SearchParcel=.

"Attorney General Kamala D. Harris Announces $241 Million Settlement with
Quest Diagnostics." https://oag.ca.gov/news/press-releases/attorney
-general-kamala-d-harris-announces-241-million-settlement-quest.

"Autumn Klein's Women's Neurology Program." Brigham and Women's
Hospital. http://www.brighamandwomens.org/Departments_and_Services
/neurology/services/WomensNeurology/autumn-klein.aspx.

"Dedication of New Research Lab." *University of Pittsburgh Neurosurgery News* 13,
no. 4 (Fall 2012). http://www.neurosurgery.pitt.edu/sites/default/files/Pdf_
Files/Newsletter/2012fall.pdf.

"Live Like Lou Center for ALS Research at Pitt Brain Institute Will Search for
Treatments, Cure." University of Pittsburgh Medical Center, February 5,
2015. http://www.upmc.com/media/NewsReleases/2015/Pages/pitt-creates
-live-like-lou-center-for-ALS-research.aspx.

Pennsylvania Department of Corrections. http://www.cor.pa.gov/Facilities
/StatePrisons/Pages/Houtzdale.aspx#.VlYtN_nMQuc.

"Quest Diagnostics to Pay U.S. $302 Million to Resolve Allegations That a
Subsidiary Sold Misbranded Test Kits." http://www.justice.gov/opa/pr
/quest-diagnostics-pay-us-302-million-resolve-allegations-subsidiary-sold
-misbranded-test-kits.

"Robert Ferrante Arrested on Homicide Warrant." City of Pittsburgh Bureau of
Police, July 25, 2013.

"Robert M. Friedlander." University of Pittsburgh, Neurological Surgery.
http://www.neurosurgery.pitt.edu/person/robert-friedlander.

"SCI Houtzdale Yard Incident Peacefully Resolved." http://www.cor.pa.gov
/_layouts/download.aspx?SourceUrl=http://www.cor.pa.gov/Administration

/Newsroom/Documents/2015%20Press%20Releases/SCI%20Houtzdale
%20Yard%20Incident%20Peacefully%20Resolved.docx.

Town of Canton Property Records. http://www.assessedvalues2.com/pdfs/50
/K002565N51931924.pdf.

"UPMC Department of Neurology 2013 Annual Report." Department of
Neurology, University of Pittsburgh School of Medicine/University of
Pittsburgh Physicians. http://www.neurology.upmc.edu/Images/Annual
_Report_2013.pdf.

Dissertations

Ferrante, Robert: "Mitochondrial Energy Impairment as a Model for
Huntington's Disease." PhD diss., Boston University, 1996.

Klein, Autumn: "Beta Amyloid Injections Cause Cortical Injury and Oxidative
Damage in the Mouse Cerebral Cortex." PhD diss., Boston University, 1998.

Journals

Feske, Steven K., MD; Bove, Riley M., MD. "Dedication to Autumn Klein
MD, PhD." *Continuum* 20, no. 1 (February 2014): 19–20. doi: 10.1212/01.
CON.0000443833.72389.57.

Roos, Karen L. "Introduction to Guest Editor." *Seminars in Neurology* 27, no. 5
(November 2007): 401. doi: 10.1055/s-002–7096.

———. "Introduction to Guest Editor." *Seminars in Neurology* 31, no. 4
(September 2011): 357–358. doi: 10.1055/s-0031–1293533.

Personal Letters

Bubrick, Ellen. Eulogy of Autumn Klein, May 10, 2013.

Kiang, Karen. Eulogy of Autumn Klein, May 10, 2013.

Klein, Autumn. E-mail messages to Karen Kiang, August 27, 2008; March 2, 2009;
March 21, 2009; December 7, 2009; July 24, 2012.

———. E-mail messages to Robert Ferrante, February 9, 2013; February 18, 2013.

———. Journal entry, July 30, 2012.

"A Service of Celebration and Remembrance for the Life of Autumn Marie
Klein, M.D., Ph.D." May 10, 2013.

Broadcast Interviews

Demolles, Diane. WTAE news. By Marcie Cipriani. http://www.wtae.com
/news/local/allegheny/Husband-of-Pittsburgh-doctor-charged-in-her
-cyanide-death/21170106.

Public Records

Commonwealth of Pennsylvania v. Robert Ferrante. Allegheny County Department
of Court Records, docket no. 13724-2013.

Diane F. Ferrante v. Robert J. Ferrante. Commonwealth of Massachusetts,
Probation and Family Court Department, Norfolk Division, docket no.
88D1330-D1.

Personal Interviews

Abney, Mike. By Paula Reed Ward, November 20, 2014.

Alberto, Enia. By Paula Reed Ward, November 2014.

Alexander, Neil. By Paula Reed Ward, November 15, 2014.

Alexander, Suzanne. By Paula Reed Ward, November 15, 2014.

Chernosky, Kevin. By Paula Reed Ward, November 24, 2014.

Cipicchio, Patricia. By Paula Reed Ward, January 2015.

Claus, Lawrence. By Paula Reed Ward, June 24, 2014.

Corcoran, Wende. By Paula Reed Ward, November 25, 2014.

De Vries, Geert. By Paula Reed Ward, December 2014.

DeWeese, Lance. By Paula Reed Ward, November 2014.

Difenderfer, William. By Paula Reed Ward, November 24, 2014.

Ewing, Helen. By Paula Reed Ward, February 4, 2015.

Eyster, Chris Rand. By Paula Reed Ward, July, August, October 2015.

Ferrante, Robert. By Paula Reed Ward, October, November 2015.

George, Stephen. By Paula Reed Ward, December 12, 2014.

Gismondi, John. By Paula Reed Ward, December 2014.

Graber, Lyle. By Paula Reed Ward, May 2014.

Green, Ray. By Paula Reed Ward, December 2014.

Hand, Leslie. By Paula Reed Ward, December 29, 2014.

Harmon, Brittany. By Paula Reed Ward, June 12, 2014.

Jarvis, F. Washington. By Paula Reed Ward, December 2014.

Kemper, Thomas L. By Paula Reed Ward, December 2014.

Kenzie, Bette. By Paula Reed Ward, January 8, 2015.

Kiang, Karen. By Paula Reed Ward, December 27, 2014

King, Jeff. By Paula Reed Ward, January 7, 2015.

King, Sharon. By Paula Reed Ward, November and December 2014;
January 7, 2015.

Klein, Lois. By Paula Reed Ward, January 7, 2015.

Luckasevic, Todd. By Paula Reed Ward, June 12, 2014.

Ludwig, Emmy. By Paula Reed Ward, December 4, 2014.

Maitz, Brian. By Paula Reed Ward, November 7, 2014.

McGee, James. By Paula Reed Ward, June 11, 2014.

Monahan, Leigh. By Paula Reed Ward, November 2014.

Pellegrini, Lisa. By Paula Reed Ward, June 25, 2014.

Poccia, Dick. By Paula Reed Ward, December 12, 2014.

Provident, Robert. By Paula Reed Ward, June 11, 2014.

Roos, Karen. By Paula Reed Ward, November 13, 2014.

Schafer, Marianne. By Paula Reed Ward, November 12, 2014.

Silverman, Rick. By Paula Reed Ward, October 14, 2014.

Smith, Alesia. By Paula Reed Ward, May 19, 2014.

Tellish, Jeannette. By Paula Reed Ward, November 25, 2014.

Weibel, Jackelyn. By Paula Reed Ward, May 2014.

Wu, Harmony. By Paula Reed Ward, December 11, 2014.

Index

Note: RF refers to Robert Ferrante; AK refers to Autumn Klein.